Computational Intelligence and its Applications

Edited by

Vikash Yadav
Government Polytechnic Bighapur Unnao, Department of Technical Education, Uttar Pradesh, India

Vimal Kumar
Galgotias University, Greater Noida, Uttar Pradesh, India

Sonam Gupta
Ajay Kumar Garg Engineering College, Ghaziabad, Uttar Pradesh, India

&

Vandana Dixit Kaushik
Harcourt Butler Technical University, Kanpur, Uttar Pradesh, India

Computational Intelligence and its Applications

Editors: Vikash Yadav, Vimal Kumar, Sonam Gupta & Vandana Dixit Kaushik

ISBN (Online): 978-981-5313-32-1

ISBN (Print): 978-981-5313-33-8

ISBN (Paperback): 978-981-5313-34-5

First published in 2025.

need for a court order if at any point you breach any terms of this License Agreement. In no event will any delay or failure by Bentham Science Publishers in enforcing your compliance with this License Agreement constitute a waiver of any of its rights.

3. You acknowledge that you have read this License Agreement, and agree to be bound by its terms and conditions. To the extent that any other terms and conditions presented on any website of Bentham Science Publishers conflict with, or are inconsistent with, the terms and conditions set out in this License Agreement, you acknowledge that the terms and conditions set out in this License Agreement shall prevail.

Bentham Science Publishers Pte. Ltd.
80 Robinson Road #02-00
Singapore 068898
Singapore
Email: subscriptions@benthamscience.net

BENTHAM
SCIENCE

CONTENTS

PREFACE

In the rapidly evolving landscape of technology, where the boundaries between the digital and physical worlds blur, computational intelligence stands as a beacon of innovation and problem-solving process. As the digital era continues to permeate every facet of our lives, the need for intelligent systems that can adapt, learn, and make decisions becomes increasingly vital. This book, "Computational Intelligence & its Applications", delves deep into the heart of this transformative field, exploring its theoretical foundations and practical applications that are reshaping industries, societies, and the very nature of human-machine interaction.

Computational intelligence, an interdisciplinary domain drawing from computer science, mathematics, engineering, and cognitive sciences, encompasses a rich tapestry of techniques inspired by nature, evolution, and human cognition. From neural networks that emulate the workings of the human brain to evolutionary algorithms that mimic the process of natural selection, computational intelligence methodologies empower machines to solve complex problems, optimize processes, and learn from data in ways that were once deemed the exclusive realm of human intelligence.

From healthcare and finance to manufacturing and transportation, the impact of computational intelligence is profound and multifaceted. In the pages that follow, readers will encounter compelling case studies and examples showcasing how computational intelligence algorithms are revolutionizing medical diagnosis, enabling autonomous vehicles, predicting market trends, optimizing supply chains, and enhancing the overall quality of life. Each chapter is crafted to provide a balance between theoretical knowledge and practical insights, making this book an invaluable resource for students, researchers, and practitioners alike.

Additionally, this book explores the ethical dimensions of computational intelligence, addressing the societal implications of intelligent systems, including privacy concerns, bias in algorithms, and the ethical responsibility of AI developers. As we venture deeper into the era of artificial intelligence, understanding these ethical considerations is paramount to ensuring that computational intelligence serves humanity's best interests.

We invite readers to embark on a journey through the realms of computational intelligence and witness firsthand the transformative power of intelligent algorithms. Whether you are a student eager to explore the frontiers of AI, a researcher seeking inspiration for your next project, or a practitioner aiming to harness the potential of computational intelligence in your industry, this book offers a wealth of knowledge and insights to guide you on your intellectual quest.

Vikash Yadav
Government Polytechnic Bighapur Unnao, Department of Technical Education, Uttar Pradesh, India

Vimal Kumar
Galgotias University, Greater Noida, Uttar Pradesh, India

Sonam Gupta
Ajay Kumar Garg Engineering College, Ghaziabad, Uttar Pradesh, India

&

Vandana Dixit Kaushik
Harcourt Butler Technical University, Kanpur, Uttar Pradesh, India

List of Contributors

Anshu	Amity Institute of Information Technology, Uttar pradesh, India
Aditya Verma	Amity Institute of Information Technology, Uttar pradesh, India
Anil Kumar Yadav	VIT Bhopal University, Madhya Pradesh, India
Ashok Kumar Rai	Galgotias University, Greater Noida, India
Ayushi Prakash	Ajay Kumar Garg Engineering College, Ghaziabad, India
Abdul Aleem	Galgotias University, Uttar pradesh, India
Bably Dolly	Integral University, Lucknow, UP, India
Bosco Paul Alapatt	Christ (Deemed to be University), Delhi NCR Campus, Ghaziabad, India
Gurpreet Kaur	Amity Institute of Information Technology, Uttar pradesh, India
Lakshay Singh Mahur	Raj Kumar Goel Institute of Technology, Ghaziabad, India
Mayur Rahul	CSJM University, Kanpur, Uttar pradesh, India
Manoj Kumar	VIT Bhopal University, Madhya Pradesh, India
Manish Kumar Gupta	Buddha Institute of Technology, Gorakhpur, India
Martand Ratnam	AKTU, Lucknow, UP, India
Namita Tiwari	CSJM University, Kanpur, Uttar pradesh, India
Nidhi Sindhwani	Amity Institute of Information Technology, Uttar pradesh, India
Pankaj Singh	KIET group of Institutions, Uttar pradesh, India
Pradeep Gupta	Ajay Kumar Garg Engineering College, Ghaziabad, India
Rohit Anand	G. B pant DSEU, Okhla Campus 1, New Delhi, India
Rohit Vashisht	KIET group of Institutions, Uttar pradesh, India
Radhey Shyam	Department of Information Technology, SRMCEM, Lucknow, India
Sonia Deshmukh	KIET group of Institutions, Uttar pradesh, India
Sonam Gupta	Ajay Kumar Garg Engineering College, Ghaziabad, India
Shivani Saxena	Ajay Kumar Garg Engineering College, Ghaziabad, India
Sneha Maurya	Ajay Kumar Garg Engineering College, Ghaziabad, India
Sandhya Avasthi	ABES Engineering College, Ghaziabad, India
Shilpi Khanna	Department of Information Technology, SRMCEM, Lucknow, India
Smita Singh	Department of Information Technology, SRMCEM, Lucknow, India
Tarun Jaiswal	National Institute of Technology, Raipur, India
Tanvi Jaiswal	Department of Information Technology, SRMCEM, Lucknow, India
Utkarsh Dixit	ABES Engineering College, Ghaziabad, India
Vivek Kumar	Koneru Lakshmaiah Education Foundation, Vijayawada, Andhra Pradesh, India
Vikash Yadav	Government Polytechnic Bighapur, Unnao, Department of Technical Education, Uttar Pradesh, India

Vikash Kumar Mishra	Galgotias University, Uttar pradesh, India
Vimal Kumar	Galgotias University, Uttar pradesh, India

CHAPTER 1

Emerging Frontiers: Post-Quantum Cryptography and Secure Communication

Namita Tiwari[1,*], **Mayur Rahul**[1] and **Vikash Yadav**[2]

[1] *CSJM University, Kanpur, Uttar pradesh, India*

[2] *Government Polytechnic Bighapur, Unnao, Department of Technical Education, Uttar Pradesh, India*

Abstract: The field of cryptography is facing a significant challenge due to fast updates in computer history. This chapter explores the key concepts, techniques, and challenges associated with post-quantum cryptography (PQC). The chapter begins by introducing the fundamental principles of quantum computing and the threats it poses to traditional cryptography systems. Each family is examined in detail, highlighting its underlying mathematical foundations, security assumptions, and implementation considerations. The chapter also discusses the ongoing standardization efforts in post-quantum cryptography led by organizations such as the "National Institute of Standards and Technology" (NIST). Furthermore, the chapter explores the challenges and open research questions in the field, such as the efficient implementation of post-quantum algorithms, the impact on existing protocols and systems, and the integration of post-quantum cryptography into real-world applications.

Keywords: Cryptography protocols, Message authentication codes (MACs), NIST, Post-quantum cryptography, Post-quantum algorithms, Quantum computers.

INTRODUCTION

PQC is a field of study and research focusing on cryptography protocols that can withstand quantum computers. Quantum computers can potentially solve the underlying mathematical problems upon which current encryption algorithms are based, rendering them ineffective. PQC's goal is to develop new cryptography algorithms that can resist attacks by quantum computers. These algorithms are designed to provide security against both classical and quantum computers, ensuring that encrypted data remains protected in a post-quantum computing era. Secure communication involves protecting the content of the communication from unauthorized access, preventing any unauthorized modifications or tampering with the data, and verifying the identity of the communicating parties. To achieve secure communication, various cryptography techniques and protocols are employed. These techniques involve the use of encryption, which transforms the original message into an unintelligible form, making it difficult for eavesdroppers

* **Corresponding author Namita Tiwari:** CSJM University, Kanpur, Uttar pradesh, India;
E-mail: namitatiwari@csjmu.ac.in

Vikash Yadav, Vimal Kumar, Sonam Gupta & Vandana Dixit Kaushik (Eds.)

to understand. Only authorized recipients with the necessary decryption keys can decipher the encrypted message and retrieve the original information. Secure communication protocols also address the issue of data integrity. They ensure that the message remains unaltered during transit by employing message authentication codes (MACs) or digital signatures. These techniques verify the integrity of the data by attaching a small piece of information that is computed using cryptography algorithms [1].

Furthermore, secure communication involves establishing the authenticity of the communicating parties. This is achieved through techniques like digital certificates and public key infrastructure (PKI), where each participant is issued a unique digital certificate that binds their identity to a public key. By verifying the digital certificate, the recipient can be assured of the sender's identity and establish a secure channel for communication. Secure communication is crucial in various contexts, including online banking, e-commerce, government communications, and sensitive data exchanges. It protects against eavesdropping, data tampering, impersonation attacks, and other forms of cyber threats, ensuring that sensitive information remains confidential and trustworthy throughout the communication process.

Key Concepts: Fundamental Techniques and Cryptography Protocols

There are several fundamental techniques and cryptography protocols used to achieve secure communication [2]. Here are some commonly employed techniques:

1. Encryption: It is the process of coding plaintext (original message) into ciphertext (encrypted message) using an encryption algorithm and a secret key. It ensures that even if intercepted, the message cannot be understood without the corresponding decryption key. Popular encryption algorithms include AES and RSA.
2. Symmetric Key Cryptography: It uses the common key for both coding and decoding, and the key must be shared through the proper channel. This approach is efficient for encrypting big data. Examples are AES, DES, and Blowfish.
3. Asymmetric Key Cryptography: It involves a public and private key for encryption and decryption, respectively. It is used in secure key exchange and digital signatures. Examples are RSA, ECC, and Diffie-Hellman key exchange.
4. Hash Functions: It converts the input of an arbitrary string to an output of a fixed string known as a message digest. Popular hash function algorithms are SHA-2, SHA-3, and message digest algorithm (MD5).
5. Digital Signatures: These use asymmetric key cryptography to provide data

integrity and non-repudiation. The sender uses its private key to make a unique digital signature, and the verifier verifies it using the corresponding public key.

6. Transport-Layer Security TLS or Secure-Sockets Layer (SSL): These protocols provide secure communication over the Internet. SSL/TLS is commonly used in web browsing, email, *etc.*
7. Virtual Private Networks (VPNs): VPNs create secure communication over public networks. VPNs are widely used for remote access, securing Wi-Fi connections, and maintaining privacy online.

These techniques and protocols can be combined and tailored to specific communication needs, providing layers of security to protect sensitive information and ensure secure communication between parties [3].

The following section examines the techniques and challenges associated with post quantum cryptography [4 - 7].

Techniques/Challenges in Post-Quantum Cryptography

Researchers are exploring various mathematical problems and cryptographic primitives believed to be intractable against quantum computers. Some of the promising approaches include:

1. Lattice-based Cryptography: It includes Learning with Errors (LWE) and Ring Learning with Errors (RLWE) schemes, which offer security against attacks by both classical and quantum computers.
2. Code-based Cryptography: It employs error-correcting codes to provide security. Schemes like McEliece and Niederreiter cryptosystems utilize the difficulty of decrypting the linear codes to achieve resistance against quantum attacks.
3. Multivariate Cryptography: It is based on the hardness of solving multivariate polynomial equations. It involves schemes like Rainbow and the Unbalanced Oil and Vinegar (UOV) cryptosystems.
4. Hash-based Cryptography: It employs cryptographic hash functions to construct digital signatures and key exchange protocols. Merkle trees and the Lamport signature scheme are examples of hash-based post-quantum cryptographic techniques.
5. Supersingular isogeny-based cryptography: These schemes are based on elliptic curves and isogenies, and security relies on the hardness of certain isogeny problems.

Lattice-based Cryptography

It offers a promising alternative to traditional cryptographic systems, such as those based on number theory or elliptic curves, which may be vulnerable to quantum attacks.

The main advantages of lattice-based cryptography include:

1. Security: Lattice-based schemes are provable and secure based on the hardness of lattice problems, even against quantum computers.
2. Post-quantum resistance: Lattice-based cryptography is considered a leading candidate for post-quantum cryptography, as the underlying lattice problems are not efficiently solvable by quantum algorithms.
3. Versatility: Lattice-based techniques can be applied to various cryptographic primitives, including encryption, digital signatures, key exchange protocols, and secure multiparty computation.
4. Efficiency: While lattice-based cryptography typically involves larger key sizes compared to traditional cryptographic systems, advances in lattice reduction algorithms and optimization techniques have improved the efficiency of lattice-based schemes.

Some commonly used lattice-based cryptographic primitives include:

1. Lattice-based encryption schemes (*e.g.*, Learning With Errors Encryption, Ring-Learning With Errors Encryption).
2. Lattice-based signature schemes (*e.g.*, BLISS, Dilithium).
3. Lattice-based key exchange protocols (*e.g.*, New Hope, Frodo).
4. Lattice-based fully homomorphic encryption (*e.g.*, TFHE).

As with any cryptographic system, it is essential to stay up to date with the latest advancements and rely on standardized and vetted implementations for secure deployment.

Code-based Cryptography (CBC)

It relies on error-correcting codes for providing security. The security of code-based cryptographic schemes is based on the hardness of certain decoding problems associated with error-correcting codes.

In code-based cryptography, encryption, digital signatures, and key exchange protocols are constructed using error-correcting codes. These codes introduce redundancy into the transmitted data to detect and correct errors caused by noise or interference during transmission.

Advantages of code-based cryptography include:

1. Post-quantum resistance: CBC is considered a promising post-quantum alternative as the decoding problem used in these schemes.
2. Well-studied and understood: Error-correcting codes have been extensively studied and used in various engineering applications, making the theoretical foundations of code-based cryptography well-developed.
3. Relatively efficient: Code-based schemes can provide a good balance between security and efficiency, with practical implementations available.
4. Compatibility with existing systems: Code-based cryptography can be implemented using existing infrastructure and protocols without major modifications, making it easier to integrate into existing systems.

However, there are also some challenges and limitations associated with code-based cryptography:

1. Key size: Code-based schemes typically require larger key sizes compared to traditional cryptographic systems, which may impact the efficiency and performance of the cryptographic operations.
2. Key management: Key management in code-based cryptography can be more complex due to the large key sizes and potential vulnerabilities if key update procedures are not properly implemented.
3. Limited deployment: Despite its post-quantum security, code-based cryptography has not yet been widely deployed, and the adoption of code-based schemes in real-world applications is still limited.

Some well-known code-based cryptographic schemes include:

1. McEliece cryptosystem.
2. Niederreiter cryptosystem.
3. RQC (Ring-LWE-based Quasi-Cyclic) cryptosystem.

Multivariate Polynomial Cryptography (MPC)

It relies on the computational hardness of solving systems of multivariate polynomial equations. Unlike traditional cryptographic systems that are based on number theory or elliptic curves, MPC utilizes the algebraic properties of polynomials to provide security.

In MPC, algorithms are based on the evaluation of multivariate polynomial equations. These equations involve multiple variables and coefficients, and the security of the system depends on the difficulty of solving these equations to recover the original input.

Solving systems of multivariate polynomial equations is a computationally difficult problem, even for powerful computers.

There are several constructions and schemes within MPC, each with its own strengths and characteristics. Two notable examples of MPC schemes are:

1. Rainbow: This scheme is a multivariate polynomial signature scheme. It uses a layered structure of polynomial equations and employs specific techniques to increase security while maintaining efficiency. Rainbow signatures are resistant to forgery and tampering attacks.
2. Unbalanced Oil and Vinegar (UOV): This is another multivariate polynomial signature scheme. It is based on the concept of oil and vinegar mixing, where the polynomials are divided into two types: the "oil" polynomials that provide security and the "vinegar" polynomials that act as public information. UOV signatures offer high resistance against known attacks.

The main challenge in implementing MPC is the efficiency and scalability of the cryptographic operations. Multivariate polynomial systems tend to have large equation sizes and require computationally intensive operations. Therefore, optimizing the performance of MPC schemes is an ongoing area of research.

It is worth noting that while MPC has shown promising resistance against attacks, it may have some limitations compared to other post-quantum cryptography approaches. For example, MPC may be vulnerable to certain algebraic attacks or advancements in solving multivariate polynomial systems. Therefore, ongoing research and analysis are crucial to ensure the security of MPC in the face of evolving attacks and computational advancements.

Hash-based Cryptography

It is also known as hash-based digital signatures or one-time signatures. It is based on the computational hardness of finding collisions or per-image resistance in hash functions [3].

In hash-based cryptography, a one-way hash function is used to derive a short fixed-length digest or hash value from an arbitrary-sized input message. The security of hash-based schemes is based on the assumption that finding collisions (two different inputs producing the same hash) or inverting the hash function (finding the original input from a given hash value) is computationally difficult.

The main idea behind hash-based cryptography is to use a one-time signature scheme, where a different key pair is used for each signature. The public key is derived from the private key using the hash function, and the signature is generated by including the hash value of the message along with the private key. Verification is performed by hashing the received message and comparing it with the derived public key and the signature.

Advantages of Hash-Based Cryptography

Post-quantum resistance: Hash-based schemes are considered post-quantum secure, as their security is based on the hardness of finding collisions or inverting hash functions, which is believed to be resistant to quantum algorithms.

1. Simplicity and efficiency: Hash functions are widely available, well-studied, and efficient cryptography primitives, making hash-based schemes relatively simple and efficient.
2. Compatibility with existing systems: Hash-based cryptography can be integrated into existing protocols and systems with minimal modifications, as hash functions are already widely used in various applications.
3. Minimal key management: In hash-based cryptography, the key management is relatively simple since new key pairs are generated for each signature. This eliminates the need for complex key distribution or revocation mechanisms.

However, there are some challenges and limitations associated with hash-based cryptography:

1. Signature size: Hash-based signatures can be significantly larger than traditional digital signatures, which may impact the efficiency and bandwidth requirements for signature generation and verification.
2. Limited signature reuse: Hash-based signatures are generally designed for one-time use and cannot be reused for multiple messages. This can be impractical in scenarios where frequent signing is required.
3. Migration challenges: Adopting hash-based cryptography may require significant changes in existing cryptography systems and protocols, which can be challenging to deploy and integrate.

Some well-known hash-based signature schemes include:

1. Lamport signatures.
2. Winternitz signatures.
3. Merkle signatures.

Supersingular Isogeny-Based Cryptography

It is based on the computational hardness of the isogeny problem in supersingular elliptic curves. It offers an alternative to traditional cryptography systems that may be vulnerable to attacks by quantum computers. In supersingular isogenylbased cryptography, the security of the cryptographic schemes is based on the difficulty of finding the isogeny between two given elliptic curves. The main idea behind supersingular isogeny-based cryptography is to use the isogeny function as a trapdoor function. By starting with a known base curve and applying a sequence of isogenies, a public key is derived from the private key. The security lies in the computational hardness of computing the isogeny in the reverse direction, *i.e.*, finding the private key from the public key.

Advantages of supersingular isogeny-based cryptography include:

1. Post-quantum resistance: Supersingular isogeny-based cryptography is designed to be resistant to attacks by both classical and quantum computers, as the underlying computational problem is believed to be hard even for quantum algorithms.
2. Smaller key sizes: Supersingular isogeny-based cryptographic schemes often have smaller key sizes compared to some other post-quantum alternatives, which can be advantageous in terms of efficiency and storage requirements.
3. Potential for efficient implementations: Advances in algorithmic techniques and efficient arithmetic on elliptic curves have led to more practical and efficient implementations of supersingular isogeny-based schemes.
4. Compatibility with existing systems: Supersingular isogeny-based cryptography can be integrated into existing protocols and systems with proper modifications, allowing for compatibility and interoperability.

However, there are also challenges and considerations in supersingular isogeny-based cryptography:

1. Relatively new and ongoing research: Supersingular isogeny-based cryptography is still an active and new research area, and further analysis and scrutiny are needed to ensure its security and practicality.
2. Performance trade-offs: While improvements in efficiency have been made, supersingular isogeny-based cryptography generally involves more computational overhead compared to some traditional cryptography systems.
3. Standardization and adoption: Standardization efforts are underway to evaluate and establish the security and practicality of supersingular isogeny-based schemes. Adoption may depend on widespread acceptance and interoperability.

Some well-known supersingular isogeny-based cryptographic schemes include:

1. Supersingular-Isogeny Key Encapsulation (SIKE).
2. Supersingular-Isogeny Diffie-Hellman (SIDH).
3. Commutative-Supersingular-Isogeny Diffie-Hellman (CSIDH).

As supersingular isogeny-based cryptography is a rapidly evolving field, it is essential to refer to the latest research and standardized specifications for the most up-to-date information on implementations and best practices.

Challenges in Post Quantum Cryptography

1. Security Analysis: Designing and analyzing secure post-quantum cryptographic algorithms is a significant challenge. It requires demonstrating resistance against attacks from both classical and quantum computers, ensuring provable security under various mathematical assumptions, and assessing the impact of algorithmic optimizations on security.
2. Efficiency and Performance: Post-quantum cryptographic algorithms typically involve complex mathematical operations, which can be computationally expensive and require significant computational resources. Balancing security and efficiency is crucial to ensure the practical adoption of post-quantum cryptography.
3. Standardization and Interoperability: Standardization plays a vital role in post-quantum cryptography to ensure interoperability and compatibility across different systems and platforms. Establishing standardized algorithms, protocols, and evaluation criteria requires collaboration among researchers, industry stakeholders, and standardization bodies.
4. Integration into Existing Systems: Integrating post-quantum cryptographic algorithms into existing systems presents challenges, particularly in cases where legacy systems or protocols rely on classical cryptographic primitives. Ensuring backward compatibility, migration strategies, and seamless integration without compromising security is a key consideration.
5. Key Management: Post-quantum cryptography introduces new challenges in key management. Key sizes for post-quantum cryptographic algorithms are typically larger than those used in traditional cryptography. Developing efficient and secure key management schemes, including key exchange and distribution, is essential.
6. Awareness and Education: Raising awareness and educating the cryptographic community, system administrators, and end-users about post-quantum cryptography is crucial. Understanding the risks posed by quantum computers and the need to transition to post-quantum cryptographic techniques is essential for a smooth and secure transition.

The Goal of PQC

The transition to PQC involves careful consideration and planning, as it requires updating encryption protocols, key exchange mechanisms, digital signatures, and other cryptography primitives used in various systems, including secure communication protocols, digital certificates, and secure storage systems.

Overall, the goal of post-quantum cryptography is to ensure that sensitive information remains secure even in the face of future quantum computers, providing long-term security for digital communications and data protection. Traditional cryptography systems, such as RSA and elliptic curve cryptography (ECC), rely on the difficulty of certain mathematical problems for their security. However, quantum computers have the potential to solve these problems much more efficiently, which poses a threat to the security of these traditional cryptography systems. One of the most well-known quantum algorithms, Shor's algorithm, can factor large numbers and solve the discrete logarithm problem (the foundation of RSA and ECC) in polynomial time, rendering these traditional cryptography systems insecure.

PQC aims to develop new cryptography algorithms that are resistant to attacks by both classical and quantum computers. These algorithms are based on different mathematical problems that are believed to be hard, even for quantum computers. These are just a few examples of the different classes of post-quantum cryptography algorithms that are being studied and developed. The goal is to identify and standardize algorithms that provide secure alternatives to the currently used cryptography systems, ensuring that our data and communications remain secure in the post-quantum era.

Power and Performance of Supercomputers

Supercomputers are highly powerful and high-performance computing systems designed to perform complex calculations and solve computationally intensive problems. They are built using a combination of advanced processors, large amounts of memory, high-speed interconnects, and specialized software to achieve exceptional computational capabilities. Supercomputers are typically used for scientific research, engineering simulations, weather forecasting, molecular modeling, and other tasks that require massive computational resources.

Here are some key characteristics and components of supercomputers:

1. Processing Power: Supercomputers are designed to provide extremely high processing power by utilizing multiple processors or processor cores. These processors are often high-performance CPUs or specialized accelerators, such as GPUs or FPGAs.
2. Parallelism: Supercomputers excel at parallel computing, dividing complex problems into smaller tasks that can be executed simultaneously. They employ parallel architectures and programming models to distribute computations across multiple processors or nodes, allowing for efficient parallel processing.
3. High-speed Interconnects: Supercomputers incorporate high-bandwidth interconnects to enable fast communication between processors and nodes.

These interconnects, such as Infini Band or Cray's Aries, minimize data transfer latency and maximize data throughput, facilitating efficient parallel computing.

4. Large Memory Capacity: Supercomputers often have large amounts of memory (RAM) to handle massive data sets and enable efficient processing. This allows them to perform computations on extensive datasets or hold complex simulations entirely in memory.
5. Storage Systems: Supercomputers typically have large-scale storage systems, including high-speed parallel file systems, for storing and accessing large volumes of data generated during computations. These storage systems provide fast data access to support the computational requirements of the supercomputer.
6. Cooling and Power Infrastructure: Due to their high-performance nature, supercomputers generate significant heat and consume substantial power. They require specialized cooling systems, such as liquid cooling or advanced air cooling techniques, to dissipate heat effectively and maintain stable operating temperatures.
7. System Software: Supercomputers use specialized software stacks and operating systems optimized for parallel computing. These software environments provide tools, libraries, and programming models that facilitate the development and execution of parallel applications on the supercomputer architecture.

Notable supercomputers include systems like Summit, Sierra, Fugaku, and Tianhe-2. These supercomputers often rank among the top in the world in terms of processing power and performance. However, it's worth noting that the field of supercomputing is continually advancing, with new systems and technologies being developed to push the boundaries of computational capabilities even further.

CONCLUSION

In summary, post-quantum cryptography employs various techniques to develop cryptography algorithms that resist attacks from quantum computers. However, challenges related to security analysis, efficiency, standardization, integration, key management, and education must be addressed to ensure the successful adoption and deployment of post-quantum cryptography solutions in real-world applications. PQC is still an active research area, and no standardized algorithms have been established yet. However, various candidate algorithms are being developed and evaluated by the cryptography community and standardization bodies, such as NIST in the United States. Overall, this chapter aims to provide a comprehensive overview of PQC, highlighting its significance in addressing the security threats posed by quantum computers. Examining the various families of post-quantum algorithms, standardization efforts, challenges, and deployment considerations equips readers with a solid understanding of the field and paves the way for the development and adoption of secure cartographic solutions in the post-quantum era.

REFERENCES

[1] W. Stallings, *Cryptography and Network Security: Principles and Practice.* 5th ed. Prentice Hall Press: USA, 2010.

[2] A. Menezes, P.C. Oorschot, and S.A. Vanstone, *Handbook of Applied Cryptography.*, 2018.

[3] B. Schneier, Front Matter.*Applied Cryptography.,* B. Schneier, Ed., 2nd ed. , 2015.

[4] W. Diffie, and M. Hellman, "New directions in cryptography", *IEEE Trans. Inf. Theory,* vol. 22, no. 6, pp. 644-654, 1976.
[http://dx.doi.org/10.1109/TIT.1976.1055638]

[5] C. Heinrich, Transport Layer Security (TLS).*Encyclopedia of Cryptography and Security.,* H.C.A. van Tilborg, S. Jajodia, Eds., Springer: Boston, MA, 2011.
[http://dx.doi.org/10.1007/978-1-4419-5906-5_234]

[6] D.J. Bernstein, Introduction to post-quantum cryptography.*Post-Quantum Cryptography.,* D.J. Bernstein, J. Buchmann, E. Dahmen, Eds., Springer: Berlin, Heidelberg, 2009.
[http://dx.doi.org/10.1007/978-3-540-88702-7_1]

[7] N. Tiwari, "New Proxy Signature Scheme over Elliptic Curves using Chaotic Maps Applicable during Pandemic COVID-19", *Recent Adv. Electr. Electron. Eng.,* 2023.
[http://dx.doi.org/10.2174/2352096516666230915113801]

CHAPTER 2

Chatbot with Machine Learning: Latest Advancements

Anshu[1,*], **Nidhi Sindhwani**[1] and **Rohit Anand**[2]

[1] *Amity Institute of Information Technology, Uttar pradesh, India*

[2] *G. B pant DSEU, Okhla Campus 1, New Delhi, India*

Abstract: The aim of this chapter is to enhance the conversational skills of a chatbot through the use of machine learning methods. The chatbot is going to be created in a way that it comprehends conversational input and offers suitable answers to inquiries made by users. To teach the machine learning model how to generate fitting responses, it will undergo training using an extensive collection of spoken interactions among humans for pattern recognition purposes. The Natural Language Processing (NLP) framework will serve as the foundation for the upcoming chatbot, which will utilize the Python programming language for its development. The model intends to apply advanced deep learning algorithms, including recurrent neural networks (RNN) as well as long short-term memory (LSTM), to analyze and interpret natural language and produce suitable replies. The model's accuracy will be enhanced by training it on a conversational log dataset, enabling it to learn from genuine interactions. Due to the swift advancement of technology and the emergence of the chatbot idea, the amount of time and effort can be conserved. A multitude of specialized frameworks have been developed to facilitate the creation and use of chatbots. The chatbot is dependent on artificial intelligence.

Keywords: Artificial intelligence, Chatbot, LSTM, Machine learning, NLP, RNN.

INTRODUCTION

Chatbot refers to a computer program designed to communicate with humans using everyday language. Incorporating technologies such as NLP (Natural Language Processing), which utilizes artificial intelligence, to achieve the desired outcome [1]. The chatbot should be made more engaging and trustworthy. Due to the recent epidemiological situation, there has been a rising need and dependence on electronic devices. The curfew that has been enforced is making it challenging

* **Corresponding author Anshu:** Amity Institute of Information Technology, Uttar pradesh, India;
E-mail: at834068@gmail.com

Vikash Yadav, Vimal Kumar, Sonam Gupta & Vandana Dixit Kaushik (Eds.)

to attend university and obtain an education. The university's scholars have only a restricted ability to obtain information due to this [2].

The utilization of AI chatbot programs is increasingly widespread among organizations and associations as a means of engaging with their clientele in live conversations. By using these computer programs, companies are able to address inquiries from customers and provide support in resolving any issues they may encounter. The aim of this project report is to present the development process of a real-time chat application with an automated bot using Django [3].

Our creation of an AI chatbot will enable customers to interact with companies instantly. It will be possible for customers to initiate a conversation with a business and receive responses to their inquiries. Firms will be able to receive and respond to chat messages. We will utilize Django, which is a Python-based web framework that allows for the speedy development of web applications, to develop the requested application [4].

Artificial intelligence's subbranch, machine learning, has made a significant impact on the development and utilization of chatbots. By implementing machine learning, chatbots are capable of learning from information, advancing with time, and providing users with more precise and customized answers [5].

In the past, chatbots were typically created using rule-based systems, whereby developers would manually establish guidelines for the chatbot to adhere to. The chatbots that were based on rules had constraints when it came to comprehending conversational language and providing fitting answers to user inquiries. Chatbots can learn from vast amounts of human conversational data using machine learning, and consequently, they will be capable of comprehending the context and producing correct responses.

In addition, chatbots now have the ability to tailor their answers to specific users using information such as their preferences, past interactions, and situational data, thanks to the advancement of machine learning. Customization of this degree has the ability to enhance the satisfaction of the user and increase their interaction with the chatbot. To sum up, the incorporation of machine learning into chatbots has brought about a significant change in the creation and usage of chatbots. Chatbots have become more efficient and beneficial in numerous industries due to their ability to comprehend natural language, retain context within conversations, and supply tailored answers to users, all of which have been made possible by the implementation of machine learning.

The understanding and interpretation of human language, also known as natural language processing, poses a significant obstacle in constructing AI chatbots.

Django offers various resources and collections for Natural Language Processing (NLP), such as spaCy, NLTK (Natural Language Toolkit), and Python. NLTK is a commonly used NLP library that offers multiple resources, including tokenization, anchoring, and part-of-speech tags. spaCy offers advanced functionalities like identifying names and analyzing dependencies, making it a potent NLP library [6].

NLP is a section of AI that concentrates on how computers and human language interact with each other. The technology of NLP allows computers to comprehend, analyze, and create human speech, which is crucial for constructing programs that entail interactions with people, like chatbots, virtual aides, and language conversion.

To sum up, the incorporation of machine learning into chatbots has brought about a significant change in the creation and usage of chatbots. Chatbots have become more efficient and beneficial in numerous industries due to their ability to comprehend natural language, retain context within conversations, and supply tailored answers to users, all of which have been made possible by the implementation of machine learning [7].

AI chatbots can be integrated with various other technologies to enhance their functionality [8]. For example, it can be integrated with voice assistants such as Amazon Alexa or Google Assistant to allow users to interact with the chatbot using voice commands. It can also be integrated with messaging platforms like Facebook Messenger or Slack to allow users to interact with chatbots through that platform [9]. Additionally, it can be integrated with analytics tools such as Google Analytics or Mixpanel to track user behavior and improve chatbot performance.

LITERATURE REVIEW

Machine learning has prompted substantial research and advancement in the realm of chatbots. In this field, a literature review of recent studies and developments is provided below. The Journal of Intelligent Information Systems documented a research project where scientists created a machine learning-based chatbot for customer service on the Internet. The conversational abilities of the chatbot were enhanced through deep learning algorithms by using a set of customer interactions as a training dataset. According to the research, the chatbot was capable of delivering correct and beneficial replies to clients, which boosted client contentment and reduced turnaround duration [10].

A recently released article in the Journal of Ambient Intelligence and Humanized Computing concentrated on creating an AI-powered automated chat assistant for medical assistance through the usage of machine learning techniques. The main objective of the chatbot was to give users medical advice and information according to their medical history and symptoms. According to the research, the chatbot was capable of giving precise and tailored recommendations that enhanced the healthcare experience of users [11].

The potential of chatbots with machine learning in healthcare was discussed by the authors in a review article that has been published in the Journal of Healthcare Engineering. In their study, the writers pinpointed various domains where chatbots could prove to be beneficial, such as engaging patients, managing chronic illnesses, and more. The Journal of Web Engineering and Technology has recently released a study that concentrated on constructing a chatbot for the purposes of language education through the utilization of machine learning. The main objective of the chatbot was to give users medical advice and information according to their medical history and symptoms. According to the research, the chatbot was capable of giving precise and tailored recommendations that enhanced the healthcare experience of users [12].

The potential of chatbots with machine learning in healthcare was discussed by the authors in a review article that has been published in the Journal of Healthcare Engineering. In their study, the writers pinpointed various domains where chatbots could prove to be beneficial, such as engaging patients, managing chronic illnesses, and more. However, more research is required to maximize the potential of chatbots equipped with machine learning and to confront issues such as ethical dilemmas and the privacy of data [13].

Methodology

Usually, the process of constructing a chatbot using machine learning consists of these steps:

i. Data collection: The initial stage involves accumulating an ample quantity of dialogues associated with the area of expertise of the chatbot. There are multiple channels available to obtain this information, including but not limited to customer service records, online discussions, social media, and chat records. For the chatbot to perform well, both the dataset's quality and quantity are important [14].
ii. Data Pre-processing: Prior to training the chatbot, it is necessary to pre-process the collected data. Various methods such as cleaning, tokenization, stemming, and other techniques are employed to prepare the data for machine learning algorithms [15].
iii. Training the model: After pre-processing the data, the machine learning model can undergo training. The task at hand determines which models to utilize,

which may include RNN, LSTM, or CNN. The training of the model enables it to grasp the setting of the discussion and produce responses that are appropriate.

iv. Model Evaluation: In order to measure the performance of the model, it is necessary to evaluate it on a separate dataset designed for testing purposes. The model's performance can be evaluated using different measurements, such as precision, accuracy, and recall [16].

v. Deployment: When the model has been trained and assessed, it is possible to utilize it as a chatbot. The chatbot has the capability to be incorporated into different platforms like messaging apps, websites, and mobile applications. Consistent supervision and revisions are necessary to enhance the effectiveness of the chatbot [17].

vi. Improvement: The chatbot's abilities can be enhanced by integrating methods like transfer learning, reinforcement learning, and active learning. Using these methods allows for the incorporation of new information to enhance the chatbot's performance and responses as time goes by [18].

To put it briefly, the process of creating a chatbot through machine learning includes gathering and preparing data, training and assessing the model, launching it, and ongoing enhancements. The successful performance of the chatbot is heavily reliant upon the dataset's size and quality, the selection of the appropriate machine learning model, and the use of effective evaluation metrics. In order to enhance its precision and importance, it is necessary to frequently supervise and revise the chatbot [19].

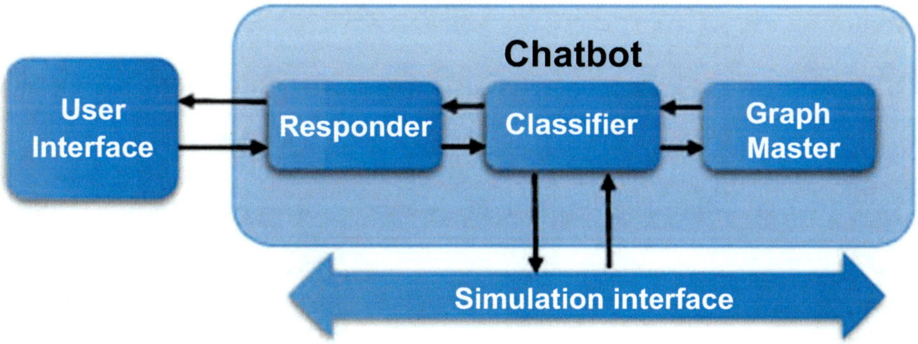

Fig. (1). Components of chatbot.

Techniques

Several techniques were used during the formation of the chatbot. Some of the common techniques are:

1. NLP is a method that empowers chatbots to comprehend and decipher human language. NLP consists of various procedures, including tokenization, identifying parts of speech, recognizing named entities, and analyzing sentiments. By utilizing these procedures, chatbots are able to comprehend the situation of a dialogue and produce appropriate replies [20].
2. Deep learning refers to a type of machine learning that entails the teaching of artificial neural networks. Deep learning is applicable in diverse fields, including but not limited to language interpretation, voice detection, and visual perception. Deep learning can enhance the precision and pertinence of responses in chatbots.
3. Reinforcement learning pertains to a methodology where an agent is trained to optimize a reward by making decisions within a particular environment. Reinforcement learning is applicable in chatbots to enhance their responses through the evaluation of user feedback [21].
4. Transfer Learning is when a pre-trained model is used again for a different task. Transfer learning can be applied to pre-trained language models in chatbots in order to adjust them for particular fields [22].
5. Active Learning Technique: The method of actively acquiring useful labeled data samples by an algorithm is known as active learning. The chatbot can benefit from active learning as it assists in identifying the most pertinent user utterances for enhancing the chatbot's training [23].
6. Transfer Learning is when a pre-trained model is used again for a different task. Transfer learning can be applied to pre-trained language models in chatbots in order to adjust them for particular fields.

Approaches

There are two primary methods of constructing chatbots utilizing artificial intelligence:

1. The rule-based approach involves creating a chatbot that follows a predetermined set of rules for its actions and responses. Domain experts, who possess comprehensive knowledge pertaining to the chatbot's domain, are usually responsible for devising the rules. One instance of this could be a chatbot designed for customer service that has established protocols to address frequently asked questions from customers, such as checking account balances or resetting passwords. These rules are utilized by the chatbot in order to answer user queries [24].
2. A technique called machine learning is utilized in designing the chatbot using the machine learning approach. By using a sizable dataset of dialogues, the chatbot is programmed to produce answers through machine learning that incorporate the current context of the conversation. Various machine learning

algorithms, such as neural networks, support vector machines and decision trees, are available for use [25].

3. The utilization of machine learning in chatbots is gaining more and more popularity as it enables them to handle a broader spectrum of queries, leading to a more authentic conversation experience for the users. With the help of user feedback, chatbots that employ machine learning techniques can keep enhancing their functioning over a period of time [26].
4. A combined method of constructing chatbots is the hybrid approach that integrates rule-based and machine learning techniques. The hybrid approach involves the use of pre-established rules for chatbots to handle easy questions while the more intricate questions can be addressed through machine learning. This method offers a combination of the authentic conversational feel of a machine learning chatbot and the dependability of a rule-based system [27].

To summarize, the rule-based method and the machine learning technique are the two primary ways of constructing chatbots using artificial intelligence. You can also use a blend of both techniques to ensure both dependable performance and an organic conversational experience.

Latest Advances

Thanks to the developments in natural language processing (NLP), machine learning, and artificial intelligence (AI) technologies, chatbots have made significant progress in recent years. Below are some of the most recent developments in chatbot technology:

1. Conversational AI refers to the use of chatbot technology that harnesses natural language processing and machine learning to allow chatbots to engage in conversations akin to those of humans. AI chatbots for conversations have the capability to grasp the context of the discussion, identify emotions, and offer appropriate and beneficial responses [28].
2. Voice-activated chatbots can be interacted with by giving voice commands through popular virtual assistants like Alexa, Siri, or Google Assistant. Chatbots that respond to voice commands utilize voice recognition technology and natural language processing (NLP) to comprehend the input and provide pertinent information in return [29].
3. Chatbots possessing Emotional Intelligence: Chatbots equipped with emotional intelligence possess the capability to identify and react to various emotions. Chatbots utilize machine learning and sentiment analysis to comprehend emotional condition of the user and react accordingly. For instance, a chatbot may give different responses to a user who is irritated versus a user who is happy.

4. Chatbots that have the ability to communicate in numerous languages are called multilingual chatbots. Chatbots utilize natural language processing (NLP) and machine learning to comprehend and reply in varied languages. Companies that have operations in different nations and require customer support services in diverse languages can make good use of chatbots that are designed to operate in multiple languages [30].

To sum up, the most recent developments in chatbot technology consist of conversational AI, voice-activated chatbots, chatbots equipped with emotional intelligence, multilingual chatbots, and chatbots tailored for personalized customer experience. The progressions in chatbot technology have resulted in their increased sophistication, ability to sound more human-like, and effectiveness in delivering customer assistance and other forms of aid.

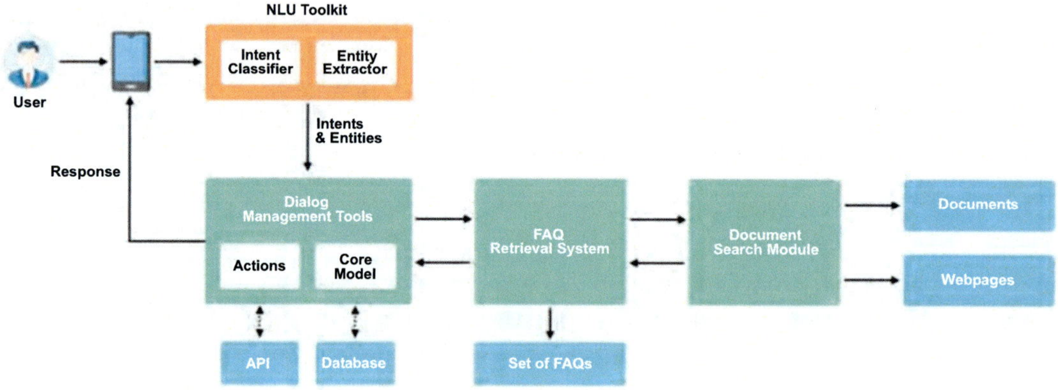

Fig. (2). Chatbot Architecture.

Benefits, Challenges and Applications

The term chatbot refers to a computer system's capacity for learning, reasoning, and decision-making based on data inputs. Chatbot can have many uses and advantages when combined with machine learning, but it also has some drawbacks.

Benefits

Chatbots with machine learning have several benefits when used together. Utilizing a chatbot equipped with machine learning provides a range of advantages, such as:

1. Personalization: Machine learning enables chatbots to study customer information and actions in order to provide personalized responses and more

precise recommendations.
2. Improved Accuracy: Machine learning helps improve the accuracy of chatbots as they are capable of learning from previous conversations and interactions, thereby enhancing their ability to offer more precise responses with time.
3. Increased Efficiency: Through the utilization of machine learning technology, chatbots are able to manage a greater quantity of customer engagements, ultimately leading to improved proficiency and reduced expenses for companies.
4. 24/7 Availability: Chatbots are capable of providing customer support all day, every day, which can help businesses offer assistance beyond their usual hours and increase overall customer satisfaction [31].
5. Multilingual support: With the aid of machine learning, chatbots can be taught various languages to communicate with clients on a global scale, enabling firms to offer multilingual assistance.
6. Scalability: Chatbots are scalable options for companies of any size, as they can effectively manage an extensive number of customer interactions.

In summary, companies can enhance customer experience, increase sales and revenue, and ensure customer satisfaction by utilizing chatbots that employ machine learning technology, thereby enabling personalized and streamlined interactions with customers.

Challenges

As chatbots with machine learning have so many advantages, they pose certain challenges, such as:

1. Data plays a significant role in the learning and performance improvement of chatbots that use machine learning techniques. Inaccurate responses and reduced effectiveness of the chatbot can result from using low-quality data.
2. Chatbots equipped with machine learning have the possibility of developing prejudice depending on the data they undergo training with. Providing flawed or biased responses may have adverse effects on both customer satisfaction and reputation. Regular maintenance and updates are necessary to ensure the proper functioning and accuracy of chatbots powered by machine learning [32].
3. For a smooth user experience, it is essential to integrate chatbots equipped with machine learning with various other systems and platforms. Businesses with intricate IT systems may face difficulties, particularly in this aspect.
4. To comprehend and reply to user inquiries, chatbots using machine learning utilize natural language processing (NLP). It can be challenging to apply NLP, which demands specific abilities and proficiency.
5. Although chatbots equipped with artificial intelligence can manage numerous

customer interactions, certain circumstances may demand human interference. It can be difficult to make the transition from a chatbot to a human representative seamless.

In summary, it is essential to have meticulous planning, consistent upkeep, and expertise in order for businesses to obtain a successful and dependable chatbot with machine learning.

Applications

Chatbots with machine learning can benefit from a variety of applications to increase their functionalities and effectiveness. Here are a few illustrations:

1. Customer Service: Chatbots are capable of offering customer assistance all day and night by managing typical inquiries and guiding customers toward relevant resources as part of customer service.
2. E-commerce: For online businesses, chatbots are useful in suggesting products, tracking orders, and processing payments, resulting in a smooth customer experience.
3. Healthcare: Chatbots can enhance healthcare by aiding in the scheduling of appointments, reminding patients to take their medications, and conducting symptom evaluations that offer patients individualized assistance and greater accessibility to healthcare services.
4. Banking and Finance: In the banking and finance industry, chatbots can be used to help customers manage their accounts, process transactions, and identify fraud, which results in a seamless and secure banking experience [33].
5. Education: The use of chatbots in education can enhance the learning outcomes of students by offering customized assistance with coursework selection, monitoring assignment progress, and preparing for assessments.
6. Human Resource: Chatbots can aid in the processes of employee engagement, onboarding, and performance management within human resources. This can lead to the enhancement of retention rates by offering personnel personalized assistance [34].

In general, chatbots using machine learning can be used in various fields and scenarios. They offer companies a convenient and customized approach to interact with clients and enhance operational effectiveness.

In conclusion, a variety of applications for intelligent computing can be used to enhance the functionality and effectiveness of cloud computing.

CONCLUSION

In conclusion, businesses can gain several advantages through the implementation of chatbots that utilize machine learning. These benefits range from customized customer assistance and higher precision to enhanced productivity, round-the-clock accessibility, multilingual aid, and adaptability. Nonetheless, there are several difficulties associated with them, such as maintaining accurate data, addressing bias, ensuring upkeep, integrating with existing systems, grappling with natural language processing (NLP) issues, and requiring human intervention.

Even though there are obstacles, chatbots that use machine learning have diverse applications across various industries and scenarios, ultimately enabling companies to interact with customers in an economical and effective manner, enhance operational efficiency, and boost earnings. Businesses of any dimension can rely on chatbots equipped with machine learning to deliver a competent and efficient solution by meticulously strategizing and consistently maintaining them.

FUTURE SCOPE AND RECOMMENDATIONS

The future scope of chatbots in relation to machine learning is vast, with many exciting opportunities for innovation and growth. Here are some potential areas of focus for the future:

1. Increased Personalization: As chatbots become more advanced in their machine learning capabilities, they will enhance their ability to analyze customer data and behavior and offer even more personalized responses and suggestions.
2. Emotion Detection: Machine learning-powered chatbots have the potential to detect and address a customer's emotions, thereby offering empathetic and customized assistance.
3. Voice Recognition: Chatbots equipped with machine learning technology may have the capability to identify and react to spoken instructions, resulting in a user-friendly and instinctive interaction.
4. Augmented Reality: To enhance customers' experience, augmented reality technology can collaborate with chatbots and machine learning to offer an immersive and interactive experience.
5. Autonomous Decision Making: Chatbots armed with machine learning can potentially make more intricate judgments and execute autonomous directives, thereby decreasing the requirement for human interference in the decision-making process.
6. Integration with IoT: It is possible to incorporate chatbots featuring machine learning into IoT gadgets, which would allow them to offer responses that are more contextual and individualized.

In general, businesses have great potential to benefit from chatbots incorporating machine learning, making the future scope of this technology very promising. In the future years, we can anticipate witnessing more inventive and complex uses of technology as it progresses further.

RECOMMENDATIONS

The following are some recommendations for maintaining chatbots with ML:

1. Determine your business goal: Establish your objectives for your enterprise: Clearly state the particular business objectives that the chatbot utilizing machine learning will uphold. Identifying the features and capabilities that are essential for your chatbot can be achieved through this technique.
2. Choose the right platform: Select an appropriate chatbot platform that is user-friendly, has the ability to expand, and can be tailored to fit your specific business requirements. Ensure that the platform is capable of accommodating machine learning functionalities.
3. Ensure High-quality data: To enable efficient machine learning, it is imperative to make certain that the data used is of high caliber. Make sure your data is precise, applicable, and current.
4. Monitor and Optimize Performance: Regularly check and enhance performance. Consistently keep track of your chatbot's performance and make use of analytics to recognize any potential areas that need improvement. To improve the efficiency of your chatbot, it is essential to regularly update and refine its algorithms.
5. Address privacy and security concerns: When creating your chatbot, it is important to consider privacy and security issues and ensure that they are addressed in the design. Make certain that the chatbot aligns with pertinent data protection regulations and that all user data is securely stored.

Make sure the chatbot offers a smooth and easy-to-use interface for users to have a seamless experience. Enhance the chatbot's human-like qualities and increase its appeal by applying conversational design strategies and natural language processing techniques.

REFERENCES

[1] F. Aslam, "The Impact of Artificial Intelligence on Chatbot Technology: A Study on the Current Advancements and Leading Innovations", *European Journal of Technology,* vol. 7, no. 3, pp. 62-72, 2023.
[http://dx.doi.org/10.47672/ejt.1561]

[2] A. Følstad, T. Araujo, E.L.C. Law, P.B. Brandtzaeg, S. Papadopoulos, L. Reis, M. Baez, G. Laban, P. McAllister, C. Ischen, R. Wald, F. Catania, R. Meyer von Wolff, S. Hobert, and E. Luger, "Future directions for chatbot research: an interdisciplinary research agenda", *Computing,* vol. 103, no. 12, pp.

2915-2942, 2021.
[http://dx.doi.org/10.1007/s00607-021-01016-7]

[3] P. Kumar, M. Sharma, S. Rawat, and T. Choudhury, "Designing and Developing a Chatbot Using Machine Learning", *2018 International Conference on System Modeling & Advancement in Research Trends (SMART),* 2018, pp. 87-91 Moradabad, India
[http://dx.doi.org/10.1109/SYSMART.2018.8746972]

[4] G. Sebastian, "Privacy and Data Protection in ChatGPT and Other AI Chatbots", *International Journal of Security and Privacy in Pervasive Computing,* vol. 15, no. 1, pp. 1-14, 2023.
[http://dx.doi.org/10.4018/IJSPPC.325475]

[5] N. Sindhwani, "Thingspeak-based environmental monitoring system using IoT", *2022 Seventh International Conference on Parallel, Distributed and Grid Computing (PDGC),* 2022.
[http://dx.doi.org/10.1109/PDGC56933.2022.10053167]

[6] G. Caldarini, S. Jaf, and K. McGarry, "A Literature Survey of Recent Advances in Chatbots", *Information (Basel),* vol. 13, no. 1, p. 41, 2022.
[http://dx.doi.org/10.3390/info13010041]

[7] A. Shakarami, M. Ghobaei-Arani, and A. Shahidinejad, "A survey on the computation offloading approaches in mobile edge computing: A machine learning-based perspective", *Computer Networks,* vol. 182, pp. 1389-1286, 2020.

[8] S. Meshram, and N. Naik, "M. VR, T. More and S. Kharche, “Conversational AI: Chatbots", *2021 International Conference on Intelligent Technologies (CONIT),* 2021, pp. 1-6 Hubli, India.
[http://dx.doi.org/10.1109/CONIT51480.2021.9498508]

[9] S.A. Abdul-Kader, and J. Woods, "“Survey on Chatbot Design Techniques in Speech Conversation Systems”, (IJACSA)", *Int. J. Adv. Comput. Sci. Appl.,* vol. 6, no. 7, 2015.

[10] A. Heryandi, "Developing Chatbot for Academic Record Monitoring in Higher Education Institution", *IOP Conference Series Materials Science and Engineering,* 2020.
[http://dx.doi.org/10.1088/1757-899X/879/1/012049]

[11] M. Choque-Díaz, J. Armas-Aguirre, and P. Shiguihara-Juárez, "Cognitive technology model to enhanced academic support services with chatbots", *2018 IEEE XXV International Conference on Electronics Electrical Engineering and Computing (INTERCON),* 2018 pp. 1-4.
[http://dx.doi.org/10.1109/INTERCON.2018.8526411]

[12] C. Chun Ho, H.L. Lee, W.K. Lo, and K.F.A. Lui, "Developing a Chatbot for College Student Programme Advisement", *2018 International Symposium on Educational Technology (ISET),* pp. 52-56, 2018.
[http://dx.doi.org/10.1109/ISET.2018.00021]

[13] S. Jain, "COVID Detection Using Chest X-Ray and Transfer Learning", *International Conference on Intelligent Systems Design and Applications,* 2021.

[14] M. Polignano, F. Narducci, A. Iovine, C. Musto, M. De Gemmis, and G. Semeraro, "Health Assistant Bot: A Personal Health Assistant for the Italian Language", *IEEE Access,* vol. 8, pp. 107479-107497, 2020.
[http://dx.doi.org/10.1109/ACCESS.2020.3000815]

[15] X. Ren, G. Spina, S. De Vries, A. Bijkerk, B. Faber, and A. Geraedts, "Understanding Physician’s Experience With Conversational Interfaces During Occupational Health Consultation", *IEEE Access,* vol. 8, pp. 119158-119169, 2020.
[http://dx.doi.org/10.1109/ACCESS.2020.3005733]

[16] M. Dharani, J.V.S.L. Jyostna, E. Sucharitha, R. Likitha, and S. Manne, "Interactive Transport Enquiry with AI Chatbot", *2020 4th International Conference on Intelligent Computing and Control Systems (ICICCS),* pp. 1271-1276, 2020.
[http://dx.doi.org/10.1109/ICICCS48265.2020.9120905]

[17] P.R. Telang, A.K. Kalia, M. Vukovic, R. Pandita, and M.P. Singh, "A Conceptual Framework for Engineering Chatbots", *IEEE Internet Comput.*, vol. 22, no. 6, pp. 54-59, 2018. [http://dx.doi.org/10.1109/MIC.2018.2877827]

[18] M. Bates, "Health Care Chatbots Are Here to Help", *IEEE Pulse,* vol. 10, no. 3, pp. 12-14, 2019. [http://dx.doi.org/10.1109/MPULS.2019.2911816] [PMID: 31135345]

[19] N. Jain, "Applications of Wearable devices in IoT", *2021 9th International Conference on Reliability, Infocom Technologies and Optimization (Trends and Future Directions) (ICRITO),* pp. 1-4, 2021. [http://dx.doi.org/10.1109/ICRITO51393.2021.9596404]

[20] V. Oguntosin and A. Olomo, "Development of an E-Commerce Chatbot for a University Shopping Mall", *Appl. Comput. Intell. Soft Comput.,* p. 14, 2021.

[21] A. Freed, *Conversational AI: Chatbots that Work.* Manning: United Kingdom, 2021.

[22] A. Singh, *Building an Enterprise Chatbot: Work with Protected Enterprise Data Using Open Source Frameworks.* Apress: Germany, 2019. [http://dx.doi.org/10.1007/978-1-4842-5034-1]

[23] N.K. Manaswi, *Deep Learning with Applications Using Python: Chatbots and Face, Object, and Speech Recognition With TensorFlow and Keras.* Apress: Germany, 2018. [http://dx.doi.org/10.1007/978-1-4842-3516-4]

[24] N.K. Manaswi, *Deep Learning with Applications Using Python: Chatbots and Face, Object, and Speech Recognition With TensorFlow and Keras.* Apress: Germany, 2018. [http://dx.doi.org/10.1007/978-1-4842-3516-4]

[25] S. Saha, and B. Mazumdar, "Towards Resolving Privacy and Security Issues in IoT-Based Cloud Computing Platforms for Smart City Applications", *Integration of IoT with Cloud Computing for Smart Applications. Chapman and Hall/CRC 53-80.* [http://dx.doi.org/10.1201/9781003319238-4]

[26] J. Kaur, Implementation of IoT in various domains. *IoT Based Smart Applications.* Springer International Publishing: Cham, 2022, pp. 165-178.

[27] A. Tripathi, Role of IoT in Smart Homes and Smart Cities: Challenges, Benefits, and Applications.*IoT Based Smart Applications.* Springer International Publishing: Cham, 2022, pp. 199-217.

[28] L. Gong, "CA (US) United States US 2003.01671.67A1 (12) Patent Application Publication c (10) Pub. No.: US 2003/0167167 A1 Gong (43)", *Intelligent Virtual Assistant,* 2003.

[29] H. Chung, M. Iorga, J. Voas, and S. Lee, "Alexa, can I trust you?", *2017 IEEE Computer Security,* 2017

[30] A. M. Weeratunga, S. A. U. Jayawardana, P. M. A. K. Hasindu, W. P. M. Prashan and S. Thelijjagoda, "Project Nethra - an intelligent assistant for the visually disabled to interact with internet services," *2015 IEEE 10th International Conference on Industrial and Information Systems (ICIIS)*, Peradeniya, Sri Lanka, 2015, pp. 55-59

[31] I. Nunes, Ed., *AHFE 2017. AISC.* vol. Vol. 592. Springer: Cham, 2018, pp. 241-250. [http://dx.doi.org/10.1007/978-3-319-60366-7_23]

[32] A. Purington, J.G. Taft, S. Sannon, N.N. Bazarova, and S.H. Taylor, "Alexa is my new BFF: social roles, user satisfaction, and personification of the amazon echo", *ACM,* 2017. ISBN 978-1-4503-4-56-6/17/05 [http://dx.doi.org/10.1145/3027063.3053246]

[33] G. López, L. Quesada, L. A. Guerrero,, "Alexa vs Siri vs Cortana vs Google assistant: a comparison of speech-based natural user interfaces", *Conference Paper,* 2018.

[34] Kepuska, V., Bohouta, G., "Next generation of virtual personal assistants (Microsoft Cortana, Apple Siri, Amazon Alexa and Google Home)", *In: IEEE Conference,* 2018.

CHAPTER 3

Stock Price Prediction: A Gateway to a Prosperous Future Using Data Science and Machine Learning

Pankaj Singh[1], **Sonia Deshmukh**[1] and **Rohit Vashisht**[1,*]

[1] *KIET group of Institutions, Uttar pradesh, India*

Abstract: Predictive analysis is a powerful tool for predicting future trends and events, and it can be useful for predicting stock prices as well. In this paper, predictive analysis for stock price prediction is done using machine learning algorithms. Predictive analysis is a kind of analytics in which we use archival data equipped with statistical models and machine learning algorithms to predict future outcomes, and it is effectively used here for stock price prediction. The intended outcome of stock forecasting is to make more briefed and calculated investment decisions. We have used a stock price prediction system that blends mathematical equations, predictive analytics, and contextual factors to enhance the accuracy of stock price predictions and generate profitable trades. For experimentation, a real-life dataset of ICICI bank is used, and the results show that our model is able to forecast future stock prices with high accuracy.

Keywords: Data science, Decision tree regression, Machine learning, Predictive analytics, Random forest regression, Regression, Support vector regression, Simple linear regression.

INTRODUCTION

Predictive analysis can be a useful tool for predicting stock prices. There are various techniques and models that can be used for this purpose. However, it is important to bear in mind that stock prices are influenced by a multitude of factors, including market trends, economic indicators, company performance, and even geopolitical events. Therefore, while predictive analysis can provide insights and help identify potential opportunities, it is not a guarantee of success.

There are different approaches to predictive analysis for stock price prediction, incorporating both technical and fundamental analysis. Technical analysis is the

* **Corresponding author Rohit Vashisht:** KIET group of Institutions, Uttar pradesh, India;
E-mail: rohitvashisht794@gmail.com

Vikash Yadav, Vimal Kumar, Sonam Gupta & Vandana Dixit Kaushik (Eds.)

process of examination of previous stock price charts and patterns in order to spot trends and projections of future price fluctuations. Fundamental analysis examines a company's financial performance and other factors, such as industry trends and competitive landscape, to determine the intrinsic value of the stock and make predictions about its future price.

A collection of recent research works on machine learning in investments includes ”Neural Networks for Portfolio Analysis With Cardinality Constraints [16]”, which focuses on optimizing portfolio allocation under constraints, enhancing diversification and risk management [16]. In ”Neural Networks for Portfolio Analysis in High-Frequency Trading [18]”, the effectiveness of neural networks in identifying optimal trading strategies in dynamic markets is explored, thereby improving portfolio performance [18]. ”A Novel Recurrent Neural Network Based Online Portfolio Analysis for High-Frequency Trading [15]” introduces a dynamic approach to portfolio analysis, leveraging recurrent neural networks to adapt to real-time market dynamics [15]. “Using Quadratic Interpolated Beetle Antennae Search for Higher Dimensional Portfolio Selection [19]” integrates nature-inspired optimization with machine learning for robust portfolio selection in complex landscapes [19]. Finally, ”A Novel Dynamic Neural System for Nonconvex Portfolio Optimization with Cardinality Restrictions [17]” develops a flexible system for optimizing portfolios under constraints, enhancing investment decision-making. These works collectively contribute to advancing machine learning applications in investment, offering insights into portfolio management, trading strategies, fraud detection, and optimization [17]. There are also various other tools and techniques used in predictive analysis, such as time series analysis, regression analysis, artificial intelligence, and machine learning. These methods can aid in the discovery of patterns and correlations in data that can be used to forecast future stock price movements.

Overall, predictive analysis can be a valuable resource for stock price prediction, but it is important to approach it with caution and keep in mind that many factors can influence stock prices. It is also important to have a solid understanding of the underlying data and analysis techniques, as well as the risks involved in investing in the stock market.

We propose to create a system for predicting stock prices that uses a combination of mathematical functions, predictive analysis, and other factors. The goal of this system is to boost stock price forecast accuracy and support traders in making lucrative transactions.

In our work, we examine various methods and models that are used to predict stock prices. We will begin by discussing the importance of stock price forecasting and the various factors that can affect stock prices. We then examine the most commonly used methods for predicting stock prices, including time series analysis, technical analysis, fundamental analysis, and machine learning. We also explore the most common algorithms used in machine learning for stock price prediction, such as ARIMA, GARCH, and LSTM [1]. We examine the performance of these methods and algorithms and evaluate their strengths and weaknesses. Finally, we discuss the future of stock price forecasting and the potential for future research. This research paper strives to give a thorough review of the current state of stock prices and to identify the most effective methods and algorithms for this task. By understanding the pros and cons of different techniques, investors and traders can make more informed decisions about investing in the stock market.

The paper is organized as follows: a description of the various techniques and models that can be used for predicting stock prices is described in Section 2. Section 3 discusses the proposed system. The fourth portion discusses the experimentation and results. Sections 5 and 6 describe the analysis and conclusion.

DATA SCIENCE AND MACHINE LEARNING: AN OVERVIEW

Predicting stock prices is an important task in finance as it can provide valuable insights to investors and traders. The ability to predict stock prices helps individuals make informed decisions about buying, selling, or holding particular stocks. In recent years, the advent of big data and advances in artificial intelligence and machine learning has greatly improved the accuracy of stock price prediction models. Various techniques and models can be used for predicting stock prices, including:

Time Series Analysis: This strategy entails looking at past pricing and volume data to find patterns and trends. Future price predictions can be made using strategies including moving averages, exponential softening, and ARIMA (autoregressive integrated moving average) models.

Machine Learning Models: To predict future prices, a variety of machine learning methods, including decision trees, neural networks, and support vector machines (SVM), can be trained on past data. These models can take into account a wide range of factors, such as market sentiment, news events, and economic indicators, to make predictions.

Sentiment Analysis: This approach involves analyzing social media and news data to gauge market sentiment and identify trends. Natural Language Processing (NLP) techniques can be used to analyze text data, and sentiment analysis algorithms can be used to predict how the market will react to news events.

Machine learning and data science are closely related fields, and their techniques and methods often overlap.

Data Science

Data Science is an area of research where information and insights are extracted from systematic and unsystematic data. It is used to analyze and interpret complex data using statistical, mathematical, and computer science techniques to make predictions, recognize patterns, and gain insights.

The process of data science involves several steps, such as data cleaning, data collection, data pre-processing, data visualization, and data analysis. It also involves the use of various tools and technologies such as programming languages like Python and R, statistical analysis software like SPSS and SAS, and big data technologies. Data science is applicable in different fields, such as machine learning, natural language processing, predictive analytics, and deep learning. Data Science is used in a variety of industries, such as healthcare, finance, marketing, and e-commerce, to make data-driven decisions and improve business outcomes [2].

Machine Learning

The primary goal of machine learning is to create models and algorithms that allow computers to learn and make predictions or judgments without being explicitly programmed. These algorithms recognize patterns and relationships in large sets of training data to learn from them and get better over time [3]. Machine learning and data science are closely related fields, and their techniques and methods often overlap. Data science is a broad field that covers many aspects of working with data, such as data collection, cleansing, exploration, and visualization [4]. Machine learning, on the other hand, is a specialized subfield of data science that focuses on building models and algorithms that can learn from them to make predictions and decisions without explicit instruction. In practice, data scientists often use machine learning techniques as part of their work to create models that can predict and discover patterns in large data sets. We also use other techniques, such as statistical analysis, data visualization, and database management. In short, machine learning is a subset of data science used to train models to make predictions and automate decision-making. Data science is broader and includes machine learning and other data-related tasks such as collecting, cleaning, and visualizing data.

Data science and machine learning can be useful for stock price prediction in several ways:

Data Acquisition

Data scientists can collect and clean large amounts of historical stock market data. B. Financial reports, news articles, and social media sentiment can be used to train machine learning models.

Feature Engineering

Data scientists can find the most important aspects affecting stock prices and develop new features that can be utilized as inputs to machine learning models by using methods like feature selection and dimensionality reduction.

Model Building

By using clean and pre-processed data, we can train machine learning algorithms like regression, decision trees, and neural networks to develop models that can make predictions about future stock prices.

Evaluation

Data scientists can use techniques such as cross-validation and back-testing to evaluate model performance and refine it for greater accuracy.

Deployment

Once your model is trained and tested, you can deploy it to production to predict new unseen data. In short, data science techniques are used to collect, cleanse, and prepare data, while machine learning algorithms are used to train models that can predict new, unseen data. These forecasts are useful for stock price forecasting and other financial forecasting tasks. However, forecasting stock prices is a difficult process affected by a wide range of variables, and it is difficult to anticipate a stock price with a high degree of precision.

Regression

Regression analysis is a statistical method that can be utilized to predict stock prices. It involves analyzing the correlation between stock prices and other factors. This approach is commonly used for long-term predictions and can provide useful information about the stock's future performance. Regression analysis is a useful tool for modeling complex relationships because it can take multiple variables into consideration, which is one benefit of using it to predict stock prices. To build a trustworthy model, though, a large quantity of historical data is also necessary, and predictions for the near future might be less precise. The correlation between historical stock data and other pertinent variables, such as economic indicators or company-specific data, is identified and examined by the regression model in order to determine how well it performs.

Cross-validation

A machine learning method called cross-validation is used to evaluate a model's efficacy. It entails dividing the information into several pieces, using one for training and the others for testing. To make sure the model is accurate and reliable, this procedure is repeated many times. Cross-validation aids in selecting the most appropriate model parameters, features, and methods for stock price prediction. Additionally, it can spot issues with the model's over- or under-fitting. Cross-validation ultimately makes sure that the algorithm produces precise predictions for fresh data.

PROPOSED SYSTEM

A stock market forecast is an effort to predict the value of a company's stock or other exchange-traded financial instruments in the future. This paper provides stock quotes for the company based on history and helps interested parties to invest in their shares or acquire shares from the company. Time series forecasting is a widely used concept in many everyday implementations, such as climate forecasting and financial market forecasting [5]. Regression analysis is a common technique used for forecasting. Use continuous data over a period of time to predict the next unit time result. Many time series forecasting algorithms have proven their effectiveness in practice. Only the opening price is considered for processing.

Input Data

First we select any real-life dataset and extract the information about the dataset.

Pre-processing

Pre-processing means cleaning and visualizing the dataset. The unnecessary columns are removed from the dataset using the command drop, and then the dataset is visualized using the matplotlib.pyplot library in Python.

Algorithm Selection

Various algorithms like LR, SVR, DTR, and RFR are applied using Sklearn Modulo.

Evaluation

Exactness of each model is computed, and then the most appropriate accuracy model for the prediction of the stock price is chosen.

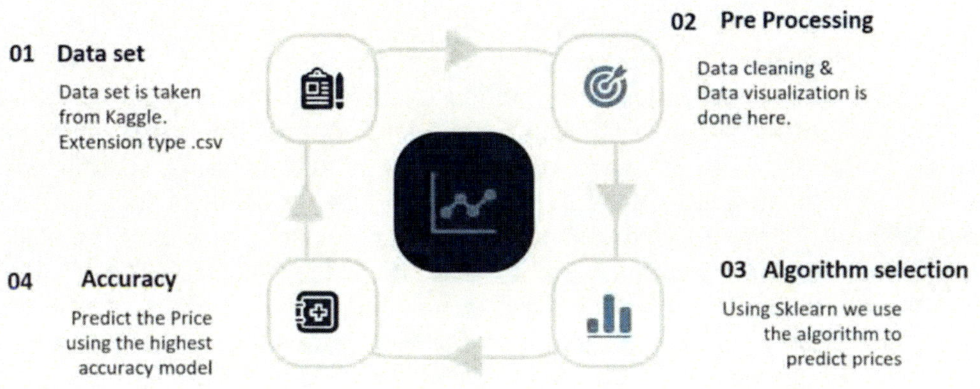

Fig. (1). Flowchart for stock price prediction.

Steps involved in stock price prediction are explained as follows (Fig. **1**):

Input Data

There are numerous sources of information that can be used to forecast stock prices. Online financial news sources like Yahoo Finance, CNBC, and Bloomberg provide up-to-the-minute information and professional commentary. Historical statistics can be found on stock exchanges like the NYSE, LSE, and NASDAQ. Real-time and archived statistics are available from financial data providers like FactSet, Reuters, and Morningstar. Twitter and Facebook are two examples of social media sites that can shed light on market opinion. Government websites provide economic statistics, while business websites provide financial reports and earnings announcements. To make precise predictions, careful analysis and the use of numerous sources are crucial. In our particular scenario, we used data from Kaggle.com. We can use the pandas module in Python to read the data.

Pre-processing and Data Visualization

To guarantee the quality and relevance of the data, it must be pre-processed before using machine learning techniques to forecast stock prices. As part of this process, the data must be cleaned to remove any errors or missing values, pertinent features must be chosen, the data must be scaled and transformed, and the dataset must be divided into training and test sets. The optimal machine learning model for predicting stock prices can be found by comparing the models using cross-validation methods. To guarantee the precision of the machine learning models, pre-processing the data is a crucial step. For our dataset, we will delete the unnecessary columns present in our dataset, such as the symbol of stock, series, turnover, and other irrelevant columns. We can use the drop function in Python to do that.

Data visualization techniques are applied to show and analyze the data in stock price prediction. To show patterns, trends, and connections in the data, various charts, including candlestick charts, line charts, scatter plots, histograms, box plots, and heat maps are used. These graphs can be used to spot outliers, the distribution of variables, and other characteristics of the data. They can also show correlations between various variables and stock values. Data visualization is a useful instrument for predicting stock prices because it enables stakeholders to comprehend the conclusions drawn from the analysis in an easy-to-understand manner. For our case, we will use scatter charts to understand our data. An example of scatter charts, which we can get using a seaborn module in Python, is given below (Fig. **2**).

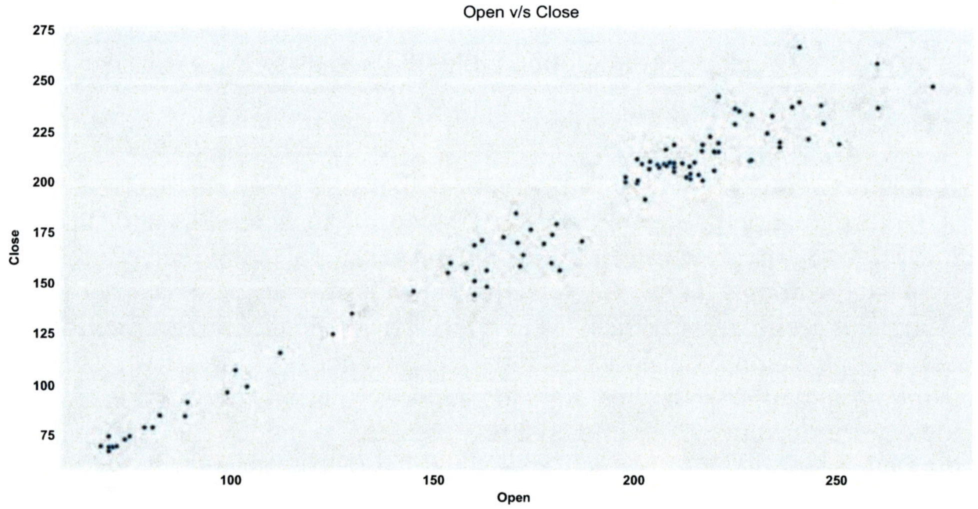

Fig. (2). Scatter Plot.

A scatter plot is used to show the relationship between two variables. They are frequently used to find relationships between financial indicators and company prices in stock price prediction. Scatter plots are essential to see the characteristics of our data and what patterns our stock is following for making the prediction. The histograms for ICICI bank stock (open and close) are shown in Fig. (**3**).

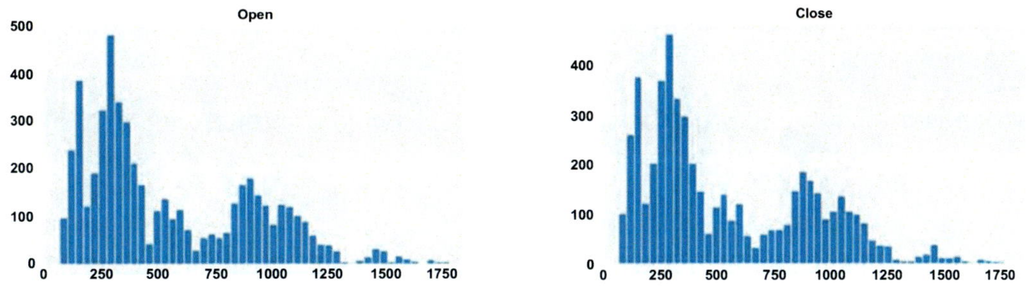

Fig. (3). Histograms for ICICI bank.

Algorithm Selection and Evaluation

Choosing and assessing algorithms for stock price prediction is a significant process that can significantly affect the precision of predictions. Moving averages, exponential smoothing, regression analysis, and neural networks are some of the widely used algorithms. When choosing an algorithm, it is crucial to account for the specific characteristics of the stock or market and historical data. Some algorithms may perform better for particular stocks or markets, and others may be more effective for forecasting short or long-term trends. After selecting an algorithm, it is vital to evaluate its accuracy using metrics such as mean squared error, root mean squared error, and mean absolute error to compare different algorithms. Besides, the overall performance of the prediction model should be considered, which may require the integration of various techniques to improve accuracy. Therefore, selecting the appropriate algorithms and effectively evaluating their performance is crucial in generating reliable and precise predictions that can guide investment decisions.

EXPERIMENTATION AND RESULTS

In this paper, we first build a model using different machine learning regression algorithms for experimentation, namely, SLR, SVR, DTR, and RFR. These algorithms are used to predict stock prices using historical data. We visualized the actual and predicted closing price of the stock for each model and tried to find the best possible model out of those.

Jupyter Notebook and Python are used for experimentation. Jupyter Notebook is a freely available web-based tool that allows users to generate and disseminate documents containing executable code, mathematical equations, graphical representations, and explanatory prose [6]. This tool has various applications, such as data cleaning, statistical and numerical modeling, data visualization, machine learning, and more. When it comes to predicting stock prices, the Jupyter Notebook can be utilized for analyzing data, creating visualizations that assist in comprehending the behavior of stock prices, and developing and training machine learning models.

Python is both a strongly typed and dynamically typed programming language. It is utilized to apply a range of models to the dataset with the assistance of the SKLEARN module. In the context of stock price prediction, Python can be beneficial in numerous ways. For instance, it can be used to process and clean stock market data, develop machine learning models for predicting stock prices, and create visualizations that help in understanding the trends and patterns in stock prices. The Pandas library is used to read the .csv file, matplotlib is used to visualize the data, and other libraries are used to clean and represent the dataset.

Simple Linear Regression

Simple linear regression is a statistical method used to examine the relationship between two variables. It involves plotting the data points on a graph and drawing a straight line that best fits the data (represented by y = b0 + b1*x). The line represents the relationship between the two variables, with one variable acting as the predictor or independent variable while the other serves as the response or dependent variable. The objective of this analysis is to understand how changes in the predictor variable affect the response variable. In essence, simple linear regression helps us to make predictions about future outcomes based on the observed relationship between the two variables.

Simple linear regression can be used for a variety of tasks like predicting future values, understanding relationships between variables, and identifying outliers. However, this method makes several assumptions, such as linearity, independence, and equal variances between predictor and outcome variables. We first split the data set into train test split in sklearn.model selection module in Python. Then, using plt.show(), we create a graph that will compare the predicted values and actual values for our dataset (Fig. **4**). Finally, we use the r2 score in sklearn.metrics to get the accuracy of the model for our dataset.

Support Vector Regression

Support vector regression (SVR) is a type of statistical algorithm that is used for regression tasks. It tries to find the best-fit line (for linear regression) or hyperplane (for nonlinear regression) that maximizes the margin between the data points and the line/hyperplane. Margin is the distance between the line/hyperplane and the closest data point, also known as the support vector [7].

The main difference between SVR and other linear regression models is that SVR allows the introduction of a "slack variable". One way to improve the model's resilience to outliers is by establishing specific bounds that some of the data points must fall within. This helps to mitigate the impact of potential outliers, making the model more robust.

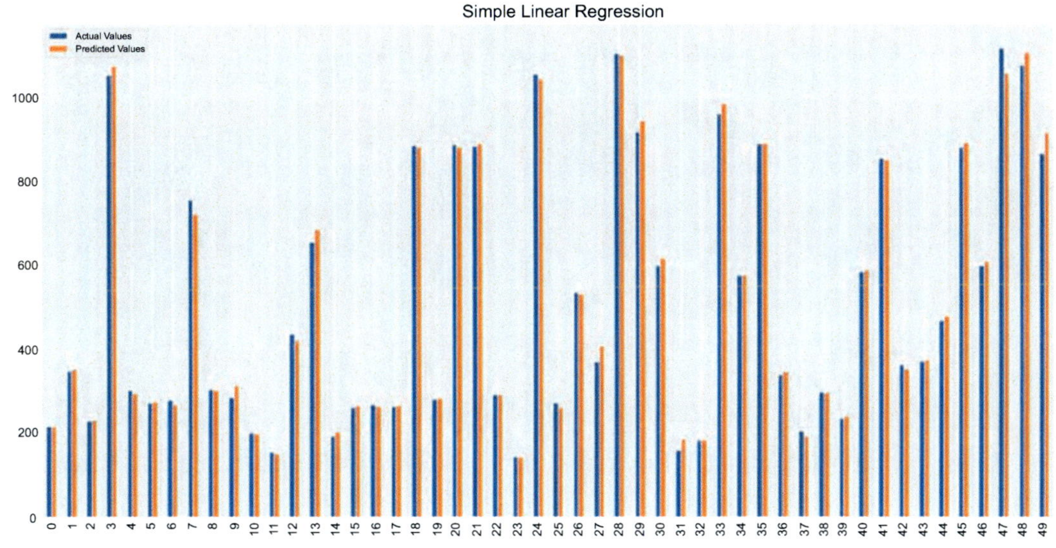

Fig. (4). Simple Linear Regression.

SVR is often used in applications with a significant amount of input variables, noisy data, or complex dependencies between input and output variables. However, the parameters should be carefully tuned as they can be sensitive to kernel choice and parameter values.

In summary, SVR is a regression algorithm based on the support vector machine principle, which aims to find the best hyperplane separating the data while maximizing the length between the data coordinates and the hyperplane. This is a robust method that can handle non-linearities and outliers but can be sensitive to the kernel and parameter choices. For our dataset, we implement the SVR using the SVR() function in the sklearn.svm module in Python [8 - 12]. Then, using plt.show(), we get the graph, as shown in Fig. (**5**).

Decision Tree Regression

Decision tree regression is a technique that involves using a decision tree to forecast a continuous target variable. A decision tree is a model that represents decisions and their outcomes in a tree-like structure. Each node within the tree represents a test of a particular attribute, and each branch represents the outcome of that test. Finally, each leaf node represents either a class label or a value [13].

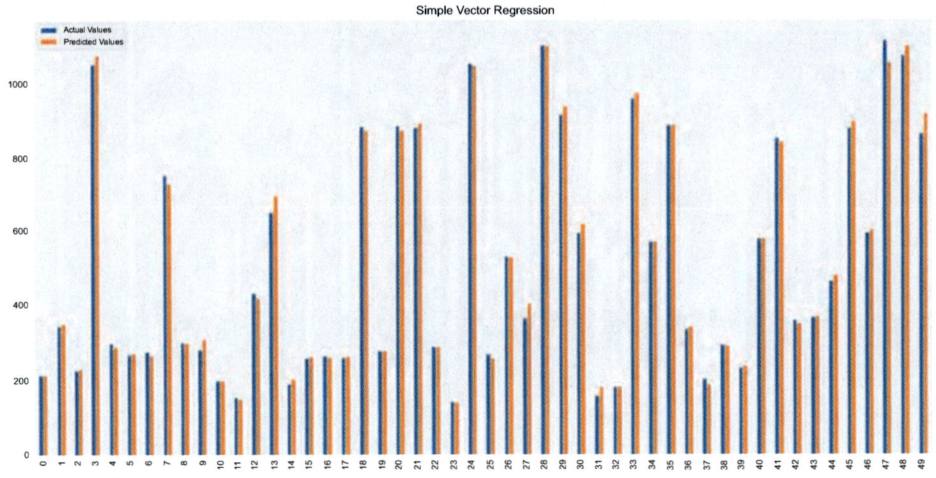

Fig. (5). Support Vector Regression.

Decision tree algorithms use metrics such as MSE (Mean Squared Error) to determine the optimal cut point for each feature. DTR is useful for tasks such as predicting future values, understanding relationships between variables, and identifying important features. However, it is important to note that decision trees are prone to overfitting, especially when the tree gets too deep. To avoid this problem, it is important to use techniques such as pruning. For our dataset, we use DecisionTreeRegressor() from the sklearn.tree module to implement the DTR (Fig. **6**).

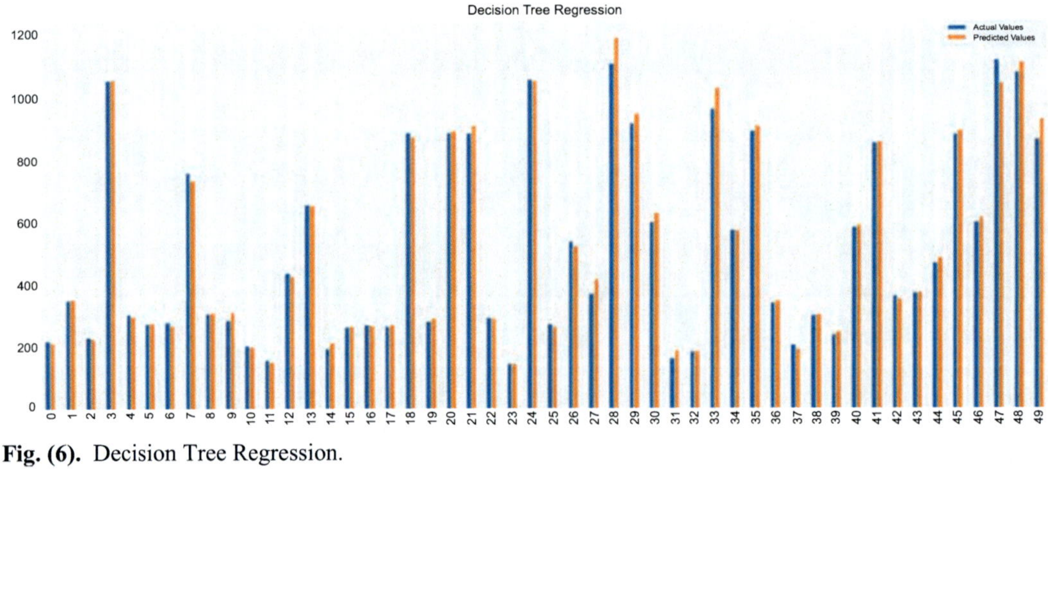

Fig. (6). Decision Tree Regression.

Random Tree Regression

Random forest regression is a statistical technique that involves combining multiple decision trees to generate predictions. This method is used in both classification and regression tasks and works by training many decision trees on different subsets of the training data. The final prediction is then made by averaging the predictions of all the individual trees [14]. All the trees in the random forests are grown on a random subset of training data and a random section of features. This process, called bootstrap aggregation or bagging, helps to decorrelate the trees, making the ensemble more robust. random forest regression models are useful for tasks such as predicting future values, understanding relationships between variables, and identifying important features. It is also a robust method of handling over-fitting, less prone to overfitting than decision tree regression, and can handle categorical variables. For our dataset, we will use RandomForestRegressor() in the sklearn.ensemble module to implement RFR, and then by using plt.show(), the graph is plotted (Fig. 7).

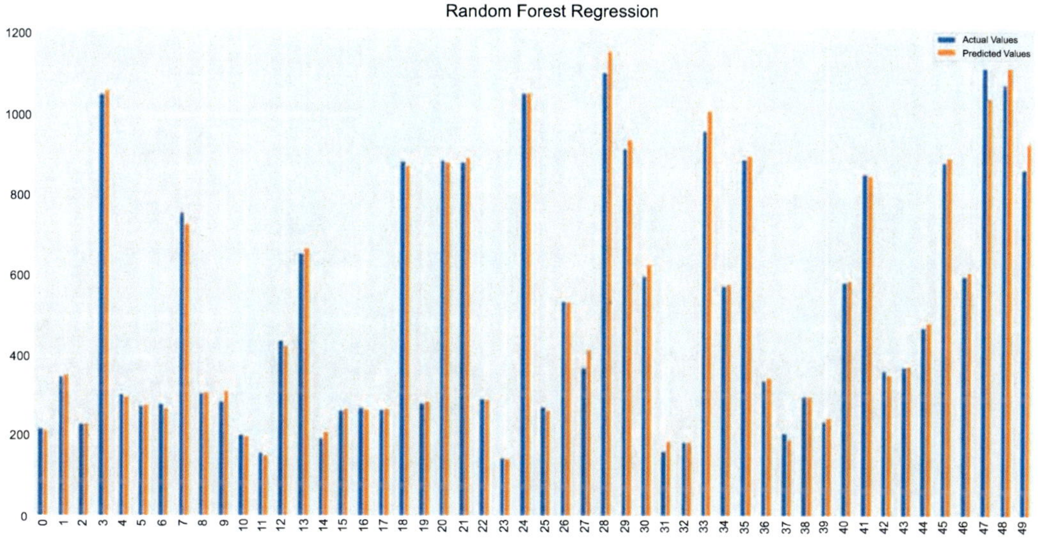

Fig. (7). Random Tree Regression.

ANALYSIS

For our stock price prediction, we use the ICICI bank stock dataset from Kaggle. We first find the predicted values and actual values for our dataset. After finding these values, model accuracies for the stock are calculated. The accuracies of all the compared algorithms are listed in Table **1**.

Table 1. Accuracy of the predicted model using different algorithms.

Algorithm	Accuracy
Simple Linear Regression.	0.998275
Support Vector Regression.	0.978254
Decision Tree Regression.	0.997234
Random Forest Regression.	0.997757

For the real-life dataset of ICICI bank, the simple linear regression model was found to be the most accurate model for predicting the ICICI bank stock price on 11 May 2022 (Fig. **8**). This result demonstrates that linear regression can be a powerful tool for stock price prediction, especially for simple datasets with a clear linear relationship between the independent and dependent variables. On May 11, 2022, the ICICI bank stock opened at 718.00. Based on the stock price prediction using the SLR algorithm, a price of 717.346 was predicted (Table **2**).

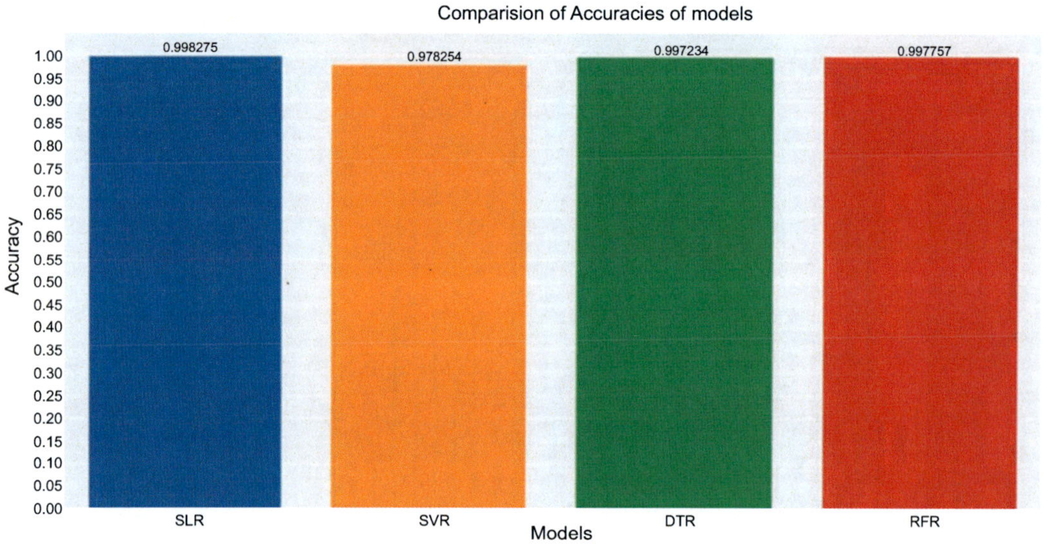

Fig. (8). Accuracy of Models.

Table 2. Predicted Values of Stocks.

S. No	Name of the Stock	Date	Open	Predicted
1.	ICICI Bank Ltd.	11-May-22	718.000000	717.346475
2.	State Bank of India.	11-May-22	475.250000	474.206118
3.	HDFC Bank Ltd.	11-May-22	1353.000000	1351.998546
4.	AXIS Bank.	11-May-22	661.700000	660.265720

This is a remarkable result as it indicates that the model was able to accurately predict the stock price within a small margin of error. It is important to note that while linear regression can be effective in some cases, it may not be the best model for every dataset [15-18]. Other models may perform better, depending on the specific characteristics of the dataset being analyzed. Similarly, we tried this method for various other stocks like SBIN, HDFC bank, Axis Bank, and others stocks and found our model to be accurate, as shown in Table **2**. The Sklearn module in Python made it a lot easier for us to apply machine learning algorithms (Regression models) to apply directly to our datasets. The success of this specific prediction serves as further evidence of how machine learning techniques can help us better comprehend complex financial systems and improve financial decision-making [19].

CONCLUSION AND FUTURE WORK

Stock price prediction is an intricate task that is affected by a wide range of factors, including economic indicators, company efficiency, and market sentiment. Several methods can be used for stock price prediction, including statistical techniques, fundamental analysis, and technical analysis. Machine learning techniques, such as SLR, SVR, DTR, and random RFR, can be used for stock price prediction. Using multiple machine learning algorithms for stock price prediction can provide several benefits. Firstly, it can improve the accuracy of the prediction by combining the strengths of different models. Secondly, it can increase the robustness of the prediction model by reducing the impact of errors or anomalies in individual algorithms. Thirdly, it can provide a better understanding of the data and underlying relationships, allowing for more informed decision-making. Fourthly, it can allow for greater adaptability to changing market conditions or unexpected events. Finally, it enables comparative analysis, allowing analysts to evaluate the performance of different models and choose the most suitable one for a given situation. These methods can learn from historical data and make predictions about future prices. However, it is important to note that stock price prediction is a challenging task, and no single method can guarantee accurate predictions all the time.

Data science is also a great tool for stock price prediction; it can be used to collect, clean, and prepare data, and machine learning algorithms can be applied to make predictions. However, it is important to keep in mind that stock price prediction is a complex task that is affected by a wide range of factors, and it is not easy to predict the exact stock price with high accuracy.

In conclusion, stock price prediction is a challenging task that requires a combination of various methods and techniques. While machine learning and data science can be useful tools, it is important to keep in mind that no single method can guarantee accurate predictions all the time. It is always better to use a combination of various approaches and to be cautious when interpreting the results.

In the future, we will extend our work for predicting cryptocurrency market trading, add sentiment analysis for better analysis, and introduce other models for predicting.

REFERENCES

[1] A. A. Ariyo, A. O. Adewumi, and C. K. Ayo.,, "Stock price prediction using the arima model", *In 2014 UKSim-AMSS 16th international conference on computer modelling and simulation, IEEE*, pp. 106-112, 2014.

[2] S. V. G. Subrahmanya, D. K. Shetty, V. Patil, B. M. Z. Hameed, R. Paul, K. Smriti, N. Naik, B. K. Somani, , "The role of data science in healthcare advancements: applications, benefits, and future prospects", *Irish Journal of Medical Science,* vol. 191, no. 4, pp. 1473-1483, 2022.

[3] T. M Mitchell, *Machine learning,* 1st ed. New York: McGraw-Hill, 2007 ,

[4] D. Cielen and A. Meysman, *Introducing data science: big data, machine learning, and more, using Python tools.* Simon and Schuster, 2016.

[5] C. Chatfield, *Time-series forecasting.* CRC press, 2000.

[6] T. Kluyver, B. Ragan-Kelley, F. Pérez, B. E. Granger, M. Bussonnier, J. Frederic, K. Kelley, J. B. Hamrick, J. Grout, S. Corlay, P. Ivanov, D. Avila, S. Abdalla, C. Willing, and the Jupyter Development Team. "Jupyter Notebooks – a publishing format for reproducible computational workflows", *in Proc. Int. Conf. Electron. Publ.,* 2016.

[7] A.J. Smola, and B. Schölkopf, "A tutorial on support vector regression", *Stat. Comput.,* vol. 14, no. 3, pp. 199-222, 2004.
[http://dx.doi.org/10.1023/B:STCO.0000035301.49549.88]

[8] V. Deshwal, and V. Kumar, "Study of Coronavirus Disease (COVID-19) Outbreak in India", *Open Nurs. J.,* vol. 15, no. 1, pp. 62-73, 2021.
[http://dx.doi.org/10.2174/1874434602115010062]

[9] V. Kumar, A.P. Singh, A.K. Rai, and M. Wairiya, "Self Alteration Detectable Image Log File for Web Forensics", *Int. J. Comput. Appl.,* vol. 975, p. 8887, 2011.
[http://dx.doi.org/10.5120/2284-2960]

[10] V. Deshwal, V. Kumar, R. Shukla, and V. Yadav, "Estimating COVID-19 Cases Using Machine Learning Regression Algorithms", *Recent Advances in Electrical & Electronic Engineering (Formerly Recent Patents on Electrical & Electronic Engineering),* vol. 15, no. 5, pp. 390-400, 2022.

[11] V. Kumar, and R. Kumar, "Detection of Phishing Attack Using Visual Cryptography in Ad Hoc Network", *2015 International Conference on Communications and Signal Processing (ICCSP),* IEEE, pp. 1021-1025, 2015.
[http://dx.doi.org/10.1109/ICCSP.2015.7322654]

[12] P. Gupta, V. Kumar, and V. Yadav, "Student's Perception towards Mobile learning using Interned Enabled Mobile devices during COVID-19", *EAI Endorsed Transactions on Industrial Networks and Intelligent Systems,* vol. 8, no. 29, p. 170958, 2021.
[http://dx.doi.org/10.4108/eai.16-9-2021.170958]

[13] M. Xu, P. Watanachaturaporn, P. Varshney, and M. Arora, "Decision tree regression for soft classification of remote sensing data", *Remote Sens. Environ.,* vol. 97, no. 3, pp. 322-336, 2005.

[http://dx.doi.org/10.1016/j.rse.2005.05.008]

[14] L. Breiman, "Random forests", *Mach. Learn.,* vol. 45, no. 1, pp. 5-32, 2001. [http://dx.doi.org/10.1023/A:1010933404324]

[15] X. Cao, A. Francis, X. Pu, Z. Zhang, V. Katsikis, P. Stanimirovic, I. Brajevic, and S. Li, "A novel recurrent neural network based online portfolio analysis for high frequency trading", *Expert Syst. Appl.,* vol. 233, p. 120934, 2023. [http://dx.doi.org/10.1016/j.eswa.2023.120934]

[16] X. Cao, and S. Li, "Neural networks for portfolio analysis with cardinality constraints", *IEEE Trans. Neural Netw. Learn. Syst.,* 2023. [PMID: 37672371]

[17] X. Cao, and S. Li, "A novel dynamic neural system for nonconvex portfolio optimization with cardinality restrictions", *IEEE Trans. Syst. Man Cybern. Syst.,* vol. 53, no. 11, pp. 6943-6952, 2023. [http://dx.doi.org/10.1109/TSMC.2023.3288224]

[18] X. Cao, C. Peng, Y. Zheng, and S. Li, "Tran Thu Ha, Victor Shutyaev, Vasilios Katsikis, and Predrag Stanimirovic. Neural networks for portfolio analysis in high-frequency trading", *IEEE Trans. Neural Netw. Learn. Syst.,* 2023.

[19] A.T. Khan, X. Cao, and S. Li, "Using quadratic interpolated beetle antennae searchfor higher dimensional portfolio selection under cardinality constraints", *Comput. Econ.,* vol. 62, no. 4, pp. 1413-1435, 2023. [http://dx.doi.org/10.1007/s10614-022-10303-0]

CHAPTER 4

Cloud, Edge, and Fog Computing: A Study on their Broader Scope

Aditya Verma[1] and **Gurpreet Kaur**[1,*]

[1] *Amity Institute of Information Technology, Uttar pradesh, India*

Abstract: This paper presents comprehensive evaluations and assessments of cloud, fog, and edge computing platforms. The main objective of the study is to evaluate and compare the characteristics, advantages, and disadvantages of these platforms and to identify the most suitable platform for various use cases. The paper begins by providing an overview of cloud computing and the various deployment techniques that are available. The concept of fog computing is then discussed, including its architecture and key components. Finally, this study examines the benefits of computing, including its architecture, advantages, and limitations. The study also compares the three platforms based on various criteria, such as scalability, latency, reliability, security, and cost. The results of the study demonstrate that the platform choice is impacted by the specific requirements of the application and that each platform has its own strengths and weaknesses. The study concludes by highlighting the importance of considering the trade-off between performance and cost when choosing the most appropriate platform for a particular use case.

Keywords: Cloud computing, Edge computing, Fog computing, Networking and resource management, QoS of cloud computing, QoS of fog computing, QoS of edge computing.

INTRODUCTION

Cloud computing has been an essential part of the modern era, but with increasing demands for low-latency, high-bandwidth applications, and data processing, fog and edge computing have emerged as complementary technologies. In this literature review, we analyze the latest research on cloud, fog, and edge computing platforms and their applications. Additionally, the background of the study section should provide a brief overview of the current trends and developments in cloud, fog, and edge computing. This can include the increasing demand for these platforms, the growth of the market, and the innovations in technology. The section will also provide a brief overview of the key players in the industry, such as major technology companies that offer cloud, fog, and edge computing services and products. It is also important to mention the challenges and limitations associated with each platform and how these challenges are being

* **Corresponding author Gurpreet Kaur:** Amity Institute of Information Technology, Uttar pradesh, India; E-mail: gkaur10@amity.edu

addressed. Problems with security, data privacy, scalability, and a lack of standards could be a few of these.

Finally, the background of the study will outline the objectives and research questions that the study aims to answer. This section will clearly state the study's purpose and objectives. The background of the study will be comprehensive enough to provide a clear understanding of the context and significance of the title of this review work.

The key issues associated with third-party data storage and computation (Cloud, fog, and edge computing) are discussed in this review. Some of the major issues are mentioned below:

i. Inadequate understanding of the key differences between cloud, fog, and edge computing, including their respective benefits and limitations.
ii. This is only a brief comparison of cloud, fog, and edge computing platform types, which makes it difficult for organizations to make informed decisions about which platform to use for different applications and workloads.
iii. The lack of standardization and compatibility across cloud, fog, and edge computing platforms creates challenges for organizations looking to integrate these platforms into their existing IT infrastructure.
iv. The need for improved scalability, performance, and cost-effectiveness of cloud, fog, and edge computing platforms to meet the demands of organizations of all sizes.

Highlights of the Study

i. To compare the key characteristics, benefits, and limitations of cloud, fog, and edge computing platforms.
ii. To evaluate the security, privacy, and reliability of cloud, fog, and edge computing platforms and recommend measures to improve these aspects.
iii. To assess the scalability, performance, and cost-effectiveness of cloud, fog, and edge computing platforms and identify ways to improve these aspects.
iv. To identify the key players in the cloud, fog, and edge computing market and analyze their offerings.
v. To provide recommendations for organizations looking to adopt cloud, fog, or edge computing platforms based on their specific needs and requirements.

Scope of the Study

i. The study will primarily focus on the technical aspects of cloud, fog, and edge computing, including security, privacy, reliability, scalability, performance, and cost-effectiveness. It will not include an in-depth analysis of the legal and regulatory aspects of these platforms, as shown in Fig. (**1**).

ii. The study will compare and contrast the key characteristics, benefits, and limitations of cloud, fog, and edge computing platforms and will not provide a detailed analysis of individual platforms or companies.

iii. The study will be limited to the examination of cloud, fog, and edge computing platforms in a general sense and will not include an analysis of specific applications or use cases.

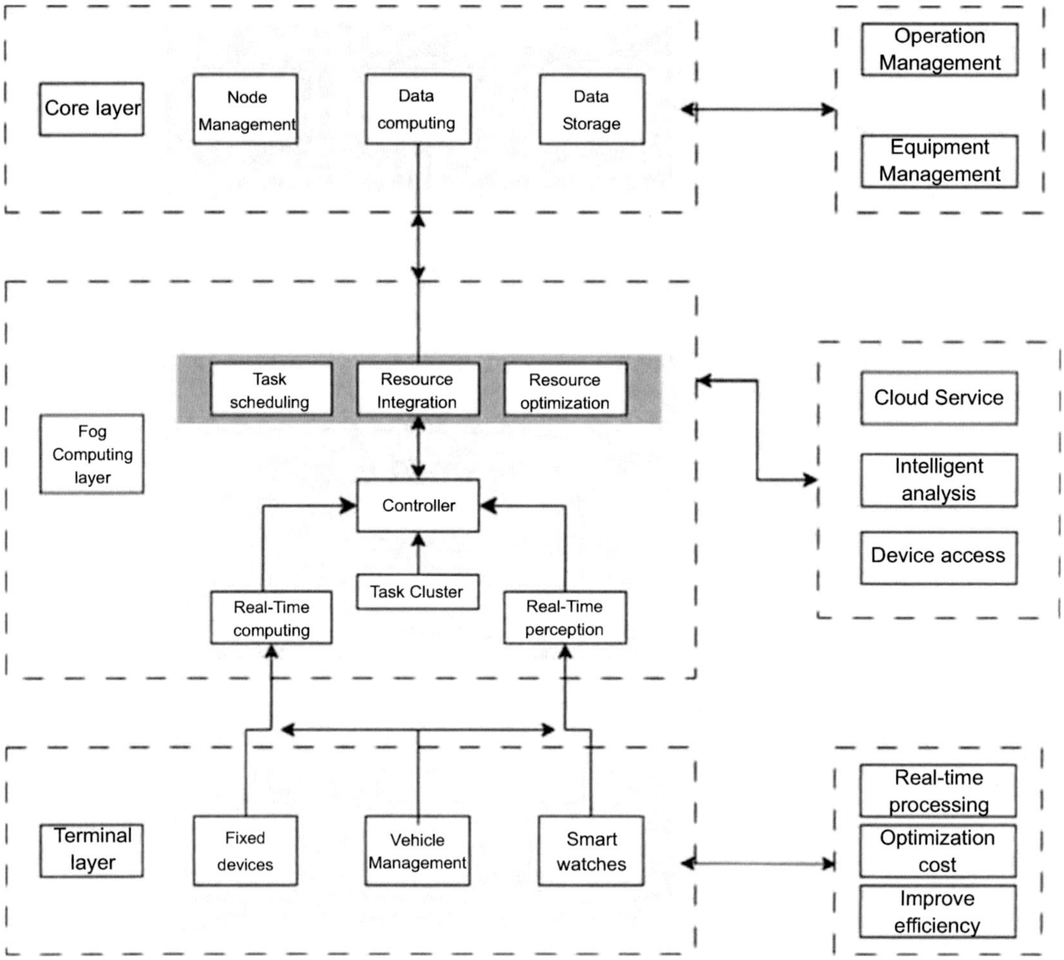

Fig. (1). Cloud-fog computing architecture.

LITERATURE REVIEW

Overview of Cloud Computing

The architecture for cloud-fog-based computing is illustrated in Fig. (**1**). A cloud-fog is a virtual resource paradigm that resides amongst smart end devices and the conventional cloud or data centers. Such a paradigm supports latency-sensitized and vertically isolation-based applications by providing scalable, pervasive, distributed computing, storage, and connectivity. "Fog" refers to its cloud-like properties, but still closer to ground level, such as IoT devices.

As shown in Fig. (**1**), there are three layers in this architecture: the core layer, the fog-computing layer, and the terminal layer. The core layer is a basic layer in fog architecture that includes devices like sensors, smart vehicles, mobile phones, smartcards, *etc*. Such devices have the property of operations in heterogeneous environments (devices from various technologies and modes of communication). The fog layer includes other devices like routers, access gateways, and points commonly known as fog nodes. These are located at the edge of a network, and they ensure the services to end devices. Thus, fog nodes are in between the end devices and cloud data centers. The terminal layer consists of devices that are able to provide huge storage and machines/servers with high performance. The computation analysis is done within this layer, and the data is permanently stored as a backup for the users.

Fig. (**2**) illustrates fog computing as an intermediate between the huge cloud storage and the end users. Online access to software, processing, and storage services is made possible *via* a method of on-demand computing known as cloud computing. It helps companies to reduce the cost of their IT infrastructure while focusing on their core competencies. Cloud computing platforms like Amazon Web Services (AWS), Microsoft Azure, and Google Cloud Platform (GCP) have become more popular due to their scalability, flexibility, and cost.

Krumm [1] explores the organizational and technical security considerations that laboratories should take into account when implementing cloud computing solutions. The article discusses organizational considerations such as developing a cloud computing strategy, assessing risk, and establishing governance and compliance frameworks. The technical security considerations include network security, data encryption, access control, and disaster recovery planning. Krumm emphasizes the importance of continuous monitoring and evaluation of cloud computing solutions to ensure they remain secure and effective over time.

Bharany *et al.* (2022) [2] provide a comprehensive review of the research on fault tolerance in cloud computing and provide a taxonomy of fault tolerance techniques based on their energy efficiency. The survey includes a review of over 70 research articles published between 2010 and 2021 and identifies several trends, such as the increasing use of virtualization-based techniques and hybrid techniques. It also highlights the need for more accurate modeling and prediction of energy consumption and more efficient fault detection and recovery techniques. The article provides a valuable resource for researchers and practitioners in the field and highlights the importance of energy efficiency in cloud computing.

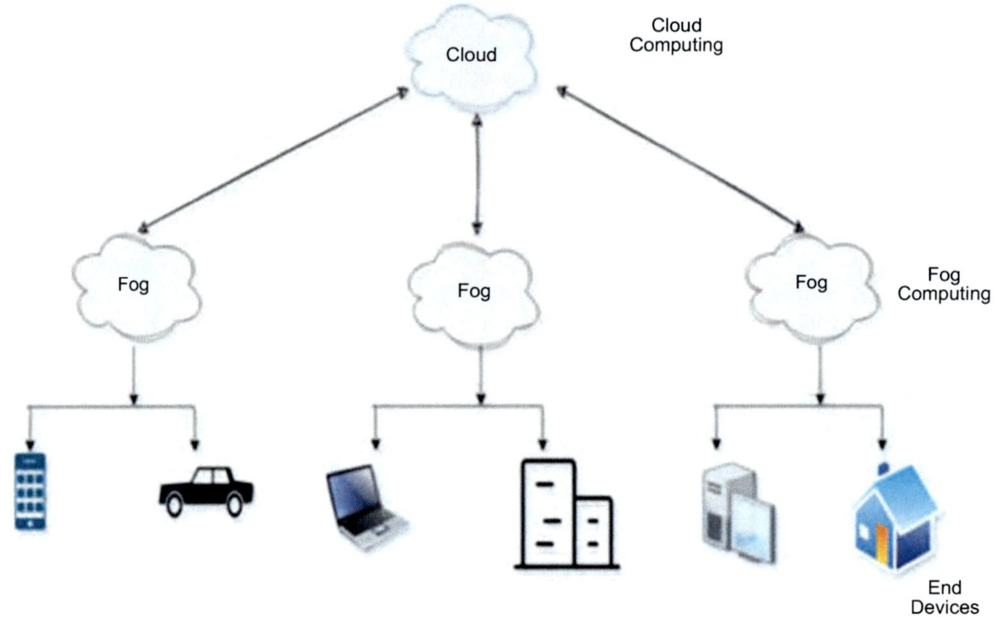

Fig. (2). Fog computing as an interface between the cloud and the end user.

Heidari, Arash *et al.* (2022) [3] provide a comprehensive review of the research on service discovery mechanisms. The authors follow a systematic literature review methodology to identify and analyze relevant research articles. They use a standardized data extraction form to extract relevant data from each article and then analyze the data to identify common themes and trends. The article also presents a taxonomy of service discovery mechanisms based on their functionality and identifies several challenges and opportunities in the research. Overall, the article provides a valuable resource for researchers and practitioners in the field.

In the context of the Internet of Things, this work by Ketu *et al.* [4] and Pramod Kumar Mishra gives an extensive literature analysis on cloud, fog, and mist computing (IoT). It introduces the concept of IoT and the challenges associated with it, as well as the different computing paradigms that can be used to address these challenges. The paper provides a detailed review of the literature on cloud computing, including its architecture, deployment models, and applications in IoT. Also, it examines the advantages and difficulties of fog computing, which extends cloud computing to the network's edge, and the newly developing mist computing paradigm, which enables Internet of Things devices to process data locally. The assessment of the newest prospects and difficulties related to cloud and fog computing in IoT finishes the study.

Overview of Fog Computing

A distributed computing concept called fog computing takes cloud computing out to the network's edge. Relocating the computer resources closer to the data-generating devices provides quicker data processing, low latency, and increased network efficiency. Platforms for fog computing, such as Cisco IOx, IBM Edge, and Huawei Agile IoT, have been deployed in various applications, such as smart cities, industrial automation, and healthcare.

Das Resul *et al.* [5] suggest an overview of fog computing, its key features, and its potential applications in various fields. The proximity to end users, low-latency data processing, and real-time data analysis are highlighted as the salient characteristics of fog computing. The next section of the article examines the possible uses of fog computing in several industries, including healthcare, transportation, smart cities, and the Internet of Things (IoT). It then delves into the challenges faced by fog computing, such as security, privacy, scalability, and interoperability. Finally, the article concludes by summarizing the key points discussed in the article and highlighting the potential benefits of fog computing.

Intrusion detection systems (IDS) for fog and cloud computing are the subject of a survey by Chang *et al.* (2022) [6] to give an overview of the state-of-the-art at the time and identify challenges and research directions for future development. They discuss the importance of IDS for these environments, such as detecting and mitigating attacks, as well as the advantages and disadvantages of traditional and machine learning-based approaches. They also discuss the challenges and open research directions for IDS, such as the need for scalable and efficient IDS, the need for IDS that can handle the dynamic nature of cloud and cloud computing environments, and the need to deal with the huge capacities of data generated by these environments.

Ariavazhagan *et al.* [7] offer a thorough analysis of the ideas, issues, and possibilities of fog computing in the context of the Internet of Things (IoT). It talks about the different difficulties with fog computing, such as security and privacy concerns, resource constraints, and interoperability issues, as well as the use of blockchain technology for enhancing security and privacy. It also offers opportunities such as improved data processing capabilities, reduced latency, and increased scalability.

In a study by Singh *et al.* [8], fog computing and its associated technologies are thoroughly discussed in this overview of the literature, along with its taxonomy, research trends, and difficulties. The authors discuss the motivation for fog computing, its architecture, deployment models, and application domains, its research areas, and its current trends. They also discuss the challenges associated with these trends, such as privacy and security concerns, data management, and interoperability. The paper emphasizes the need for more research on fog computing architectures, resource management, security, and application development.

Overview of Edge Computing

A decentralized computing approach called edge computing moves processing and data storage closer to the gadgets and sensors that provide the data. It provides real-time data processing, reduces data transmission, and improves network security. Edge computing platforms, such as Microsoft Azure IoT Edge, Amazon Greengrass, and Google Edge TPU, have been widely used in IoT applications such as autonomous vehicles, smart homes, and wearables.

Tian *et al.* [9] provide a comprehensive overview of the concepts of edge computing and sensor-cloud networks, and a distributed computing environment is created by combining them. They discuss the benefits of edge computing, such as reduced latency, improved bandwidth, and enhanced user experience, and the challenges of integrating them. It also presents proposed solutions for overcoming the challenges, such as intelligent resource management, data analytics, machine learning algorithms, and blockchain technology. Future research in the field should focus on efficient resource allocation algorithms, enhancing security and privacy, and improving scalability and reliability.

Nadjib Achir *et al.*'s (2022) [10] survey paper provides an extensive review of the state of the art in MEC. It discusses the current landscape of MEC and its potential applications in various domains, as well as the difficulties and chances that MEC offers. The paper also provides an overview of MEC architecture, including access points, edge servers, and cloud resources, as well as the different types of networks that can be used for MEC. The paper concludes with a discussion of future research directions in MEC, highlighting the need for research in areas such as resource allocation, security and privacy, and standardization.

The article by Shou Li *et al.* [11] gives an in-depth analysis of the multi-access edge computing (MEC) foundations, services, enablers, and obstacles. It covers the key features of MEC, such as low latency, high bandwidth, and high reliability, as well as its architecture, protocols, and standards. It also addresses the challenges associated with MEC, including resource management, security, and privacy, and it emphasizes the next avenues for MEC research. It is a useful tool for academics and professionals who want to learn more about the condition of MEC right now and its possible uses in the future.

A review of the literature on edge computing is included in the study by Sulieman *et al.* [12]. The idea of edge computing is introduced, and the architecture of edge nodes, edge devices, and the cloud is described in depth. It then describes the various research efforts in the field of edge computing, such as resource management, security, and privacy. It also provides examples of edge computing implementations in each of these use cases and discusses the benefits and challenges associated with each of them. The authors use a systematic approach to gather and provide information about edge computing, making it a useful tool for academics and industry professionals.

COMPARISON BETWEEN DIFFERENT COMPUTING TECHNIQUES

By comparing different research papers on cloud, fog, and edge computing, as shown in Fig. (**3**), a hierarchy can be seen where the cloud data center is on the top, the fog node is just below, and edge computing is at the bottom, showing the connection on devices.

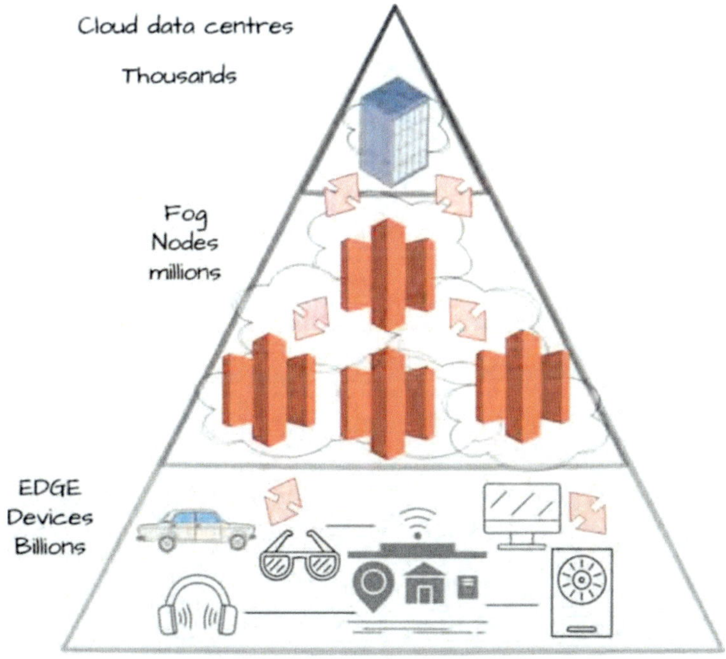

Fig. (3). Cloud, Fog, and Edge Computing layers.

Definition and Characteristics

The definitions and traits of cloud, fog, and edge computing have been contrasted in studies. According to research by Buyya *et al.* (2015) [13], edge computing is a computing paradigm that enables data processing at the network's edge, whereas fog computing and cloud computing are complementing paradigms. Cloud computing is a delivery strategy for IT services. The authors also contrast each paradigm's attributes, such as the location of data processing and storage, the type of computer resources used, and the latency of communication.

USE CASES AND APPLICATIONS

The use cases and applications of cloud, fog, and edge computing have been contrasted in studies. 2012 research by Bonomi *et al.* [14] looks at whether cloud, fog, and edge computing are appropriate for IoT applications. The authors assess the capabilities of each paradigm against the needs of IoT applications and come to the conclusion that edge and fog computing are more suited than cloud computing for IoT applications that call for low latency and real-time data processing.

Networking and Resource Management

The networking and resource management issues in cloud, fog, and edge computing have been compared in studies. A study by Chen *et al.* (2018) [15] analyze the trade-offs of centralized and decentralized resource management strategies and compares the networking topologies of cloud, fog, and edge computing. The authors also compare the resource management challenges of each paradigm, including the limitations of computing resources at the edge of the network in edge computing and the scalability and reliability challenges in cloud computing.

Security and Privacy

The difficulties with security and privacy in cloud, fog, and edge computing have been contrasted in studies. A study by Liu *et al.* (2016) [16] discusses the security and privacy challenges posed by the decentralized nature of edge computing and compares these challenges with those in cloud and fog computing. In order to solve the security and privacy issues in edge computing settings, the authors also provide secure edge computing designs.

PERFORMANCE AND QUALITY OF SERVICE (QOS)

The effectiveness and QoS of cloud, fog, and edge computing have been compared in studies. In a 2019 [17] research, Wang *et al.* analyze the effectiveness and quality of service (QoS) of edge computing, cloud computing, and fog computing in multimedia streaming applications. The authors also discuss the challenges of delivering high performance and QoS in each paradigm, including the limited resources and network heterogeneity at the edge of the network in edge computing, as well as the scalability and reliability challenges in cloud computing. Table **1** shows the comparative analysis between various existing works.

Table 1. Comparative Analysis.

Reference	Methodology	Key Findings	Limitations
[1] Krumm *et al.*	The article emphasizes the importance of a comprehensive, risk-based approach to laboratory cloud computing security to identify risks, implement appropriate security controls, monitoriand test those controls, and continuously improve security practices.	1. It poses unique security risks that need to be addressed. 2. Both lab managers and cloud service providers must take measures to ensure the security and confidentiality of data. 3. The benefits of cloud computing can be realized while addressing security concerns.	1. Laboratories should consider the specific needs and context of their own operations when implementing security controls and assessing risk. 2. This is important for ensuring that the security measures put in place are effective and appropriate for the laboratory's unique situation.
[2] Bharany *et al.*	The authors follow a structured approach to ensure that their review is comprehensive and unbiased. The taxonomy developed by the authors provides a useful framework for categorizing and comparing fault tolerance techniques in green cloud computing.	1. The study highlights the importance of integrating energy efficiency. 2. The fault tolerance techniques to achieve sustainable and reliable cloud computing systems.	1. Lacks empirical evidence and limited discussion of trade-offs between energy efficiency and fault tolerance.
[3] Heidari *et al.*	The review conducted by the authors employs a systematic method that guarantees inclusivity and impartiality. Their taxonomy offers an advantageous structure for classifying and contrasting service discovery techniques in cloud computing.	1. Service discovery is a key part of cloud computing that allows for dynamic access to cloud services. 2. It is classified into registry, broadcast, query, and hybrid-based mechanisms.	1. It has limitations such as limited coverage, limited scope, lack of empirical evidence, language bias, and need for further research.

(Table 1) cont.....

Reference	Methodology	Key Findings	Limitations
[4] Ketu *et al.*	The authors reviewed existing literature, surveys, and case studies to gain insights into the advantages and disadvantages of cloud, fog, and mist computing in IoT and conducted case studies to understand the practical implications. They concluded with recommendations for the use of these technologies in IoT.	1. Cloud, fog, and mist computing in IoT offer significant opportunities for innovation and advancement in various domains.	1. Fog computing nodes have limited resources, scalability issues, heterogeneity, security and privacy concerns, reliability, maintenance and management, and emerging trends and opportunities.
[5] Das Resul *et al.*	The article provides a structured approach to ensure the security of laboratory data in a cloud computing environment. Laboratory managers and IT professionals ensure compliance with regulatory requirements.	1. It has advantages like increased bandwidth, energy efficiency, and latency, 2. Transportation, healthcare, and smart cities are a few potential applications.	1. Lack of comparisons, obsolete material, biased viewpoints, and a lack of empirical data may restrict its applicability in comprehending the larger technical landscape.
[6] Chang, Victor *et al.*	To advance knowledge in the area of IDS for cloud and fog computing, this survey utilized a methodology that encompassed a thorough literature review, stringent selection criteria, meticulous analysis of articles, and a systematic presentation of findings.	1. IDS are essential for security in fog and cloud computing. 2. Classified into signature-based, anomaly-based, and hybrid.	1. Limited coverage, bias towards certain IDS, lack of empirical evidence, quickly changing technology, and linguistic biases. 2. It is crucial to take into account the study's limitations, even though they are useful insights.
[7] Arivazhagan *et al.*	The article is based on a comprehensive and critical review of the existing literature on fog computing in IoT, supplying an invaluable resource for specialists and researchers interested in this area.	1. Fog computing takes cloud computing to the network edge, providing improved latency, reduced network congestion, and enhanced user experience.	1. Drawbacks, including low processing power, little storage space, a reliance on network access, security concerns, interoperability issues, and high deployment and maintenance costs.
[8] Sukh pal Singh Gill *et al.*	The paper's methodology involves a systematic and meticulous approach to examining the existing literature on fog computing. The authors adopted a well-structured process to identify pertinent papers, scrutinize the data, and consolidate the outcomes.	1. It provides a taxonomy of Fog computing, a systematic review of the existing literature, current trends in Fog computing, research challenges, and potential solutions.	1. Limitations, such as limited processing capabilities, scalability issues, resource constraints, heterogeneity, security and privacy concerns, maintenance and management, and limited standardization.

(Table 1) cont.....

Reference	Methodology	Key Findings	Limitations
[9] Tian *et al.*	This article on edge computing and sensor-cloud research involves problem identification, literature review, solution design, implementation, evaluation, and iteration. This methodology helps researchers develop innovative solutions that can address the challenges of edge computing and sensor-cloud and unlock their full potential.	1. This paper provides a comprehensive overview of edge computing and sensor-cloud networks, discussing their potential applications, challenges, and solutions.	1. It has limited coverage, lacks empirical evidence, is outdated, and uses technical jargon. Therefore, more research is needed to build upon its findings.
[10] Nadjib Achir *et al.*	This survey paper included a systematic review of the literature and a meticulous analysis of the chosen articles. The authors' methodology ensured that their survey encompassed a broad range of pertinent and up-to-date research, which makes it a valuable source of information for MEC researchers and practitioners.	1. MEC intends to deliver cloud computing services and capabilities to the network's edge, improving the latency and reliability of mobile applications and services. 2. It can enable new types of applications and services, such as augmented reality, virtual reality, smart cities, and self-sufficient vehicles.	The article provides a comprehensive overview of MEC technologies but does not cover the economic, regulatory, and social implications. It focuses on MEC from the perspective of a telecommunication operator and does not cover other stakeholders.
[11] Shou Li *et al.*	The paper provides a comprehensive overview of MEC and its various aspects. The authors use a systematic approach to gather and display information on MEC, making it a useful tool for academics and industry professionals.	1. A promising technology that enables low-latency and high-bandwidth services by bringing processing and storage capabilities closer to end users is called MEC. 2. Its benefits are reducing network traffic, improving the quality of service, enhancing security and privacy, and supporting new and innovative services.	1. Limitations include limited scope, lack of empirical evidence, limited generalizability, lack of practical implementation examples, and limited discussion on regulatory issues.

(Table 1) cont.....

Reference	Methodology	Key Findings	Limitations
[12] Sulieman *et al.*	The paper offers significant value to researchers and experts in the area of edge computing as the authors employed a rigorous and systematic method to collect and evaluate existing literature on the subject.	1. Edge-oriented computing allows services with high bandwidth and low latency. 2. The paper provides a comprehensive overview of EOC, its applications, challenges, and future research directions.	1. Its limitations are such as limited scope, lack of empirical evidence, limited generalizability, lack of practical implementation examples, and limited discussion on regulatory issues.

DISCUSSION

Below is a summary of the conclusions from the literature review on the comparison of cloud, fog, and edge computing:

Definition and Characteristics

Edge computing is described as a computing paradigm that enables data processing at the edge of the network, while fog computing is described as a complementary paradigm to cloud computing. Cloud computing is described as a delivery mechanism for IT services [13, 14]. The location of data processing and storage, the type of computer resources used, and the communication latency are some of each paradigm's essential characteristics [15].

Applications and use cases

Different use cases and applications can benefit from cloud, fog, and edge computing in different ways [25]. IoT applications that need low latency and real-time data processing are better suited to fog and edge computing than to cloud computing [16, 17].

Networking and Resource Management

There are transfers between centralized and decentralized resource management strategies, and there are differences in the networking topologies of cloud, fog, and edge computing [18, 19]. The issues of resource management in each paradigm include those related to scalability and dependability in cloud computing as well as restrictions on computing resources at the network's edge [20, 21].

Security and Privacy

Edge computing has different security and privacy issues than cloud and fog computing due to its decentralized nature. To deal with these issues, secure edge computing architectures have been put forth [22 - 25].

RESULTS ANALYSIS

The comparison of cloud, fog, and edge computing using the results of the literature review reveals that each paradigm has advantages and disadvantages of its own, it can be shown in Fig. **(4-6)** consecutively. Cloud computing is well-suited for large-scale, data-intensive applications that require centralized processing and storage, but it may not be the best choice for applications that require real-time processing and low latency [26 - 28].

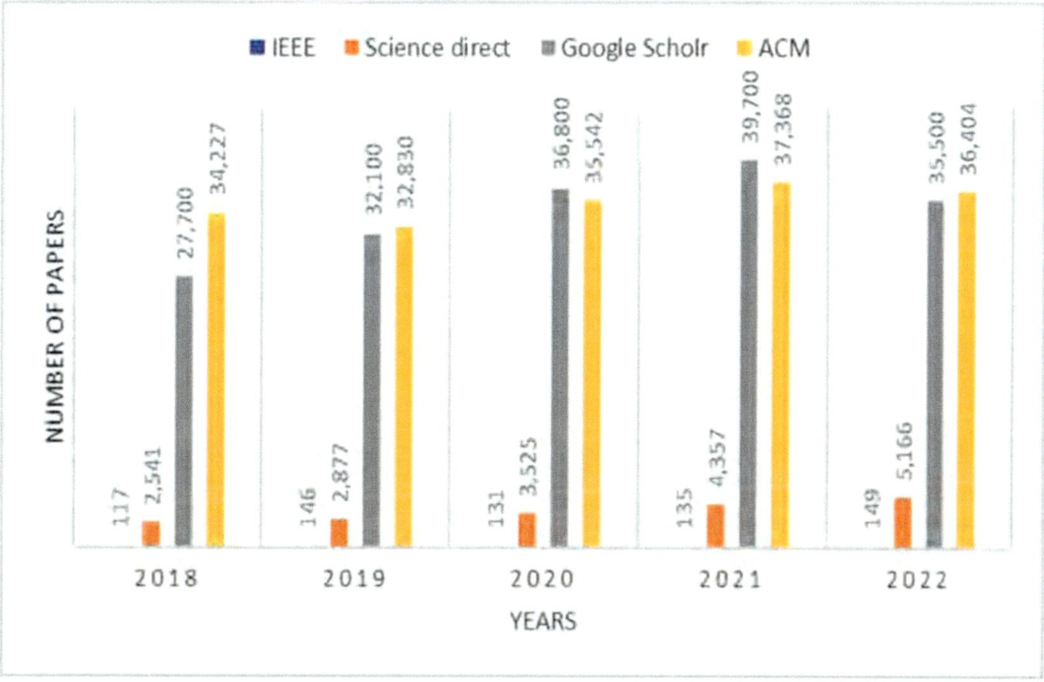

Fig. (4). Bar-graph of various security for cloud computing papers.

By enabling data processing closer to the end devices, fog computing, as a complementary paradigm to cloud computing, can improve cloud computing's performance and quality of service. Edge computing is ideal for IoT and real-time applications that require low latency and real-time processing, but it may face challenges in terms of limited computing resources and network heterogeneity at the edge of the network. Security and privacy are important considerations in each paradigm, but edge computing poses unique challenges due to its decentralized nature [29, 30]. In summary, the choice of cloud, fog, or edge computing depends on the specific requirements and constraints of the application or use case. To determine the most suitable paradigm, it is necessary to consider factors such as data processing and storage, resource management, security, performance, and QoS [31, 32]. Table **2** shows the recent publications in the area of cloud computing, whereas Table **3** in the area of fog computing and Table **4** in the area of edge computing.

Table 2. Recent publications in cloud computing.

Methodology	Year of papers	IEEE	Science- Direct	Google Scholar	ACM
Technical security for cloud computing.	2018	117	2,541	27,700	34,227
	2019	146	2,877	32,100	32,830
	2020	131	3,525	36,800	35,542
	2021	135	4,357	39,700	37,368
	2022	149	5,166	35,500	36,404

Table 3. Publications in Fog Computing-based Architecture.

Methodology	Year of papers	IEEE	Science- Direct	Google Scholar	ACM
Fog computing in IOT.	2018	491	308	9,560	33,776
	2019	584	523	13,200	32,390
	2020	531	691	16,400	35,168
	2021	492	922	20,300	37,068
	2022	484	1,152	22,400	35,999

Table 4. Recent publications in Multi-access Edge Computing.

Methodology	Year of papers	IEEE	Science- Direct	Google Scholar	ACM
Multi-access Edge Computing.	2018	132	3,000	1,270	34,010
	2019	212	3,418	2,230	32,661
	2020	336	4,447	3,070	35,442
	2021	474	5,306	3,720	37,259
	2022	639	6,603	4,900	36,302

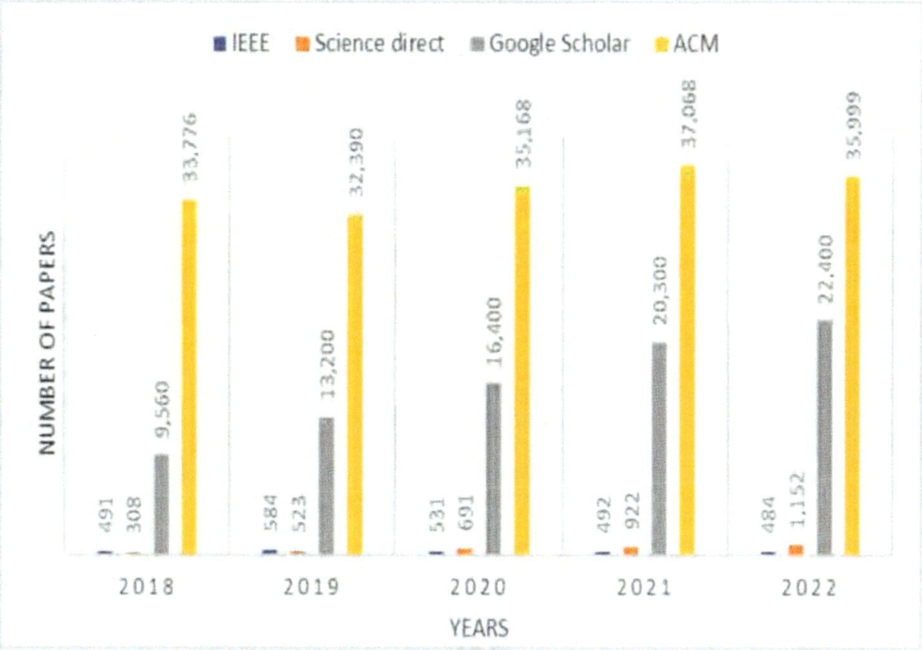

Fig. (5). Bar-graph of various papers on Fog computing in IOT.

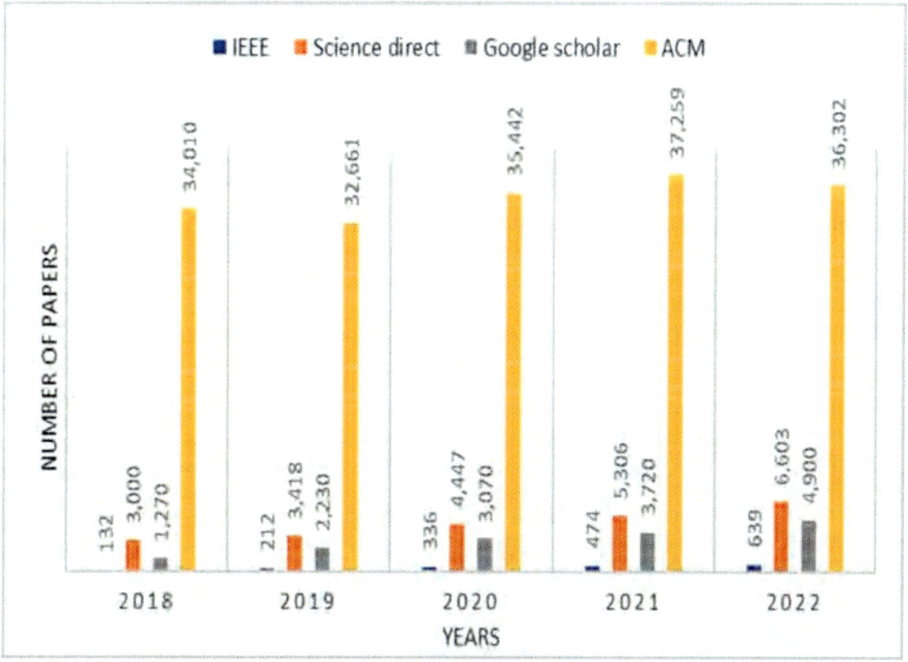

Fig. (6). Bar-graph of various papers on multi-access edge computing.

The findings from the review of the literature comparing cloud, fog, and edge computing emphasize the trade-offs and difficulties involved with each paradigm. Cloud computing has proven to be a popular and successful paradigm for delivering IT services, but it may not be well-suited for real-time, low-latency applications. Fog computing has the potential to enhance cloud computing by enabling data processing closer to the end devices, but it also has its own set of challenges, such as resource allocation and management, that need to be addressed. Edge computing is gaining popularity for its ability to process data at the edge of the network, but it may face limitations in terms of computing resources and network heterogeneity.

Security and privacy are important considerations in each paradigm, but edge computing has unique challenges due to its decentralized nature. In a broad spectrum, the comparison of cloud, fog, and edge computing demonstrates that each has advantages and disadvantages of its own, and the selection of a paradigm depends on the requirements and limitations of the application or use case. To address the issues with each paradigm and determine optimum practices, more study is required.

CONCLUSION

The literature review on the comparison of cloud, fog, and edge computing aimed to provide an overview of the key characteristics, use cases, and challenges associated with each paradigm. The study found that cloud computing is well-suited for large-scale, data-intensive applications but may not be the best choice for real-time, low-latency applications. Fog computing has the potential to enhance cloud computing by enabling data processing closer to the end devices, but it also has its own set of challenges that need to be addressed. Edge computing is ideal for IoT and real-time applications that require low latency and real-time processing but may face limitations in terms of computing resources and network heterogeneity. The study highlighted the importance of privacy and security in each paradigm, with edge computing posing particular difficulties because of its decentralized nature. The advantages and disadvantages of each paradigm vary, and the choice of paradigm is influenced by the particular needs and limitations of the application or use case. Best practices for utilizing cloud, fog, and edge computing across a range of applications and use cases require more study.

RECOMMENDATIONS FOR FUTURE WORK

Resource allocation and management: Future work should focus on developing effective algorithms and protocols for resource allocation and management in fog computing, taking into account the dynamic nature of fog nodes and the heterogeneity of edge devices.

Security and privacy: Future research should concentrate on creating secure and privacy-preserving protocols and algorithms that can be successfully used in cloud, fog, and edge computing, given how important security and privacy are in these paradigms.

Performance and QoS: Future work should focus on evaluating the performance and QoS of cloud, fog, and edge computing in different use cases and applications, as well as developing techniques to enhance the performance and QoS of these paradigms.

Interoperability: Given the decentralized nature of edge computing and the complementary relationship between cloud and fog computing, future work should focus on developing techniques to ensure interoperability and seamless integration between these paradigms.

Case studies and empirical evaluations: Further case studies and empirical evaluations of cloud, fog, and edge computing are needed to validate the advantages and disadvantages of each paradigm in different use cases and applications.

In conclusion, there are several prospects for future research in the fields of resource allocation and management, security and privacy, performance, QoS, and interoperability, as well as case studies and practical assessments of cloud, fog, and edge computing. These areas of research have the potential to significantly advance our understanding of these paradigms and to inform the development of effective solutions for real-world applications and use cases.

REFERENCES

[1] N. Krumm, "Organizational and Technical Security Considerations for Laboratory Cloud Computing", *J. Appl. Lab. Med.,* vol. 8, no. 1, pp. 180-193, 2023. [http://dx.doi.org/10.1093/jalm/jfac118] [PMID: 36610429]

[2] S. Bharany, S. Badotra, S. Sharma, S. Rani, M. Alazab, R.H. Jhaveri, and T. Reddy Gadekallu, "Energy efficient fault tolerance techniques in green cloud computing: A systematic survey and taxonomy", *Sustain. Energy Technol. Assess.,* vol. 53, p. 102613, 2022. [http://dx.doi.org/10.1016/j.seta.2022.102613]

[3] A. Heidari, and N. Jafari Navimipour, "Service discovery mechanisms in cloud computing: a comprehensive and systematic literature review", *Kybernetes,* vol. 51, no. 3, pp. 952-981, 2022. [http://dx.doi.org/10.1108/K-12-2020-0909]

[4] O. Jayeola, S. Sidek, and J. Hu, "Cloud computing adoption in small and medium enterprises (SMEs): A systematic literature review and directions for future research", *International Journal of Business and Society,* vol. 23, no. 1, pp. 226-243, 2022. [http://dx.doi.org/10.33736/ijbs.4610.2022]

[5] R. Das and M. M. Inuwa, "A review on Fog Computing: Issues, Characteristics, Challenges, and Potential Applications," *Telemat. Informat. Rep.*, p. 100049, 2023. ,

[6] V. Chang, "survey on intrusion detection systems for fog and cloud computing", *Future Internet,* p. 89, 2022.
[http://dx.doi.org/10.3390/fi14030089]

[7] C. Arivazhagan, and V. Natarajan, "A Survey on Fog computing paradigms, Challenges and Opportunities in IoT", *2020 International Conference on Communication and Signal Processing (ICCSP),* 2020.
[http://dx.doi.org/10.1109/ICCSP48568.2020.9182229]

[8] J. Singh, P. Singh, and S. S. Gill, "A taxonomy, systematic review, current trends and research challenges", *Journal of Parallel and Distributed Computing,* vol. 157, pp. 56-85, 2021.
[http://dx.doi.org/10.1016/j.jpdc.2021.06.005]

[9] T. Wang, Y. Liang, X. Shen, X. Zheng, A. Mahmood, and Q.Z. Sheng, "Edge Computing and Sensor-Cloud: Overview, Solutions, and Directions", *ACM Comput. Surv.,* vol. 55, no. 13s, pp. 1-37, 2023.
[http://dx.doi.org/10.1145/3582270]

[10] P. Cruz, N. Achir, and A.C. Viana, "On the edge of the deployment: A survey on multi-access edge computing", *ACM Comput. Surv.,* vol. 55, no. 5, pp. 1-34, 2023.
[http://dx.doi.org/10.1145/3529758]

[11] B. Liang, M.A. Gregory, and S. Li, "Multi-access Edge Computing fundamentals, services, enablers and challenges: A complete survey", *J. Netw. Comput. Appl.,* vol. 199, p. 103308, 2022.
[http://dx.doi.org/10.1016/j.jnca.2021.103308]

[12] N. A. Sulieman, "Edge-oriented computing: A survey on research and use cases", *Energies,* p. 452, 2022.
[http://dx.doi.org/10.3390/en15020452]

[13] R. Buyya, C.S. Yeo, S. Venugopal, J. Broberg, and I. Brandic, "Cloud computing and emerging IT platforms: Vision, hype, and reality for delivering computing as the 5th utility", *Future Gener. Comput. Syst.,* vol. 49, pp. 167-178, 2015.

[14] F. Bonomi, R. Milito, J. Zhu, and S. Addepalli, "Fog computing and its role in the internet of things", *Proceedings of the first edition of the MCC workshop on Mobile cloud computing,* 2012 pp. 13-16.
[http://dx.doi.org/10.1145/2342509.2342513]

[15] Y. Chen, J. Ma, J. Li, and S. Wang, "Networking and resource management in edge computing: A survey", *Future Gener. Comput. Syst.,* vol. 82, pp. 551-566, 2018.

[16] J. Liu, J. Li, J. Ma, and S. Wang, "A secure edge computing architecture for the internet of things",

[17] Y. Wang, J. Li, and Y. Chen, "Quality of service and performance analysis of edge computing in multimedia streaming applications",

[18] H. Chen, L. Zhang, C. Liu, and X. Li, "A survey of fog computing: concepts, applications and issues",

[19] X. Gu, Y. Peng, and J. Liu, "A secure fog computing architecture for the internet of things", *J. Netw. Comput. Appl.,* vol. 91, pp. 1-14, 2017.

[20] X. Wang, T. Huang, Q. Li, Y. Wang, and F. Hu, "A comparative analysis of edge computing platforms: Key features, applications and challenges", *Future Gener. Comput. Syst.,* vol. 119, pp. 189-205, 2021.
[http://dx.doi.org/10.1016/j.future.2021.04.013]

[21] X. Xing, J. Li, and P.S. Yu, "Networking and resource management in fog computing: A survey", *J. Parallel Distrib. Comput.,* vol. 100, pp. 68-82, 2017.

[22] X. Zhang, Q. Li, Y. Li, L. Li, and Y. Hu, "Quality of service and performance analysis of fog computing in multimedia streaming applications",

[23] K. Zhang, H. Song, and Z. Liu, "Cloud computing platform selection: A comparative study of Amazon Web Services, Microsoft Azure, and Google Cloud Platform", *IEEE Access,* vol. 7, pp. 150990-

151005, 2019.
[http://dx.doi.org/10.1109/ACCESS.2019.2944236]

[24] S. Biswas, S.K. Datta, and S. Ruj, "A comprehensive review on fog computing: State-of-the-art and research challenges", *J. Netw. Comput. Appl.,* vol. 156, p. 102470, 2020.
[http://dx.doi.org/10.1016/j.jnca.2020.102470]

[25] M. Chen, S. Mao, and Y. Liu, "A survey of fog computing: Concepts, applications and issues", *Internet of Things,* vol. 15, p. 100452, 2021.
[http://dx.doi.org/10.1016/j.iot.2021.100452]

[26] J. Wei, J. Zhu, Y. Zhou, Z. Chen, and Y. Shang, "Fog computing: A review of research progress and open challenges", *J. Netw. Comput. Appl.,* vol. 186, p. 103064, 2021.
[http://dx.doi.org/10.1016/j.jnca.2021.103064]

[27] Y. Li, Z. Wu, and L. Wang, "A comprehensive survey of fog computing: Concepts, applications, and future directions", *Future Gener. Comput. Syst.,* vol. 123, pp. 205-228, 2021.
[http://dx.doi.org/10.1016/j.future.2021.06.023]

[28] H. Jiang, S. Huang, and S. Wu, "A review of edge computing: From technology to architecture", *IEEE Access,* vol. 8, pp. 165921-165935, 2020.
[http://dx.doi.org/10.1109/ACCESS.2020.3026883]

[29] S. Gupta, and P. Varshney, "A review on challenges and opportunities in fog computing", *J. Ambient Intell. Humaniz. Comput.,* vol. 10, no. 7, pp. 2515-2534, 2019.
[http://dx.doi.org/10.1007/s12652-018-0911-1]

[30] A. Adhikari, J. Lu, and L. Zhang, "Edge computing: Vision and challenges", *IEEE Internet Things J.,* vol. 7, no. 5, pp. 3945-3954, 2020.
[http://dx.doi.org/10.1109/JIOT.2020.3002394]

[31] Y. Huang, Y. Gao, and J. Li, "Edge computing: Recent advances and future directions", *J. Parallel Distrib. Comput.,* vol. 155, pp. 172-184, 2021.
[http://dx.doi.org/10.1016/j.jpdc.2021.08.004]

[32] P. Hu, Z. Xu, and X. Xu, "A review of cloud-edge computing systems", *J. Netw. Comput. Appl.,* vol. 162, p. 102468, 2020.
[http://dx.doi.org/10.1016/j.jnca.2020.102468]

CHAPTER 5

Data-Driven Approach of Species DNA Sequencing Based on Similar Patterns Using Machine Learning

Manoj Kumar[1,*], **Anil Kumar Yadav**[1], **Vivek Kumar**[2] and **Bably Dolly**[3]

[1] *VIT Bhopal University, Madhya Pradesh, India*

[2] *Koneru Lakshmaiah Education Foundation, Vijayawada, Andhra Pradesh, India*

[3] *Integral University, Lucknow, UP, India*

Abstract: Bioinformatics is majorly used to infer hidden information from biological datasets using advanced techniques. Genomics uses machine learning and deep learning extensively to understand hidden facts and dependencies in new biological hypotheses. Recent advancements in dataset development have increased hope in understanding biologically inherited diseases, and a lot of computational models have shown promising results in deoxyribonucleic acid (DNA) sequencing to detect similar and dissimilar kinds of species. Two sequences are called homogeneous if similarities exceed, and we can conclude that two sequences are likely to have an evolutionary relationship. It has already been proven that chimpanzees are ancestors of humans, but can we prove it based on DNA similarity? This work is an effort to understand DNA structure and species of similar kinds based on genome sequencing. We have used the human, chimpanzee, and dog datasets to interpret their DNA sequence. The result shows that humans and chimpanzees share closeness in terms of DNA sequence, which confirms that both organisms are related to each other. Naïve Bays algorithm has shown similarity between chimpanzees and humans by scoring 99.30% and 98.40%, which are the closest figures compared to the dog with a score of 92.60%. This work has a lot of future scope to testify different species and their ancestor, which will help us understand life sciences more closely.

Keywords: Bioinformatics, Deep learning (DL), DNA, Genomics, Machine learning (ML).

INTRODUCTION

Computational intelligence techniques are widely used in DNA sequencing to analyze, interpret, and understand the genetic information encoded in DNA. Sequencing of DNA is the process of getting the order of nucleotides (A, T, C, G) in a DNA molecule, which is crucial for various applications in genetics, such as

* **Corresponding author Manoj Kumar:** VIT Bhopal University, Madhya Pradesh, India;
E-mail: manojkumar@vitbhopal.ac.in

Vikash Yadav, Vimal Kumar, Sonam Gupta & Vandana Dixit Kaushik (Eds.)

diagnosing genetic disorders, tracking the spread of infectious diseases, and identifying genetic mutations related to cancer. CI techniques, such as ML and artificial neural networks, are used in DNA sequencing to identify patterns and extract meaningful information from large and complex datasets. For example, ML algorithms can be used to predict the likelihood of certain mutations occurring in each DNA sequence based on the analysis of known mutations and associated genetic features. Artificial neural networks can also be trained to recognize specific patterns in DNA sequences, which can be used to identify disease-causing mutations or to classify sequences based on their origin or function. Additionally, CI techniques are also used for DNA sequence alignment and assembly, which involve comparing and merging multiple sequences to create a complete and accurate representation of a genome. These tasks require complex algorithms that can handle errors, gaps, and variations in the data, and CI techniques such as genetic algorithms and particle swarm optimization are often used to optimize the sequence alignment and assembly process [1].

As a data-driven science, genomics extensively utilizes ML and DL approaches to find data dependency and utilize different concepts of artificial intelligence to find similar patterns among different species in the world. It is a challenging task to propose new frameworks and algorithms that can be used to predict DNA sequences more accurately in biological datasets. Bioinformatics is an interdisciplinary domain that uses mathematics, statistics, and artificial intelligence to analyze the relationship between data points of huge complex datasets. According to research, biological data is being recorded and stored at a massive rate nowadays due to the availability of simulators, sensors, and labs. It is interesting to see how ML methods and biological approaches collectively help to find hidden patterns in biological datasets and provide useful knowledge discovery [2]. Data preparation, data collection, and data analysis using recent next-generation sequencing (NGS) techniques are still major challenges in this domain. DNA sequencing has numerous applications in different fields like pathology, genetics, virology, microbiology, systematics, and forensics.

There are many applications of ML in genome sequencing, such as genetic disorder classification, gene theory, prediction of genetic disorders caused by mutations, personalized medical treatment, molecular genetics, genomic medicine, enzyme replacement, drug supply prediction, and food management. Classification, clustering, and neural network models play important roles in the prediction and analysis of DNA sequencing and coding and their side effects. With the rapid growth in artificial intelligence (AI), AI can unlock a better understanding of genome sequencing, coding, and instruction forming, with better acceleration of scientific progress and, finally, huge benefits to society.

Fig. (**1**) shows the workflow of DNA sequencing, which is still an error-prone process, although it has become cheaper and faster. A lot of next-generation sequencing (NGS) technology-based companies like Illumina have shown 1% error, while third-generation companies have shown around 15% error. Biological datasets still need to be processed and cleaned before being applied to ML and DL models. Higher-quality datasets are still a major challenge to apply in artificial intelligence fields to get better results [3]. The main motive of this article is to understand DNA structure as well as to develop a more accurate computational model that can predict DNA sequence among species.

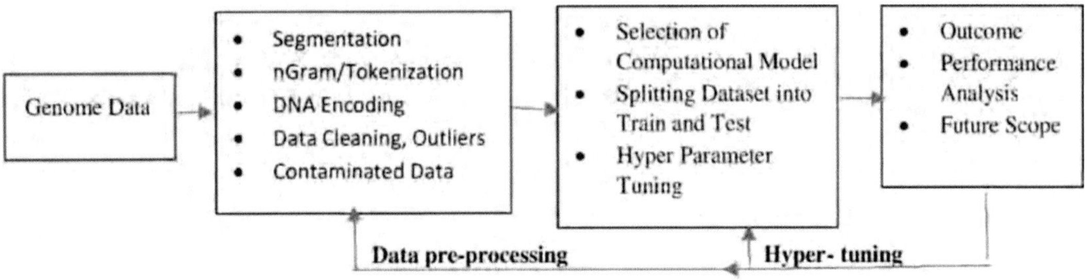

Fig. (1). Workflow of DNA sequencing using ML [1 - 3].

Background

DNA is like printed information that needs to be understood in terms of stored characters, words, or sentences. It is a language to learn. Understanding the complete glossary of DNA from A to Z is a very complex task. There are different kinds of structures possible in DNA based on base sequence. Research shows that only F, Q, U, V, and Y are the characters that are available to form a new kind of structure for the future. Several recent structures show mixed types of nature. Analysis of such a structure should be done very carefully before allocating new characters to a new structure [4]. A DNA sequence is the structure of a polynucleotide chain. DNA and RNA are genetic materials that are responsible for inheritance. A nucleotide is composed of three components called (i) Phosphate group, (ii) Five-carbon sugar or pentose, and (iii) Nitrogenous base. A nitrogenous base is made up of (i) Purines: A-Adenine and G: Guanine and (ii) Pyrimidines: Cytosine (C), Thymine (T), and Uracil (U). Genes are the building blocks of species. They give instructions to make proteins that are responsible for your physical chrematistics. DNA and RNA both perform different kinds of jobs in the human body. Genes are inherited from parents. Genes have the power to reproduce themselves again and again to form enough genes in an organism's body to fill an instructional manual. Chromosomes, which are made up of one molecule of DNA and proteins, give instructions to cells to make each unique in nature. DNA, genes, and chromosomes all work together to make a person's personality. DNA structure plays a vital role in the field of biological science in identifying and understanding the nature of living things.

Comparative study of genomics [5] of different species like humans, mice, rats, chimpanzees, dogs, cattle, and macaques has already had an impressive impact on understanding evolutionary progress and changes in biological science. Chimpanzees are very close to humans' genes. Researchers and scientists have always had a great interest in knowing how different attributes and behavioral aspects have been transferred from chimpanzees to humans. Humans and chimpanzees share almost the same number of chromosomes. Humans have 46 chromosomes, while chimpanzees have 48 chromosomes. This is one of the strong reasons for having similarities between them [6].

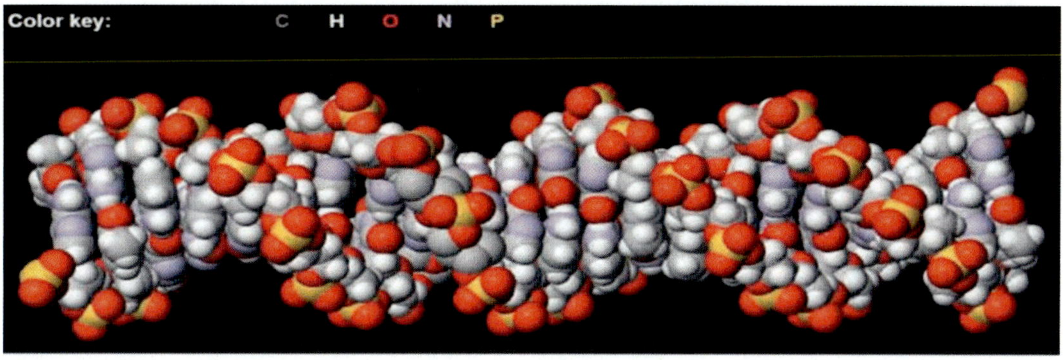

Fig. (2). DNA structure as space fill atoms and color by elements [7, 8].

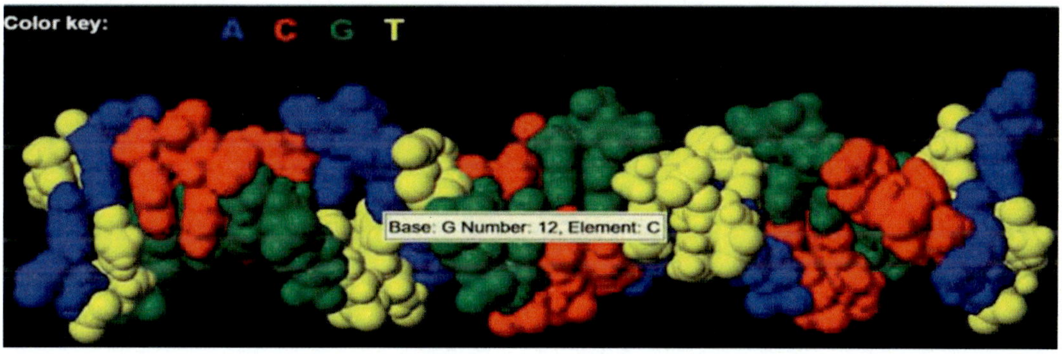

Fig. (3). DNA structure as space fill atoms and color by nucleotides (ACGT) [8].

The above images have been taken from DNA: The Double Helix Simulator (Fig. **2**). We can also show the DNA structure in the form of sticks, balls, and a ladder. DNA, or deoxyribonucleic acid, has numerous applications in various fields, including genetics, medicine, forensics, biotechnology, and agriculture (Fig. **3**). Here are some of the key DNA applications [7]:

a. **Genetic Testing and Diagnosis:** DNA analysis is used to diagnose genetic disorders and to determine whether an individual carries a specific genetic trait or mutation that increases their risk for certain diseases.
b. **Forensic Analysis**: DNA profiling is used to identify individuals and establish their presence at a crime scene or other forensic investigation.
c. **Biotechnology and Genetic Engineering**: DNA manipulation is used to create genetically modified organisms (GMOs) and develop new drugs and vaccines.
d. **Personalized Medicine**: DNA sequencing can be used to create personalized cures for diseases based on an individual's unique genetic makeup.
e. **Evolutionary Biology and Anthropology**: DNA analysis is used to study the evolution of species and trace human ancestry.
f. **Agricultural Biotechnology**: DNA testing can be used to identify and select desirable traits in plants and animals, such as drought resistance, disease resistance, and increased yield.
g. **Conservation Biology**: DNA analysis is used to study endangered species and to develop conservation strategies to preserve biodiversity.

These are just a few examples of the many ways in which DNA is used in different fields. The versatility of DNA makes it an essential tool for understanding the complexities of life and for advancing scientific research in a variety of areas.

Role of ML and DL

ML-DL is increasingly being used in DNA sequencing to develop computational models that can automatically analyze and interpret large and complex DNA datasets. Here are some specific roles that ML-DL plays in DNA sequencing:

a. **Sequence Alignment**: ML-DL algorithms can be used to develop more accurate and efficient sequence alignment methods. These algorithms can learn patterns in the data to help identify variations and differences between DNA sequences and to improve the accuracy of sequence alignment [9].
b. **Variant Calling**: Identifying genetic variants and mutations is a critical task in DNA sequencing. ML-DL techniques can be used to develop models that can automatically identify these variants with high accuracy and efficiency, enabling researchers and clinicians to identify disease-causing mutations and develop personalized treatments.
c. **Gene Expression Analysis**: ML and DL algorithms can be used to analyze gene expression data to identify patterns and trends in gene expression across different samples. This enables researchers to better understand how genes are regulated and how changes in gene expression may be related to disease.

d. **Epigenomics**: Epigenomic data, which describes how genes are regulated without changes to the DNA sequence, is complex and difficult to analyze. ML-DL can be used to develop models that can learn from epigenomic data to identify patterns and relationships between different features of the data.
e. **Drug Discovery**: ML-DL can be used to analyze DNA sequencing data to identify potential drug targets and to develop new drugs based on the genetic makeup of a patient.

Overall, ML and DL play a critical role in DNA sequencing by enabling the development of computational models that can automatically analyze and interpret large and complex DNA datasets, leading to new insights and discoveries in genetics and personalized medicine.

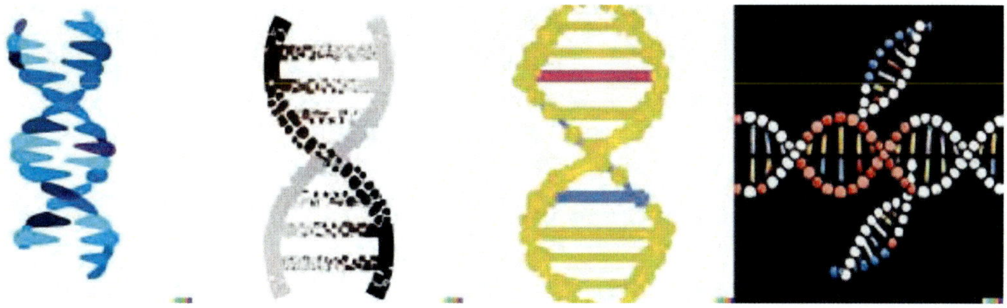

Fig. (4). Different DNA Molecule Structure Variations [3].

Pattern Matching in DNA

Pattern matching is a key aspect of DNA sequencing that involves finding matches between a known sequence and an unknown sequence. This is often done to identify genetic variants, to determine the presence of specific mutations, or to compare sequences between different individuals or species, as shown in Fig. (**4**). Here are some of the key methods used for pattern matching in DNA:

a. **Exact Matching**: Exact matching involves searching for a specific sequence of nucleotides in a DNA sequence. This is typically done using algorithms like the Knuth-Morris-Pratt algorithm (KMP algorithm) or the Boyer-Moore algorithm. These algorithms can efficiently find exact matches between a reference sequence and a query sequence [10].
b. **Approximate Matching**: Approximate matching involves finding matches between sequences that are similar but not identical. This is typically done using algorithms such as the Smith-Waterman algorithm or the Needleman-Wunsch algorithm. These algorithms use dynamic programming to find the best alignment between two sequences, considering insertions, deletions, and substitutions [10].

Pattern Discovery: Pattern discovery involves identifying frequently occurring sequences in a DNA dataset. This can be done using algorithms such as Apriori or the frequent pattern growth (FP-growth) algorithm. These algorithms can identify patterns in the data that are associated with specific genetic traits or mutations.

a. **Hidden Markov Models**: Hidden Markov Models (HMMs) can be used to identify complex patterns in DNA data. HMMs can be used to model the DNA sequence structure and to identify regions of the sequence that are associated with specific genetic traits or mutations.
b. **Machine Learning**: ML algorithms, such as support vector machines (SVMs), random forests, and neural networks, can be used to get patterns in DNA data. These algorithms can be trained on large datasets to identify patterns that are associated with specific genetic traits or mutations. Overall, pattern matching is a critical aspect of DNA sequencing that involves finding matches between a known sequence and an unknown sequence. The methods used for pattern matching in DNA are constantly evolving and improving, leading to new insights and discoveries in genetics and personalized medicine.

DNA Sequence Encoding Specific Techniques

a. **Homology search**: This involves comparing the DNA sequence of interest to a database of known DNA sequences to identify regions of homology. This can be done using tools such as BLAST (Basic Local Alignment Search Tool) or FASTA.
b. **Hidden Markov Models (HMMs)**: HMMs are statistical models that can be used to identify conserved protein domains in DNA sequences. This approach is particularly useful for identifying sequences that are not well conserved at the nucleotide level but have conserved protein domains.
c. **Position-specific scoring matrices (PSSMs):** PSSMs are another statistical approach used to identify conserved protein domains. They are generated from multiple sequence alignments and can be used to search for similar sequences in a database.
d. **ML:** Various ML algorithms can be trained on annotated datasets to identify DNA sequences encoding specific features. For example, CNNs (convolutional neural networks) have been used to identify transcription factor binding sites and other functional DNA elements.
e. **Codon usage bias**: Codon usage bias can be used to identify protein-coding regions in DNA sequences. This approach is because different organisms have different preferences for using codons to encode specific amino acids. Therefore, the codon usage pattern of a DNA sequence can be used to predict whether it encodes a protein-coding region. These techniques can be used

alone or in combination to identify DNA sequences encoding specific features or functional domains.

Structure of Paper

Section one contains an introduction and background, which will help you understand the fundamentals related to the topic. Related work and problem statements are part of section two. Section three describes the methodology, which contains a dataset description and framework used to identify similar patterns in species. The results have been discussed in section four. Section five contains the conclusion and future scope of work.

RELATED WORK

In the last four decades, a lot of work has been done in this domain, but the cost and computation time have been high. The third generation of DNA sequencing has gained a lot of popularity in terms of speed and reduced cost due to a greater number of biological datasets and different computational model availability. We have tried to capture the recent state of the art from the past few years of literature available globally. There are three major popular DNA sequence coding methods: sequential encoding, hot encoding, and k-*mer* encoding [11]. Remita, M. A. *et al.* [11] have proposed CASTOR, which is a virus classification platform inspired by molecular biology named restriction fragment length polymorphism (RFLP). CASTOR has shown very promising results for the future. Huang *et al.* [12] have used a support vector machine (SVM) to classify cancer genome data. Authors conclude that SVM is better at identifying cancer genes in genomic datasets. This article [13] presents different ML models that are used to classify gene sequences. The authors have also discussed different challenges and issues in bioinformatics in the context of applying ML. Busia A. *et al.* [14] have proposed a deep neural network (DNN), which has shown better results than other existing approaches, k-*mer*, alignment, and taxonomic binning baselines in the 16S mock community dataset. This work was the very first step in producing DL models to predict labels using short DNA sequences.

Another View of Literature Survey: A Summary

There has been a significant amount of research in the field of DNA sequencing, including the development of new technologies, methods, and algorithms. Some of the most significant related works in DNA sequencing include:

a. **Sanger Sequencing**: The Sanger sequencing method, developed by Fred Sanger in 1977, was the first method for sequencing DNA. It involves using dideoxynucleotides to terminate DNA synthesis at specific positions, resulting in a set of fragments that can be used to determine the nucleotide sequence of the original DNA [9].

b. **Next-Generation Sequencing**: Technologies of next-generation sequencing (NGS) have revolutionized DNA sequencing by enabling the parallel sequencing of millions of DNA fragments in a single run. This has dramatically increased the speed and efficiency of DNA sequencing and has led to a significant reduction in the cost of sequencing [15].
c. **Third-Generation Sequencing**: Third-generation sequencing technologies, such as PacBio and Nanopore, have shown further improvement toward the accuracy and efficiency of DNA sequencing by allowing the direct sequencing of single DNA molecules. This eliminates the need for PCR amplification and reduces the risk of sequencing errors.
d. **Computational Methods:** Computational methods, such as alignment algorithms and ML techniques, are used to analyze and interpret large amounts of data generated by DNA sequencing. These methods enable the identification of genetic variants, the prediction of gene function, and the development of personalized treatments based on an individual's unique genetic makeup.
e. **Clinical Applications:** DNA sequencing has significant clinical applications, including the diagnosis of genetic diseases, the identification of disease-causing mutations, and the development of personalized treatments. Recent studies have also shown the potential of using DNA sequencing to monitor disease progression and to detect early-stage cancers.

Overall, the related works in DNA sequencing have led to significant advances in our understanding of genetics and have opened up new avenues for research and clinical applications.

Research Challenges

DNA sequencing is the approach of getting the precise order of nucleotides, such as adenine, guanine, cytosine, and thymine, in a DNA molecule. The accurate identification of DNA sequences is crucial in various fields, including medical diagnosis, drug development, and genetic research [16]. However, DNA sequencing faces several challenges, such as:

a. **Accuracy**: The accuracy of DNA sequencing is critical, as even a single incorrect nucleotide can lead to misinterpretation of the entire sequence. Errors can occur due to various factors, such as sample contamination, sequencing technology limitations, and processing errors.
b. **Complexity**: DNA sequences are often long and complex, with millions or billions of nucleotides. Analysing and interpreting such large datasets can be challenging and require advanced algorithms and computational resources.
c. **Cost**: DNA sequencing can be expensive, particularly for large-scale projects

or studies involving many samples. Cost reductions through improvements in sequencing technology and data analysis are essential to enable wider access and adoption of DNA sequencing in research and healthcare.

d. **Ethical and privacy concerns**: DNA sequencing raises ethical and privacy concerns, as genetic data can reveal sensitive information about an individual or population. Appropriate measures are necessary to protect the confidentiality and security of DNA and ensure that it is used ethically and in compliance with regulations and guidelines.

Problem Statements of Related Work

1. Development of bioinformatics systems to minimize error rate in DNA sequencing.
2. Design of computational model to improve accuracy with minimum cost.
3. Predicting DNA Sequences using machine learning and deep learning for improved DNS Resolution in Network Systems.

RECENT DEVELOPMENT IN DNA SEQUENCING AND FUTURE TRENDS [17]

There have been several recent developments in DNA sequencing technologies that have greatly increased the speed and accuracy of DNA sequencing, as well as reduced the cost. Some of the key developments include:

a. **Third-generation sequencing**: This refers to a group of sequencing technologies that can sequence longer stretches of DNA in a single read, which can reduce the need for the assembly of short reads. Some examples of third-generation sequencing technologies include PacBio and Oxford Nanopore.
b. **High-throughput sequencing**: This refers to the ability to sequence many samples simultaneously, which has greatly increased the efficiency and speed of DNA sequencing. Some examples of high-throughput sequencing platforms include Illumina and Ion Torrent.
c. **Single-cell sequencing**: This is a technique that allows researchers to sequence the DNA of individual cells, which can provide a more detailed understanding of cellular heterogeneity and help to identify rare cell types.
d. **Metagenomic sequencing**: This is a technique that allows researchers to sequence the DNA of entire microbial communities, which can provide insights into the diversity and function of these communities.
e. **Advances in bioinformatics**: As DNA sequencing technologies have improved, so have the computational tools used to analyze the data. There have been many recent developments in bioinformatics, including improved algorithms for read alignment and assembly, as well as methods for analyzing large-scale genomic data.

f. **DNA Nanotechnology**: Global warming has always created a platform for the ZIKA(ZIKV) virus and dengue virus to spread easily. Biosensors have been used in DNA nanotechnology to minimize these viruses' effects worldwide [18]. Table **1** shows the recent DNA technological growth and its outcome.

Table 1. Recent DNA technological growth and its outcomes.

S.NO.	Key Concepts in DNA Technology	Outcome	Ref.
1.	Cytosensing	DNA structure is useful in life sciences.	[19]
2.	CRISPR-Cas based system: MPXV detection tool.	Monkeypox virus genome.	[20]
3.	Biological similarity between humans and chimpanzees	The similarity is due to the fact that both species have evolved to be similar in order to survive in their respective environments.	[21]
4.	DNA sequencing and its various applications, as well as the future trends associated with this technology.	Further advances in DNA sequencing technology and its various applications.	[22]
5.	Automatic DNA sequencer and mass spectrometry.	Speed and efficiency of DNA sequencing, chemiluminescent detection.	[23]
6.	Early detection of different variations of breast cancer in women.	NSG (Next-generation sequencing) applications in the cancer field and the role of IHC (immunohistochemistry) in patient management.	[24]
7.	Quantification of viable bacteria abundance in food by next-generation sequencing (NSG).	Possible to determine the absolute numbers of bacteria in a food sample, which can help improve food safety.	[25]
8..	Use of next-generation sequencing technologies in forensics.	A global snapshot of current opinions on the use of these technologies in forensics.	[26]
9.	Use of NSG panels to distinguish separate primary lung adenocarcinomas from intrapulmonary metastases.	This study will improve the diagnosis and treatment of lung cancer.	[27]
10.	Development of an AI nanopore device for high-throughput DNA sequencing using an ML-aided quantum-tunneling approach.	Nanopore technology, Quantum tunneling.	[28]

Application of Artificial Intelligence and Data Science in DNA Sequencing

AI and data science are being progressively used in the field of DNA sequencing to help improve the accuracy, speed, and efficiency of the process. Here are some of the applications of AI and data science in DNA sequencing:

a. **Genome assembly**: AI and data science can be used to help assemble large and complex genomes. This involves piecing together the DNA sequences obtained from sequencing machines into a coherent whole. AI algorithms can help identify overlaps between fragments of DNA, which can then be assembled into a full genome.

b. **Variant calling:** Variant calling involves identifying differences between an individual's DNA sequence and a reference genome. This is important for identifying genetic mutations that may be associated with disease. AI and data science algorithms can be used to help identify and classify these variants more accurately and efficiently.
c. **Gene expression analysis**: AI and data science can be used to analyze gene expression data, which can help researchers understand how genes are regulated and how they contribute to different biological processes. This involves analyzing large datasets and identifying patterns and correlations that may not be visible to the human eye.
d. **Drug discovery:** AI and data science can be used to help identify new drugs and drug targets. This involves analyzing large databases of chemical compounds and using ML algorithms to identify compounds that are likely to be effective against specific diseases or targets.
e. **Precision medicine:** AI and data science can be used to help develop personalized treatment plans based on an individual's genetic makeup. This involves analyzing the individual's DNA sequence and identifying genetic variants that may be associated with a particular disease or response to treatment.

Overall, AI and data science are playing an increasingly important role in DNA sequencing, helping to improve our understanding of the genome and its role in health and disease.

Research Challenges in DNA Sequencing

DNA sequencing is the approach of getting the order of nucleotides in a DNA molecule. It has revolutionized many fields, including genetics, medicine, and agriculture. However, there are still many challenges in DNA sequencing that researchers are working to overcome. Some of the key challenges include:

a. **Accuracy**: DNA sequencing technologies can produce errors, especially when sequencing long stretches of DNA. Researchers are working to improve the accuracy of sequencing technologies, which will make it easier to identify rare genetic variants and mutations.
b. **Speed**: DNA sequencing can be time-consuming, which limits its usefulness in certain applications. Researchers are developing new methods that can sequence DNA more quickly, which will enable more rapid diagnosis of genetic diseases and faster research progress.

c. **Cost**: DNA sequencing can be expensive, which limits its accessibility to many researchers and clinicians. Researchers are developing new technologies that can sequence DNA more affordably, which will democratize access to genetic information.
d. **Read length**: Some DNA sequencing technologies can only read short stretches of DNA at a time, which can make it difficult to assemble the entire genome. Researchers are developing new methods that can read longer stretches of DNA, which will make it easier to assemble complex genomes.
e. **Data analysis**: DNA sequencing generates vast amounts of data, which can be challenging to analyze and interpret. Researchers are developing new algorithms and tools that can analyze DNA data more efficiently and accurately, which will enable researchers and clinicians to make better use of genetic information.

Overall, these challenges are being addressed through ongoing research and development, and improvements in DNA sequencing technology are expected to continue to accelerate our understanding of genetics and drive progress in many fields.

Analysis of DNA Sequencing Error Correction

Nucleus is a tool for DNA sequence error correction developed by researchers at the University of California, Los Angeles (UCLA), which uses ML algorithms implemented in TensorFlow [29]. The goal of Nucleus is to improve the accuracy of DNA sequencing data by correcting errors that arise during the sequencing process. Here, we provide a critical analysis of this approach. One of the main advantages of using ML algorithms for DNA sequencing error correction is that these algorithms can learn from large amounts of sequencing data and use this knowledge to identify and correct errors. This can potentially lead to higher accuracy in DNA sequencing and reduce the cost of downstream analysis. Moreover, using TensorFlow for ML can help improve the scalability of the error correction process by enabling parallel processing. However, there are also several challenges associated with using ML for DNA sequencing error correction. One major challenge is the need for large amounts of high-quality training data, which may not always be available, especially for less well-studied organisms or rare mutations. In addition, the performance of ML algorithms can be sensitive to the quality and representativeness of the training data. Therefore, careful selection and curation of the training data is crucial for the success of the error correction process. Another challenge is the potential for overfitting, where the ML algorithm becomes too specialized to the training data and performs poorly on new data. To address this, the Nucleus team has implemented various techniques, such as dropout and early stopping, to regularize the ML model and prevent overfitting. However, it is still important to carefully validate the performance of the model on independent test datasets to ensure its generalizability.

Overall, the use of ML algorithms implemented in TensorFlow for DNA sequencing error correction has the potential to improve the accuracy and scalability of DNA sequencing. However, careful selection and curation of training data, as well as appropriate regularization techniques, are crucial for the success of the approach. Future work may focus on developing more sophisticated ML models that can better capture the complex patterns of sequencing errors and improve the accuracy of DNA sequencing even further.

Exploring the Intersection of Genomic Medicine and ML: An Introspective Analysis of Computational Models

ML has been increasingly applied in genomic medicine to help identify patterns and make predictions based on large datasets of genomic data. In this field, several computational models have been developed to facilitate the analysis of genomic data using ML techniques. One popular computational model is the neural network, which is a type of DL model that is designed to mimic the structure and function of the human brain. Neural networks have been used in genomic medicine to analyze gene expression data and predict disease outcomes. For example, a neural network can be trained on gene expression data from patients with a particular disease and used to predict the likelihood of a patient developing the disease based on their gene expression profile. Another computational model that is commonly used in genomic medicine is the support vector machine (SVM). SVMs are a type of supervised learning algorithm that can be used for classification and regression tasks. In genomic medicine, SVMs have been used to classify genomic data into different categories, such as disease versus non-disease or different subtypes of a disease. Random forests are another popular computational model in genomic medicine. They are an ensemble learning method that combines multiple decision trees to improve the accuracy of predictions. Random forests have been used to identify genetic variants that are associated with disease risk and to predict the outcomes of different treatment options.

Finally, Bayesian networks are a kind of probabilistic graphical model that can be used to show complex relationships between variables. In genomic medicine, Bayesian networks have been used to model gene regulatory networks and identify the genetic factors that contribute to the development of complex diseases. Overall, ML has the potential to revolutionize genomic medicine by enabling more accurate diagnosis and personalized treatment options. However, the field is still in its early stages, and more research is needed to validate the effectiveness of different computational models and ensure that they are used responsibly and ethically [30].

Deep Learning in Bioinformatics and its Applications in DNA Sequencing

DL is a subset of ML that utilizes neural networks to learn from large and complex datasets. In bioinformatics, DL has been applied to various tasks, including DNA sequencing. DNA sequencing refers to the process of determining the precise order of nucleotides in a DNA molecule. DL has been used in DNA sequencing to improve accuracy and speed up the process. One application of DL in DNA sequencing is error correction. Sequencing errors can arise from a variety of sources, including inaccuracies in the sequencing technology itself, sample preparation, and data processing. DL models can be trained to detect and correct these errors, improving the accuracy of the sequencing results. Another application of DL in DNA sequencing is variant calling. Variant calling refers to the process of identifying genetic variations in DNA sequences. DL models can be trained to identify these variations, which can be used to diagnose genetic diseases and develop personalized treatments.

DL has also been applied to genome assembly, which is the process of assembling a complete genome sequence from short DNA fragments. Traditional methods of genome assembly are time-consuming and computationally expensive. DL models can be trained to predict the location and orientation of DNA fragments, which can speed up the assembly process. In addition to these applications, DL has also been used in protein structure prediction, drug discovery, and gene expression analysis. Despite the promise of DL in DNA sequencing, there are still some challenges that need to be addressed. One challenge is the need for large and diverse datasets to train DL models. Another challenge is the interpretability of DL models, which can make it difficult to understand the biological insights they provide. In summary, DL has shown great promise in bioinformatics, particularly in DNA sequencing. Its ability to learn from large and complex datasets has the potential to transform our understanding of genetics and improve personalized medicine. However, further research is needed to address the challenges and limitations of DL in bioinformatics.

Applications of DNA Sequencing in Healthcare and Disease Management [31]

DNA sequencing has revolutionized healthcare and disease management by enabling precise and personalized diagnosis, treatment, and prevention of various diseases. Here are some applications of DNA sequencing in healthcare and disease management:

a. **Genetic diagnosis**: DNA sequencing can identify genetic mutations that cause inherited diseases such as cystic fibrosis, sickle cell anemia, and Huntington's disease. This information can help in early diagnosis, treatment, and genetic counseling for patients and their families.
b. **Cancer diagnosis and treatment**: DNA sequencing can detect cancer-associated genetic mutations and help in diagnosis, prognosis, and personalized treatment of cancer. It can also identify specific genetic mutations that can be targeted with precision therapies such as immunotherapy, targeted therapy, and gene therapy.
c. **Pharmacogenomics:** DNA sequencing can help in predicting an individual's response to certain drugs and their potential side effects. This information can help in selecting the most effective and safe medications for a patient based on their genetic makeup.
d. **Infectious disease diagnosis**: DNA sequencing can identify the genetic material of infectious agents such as viruses, bacteria, and fungi, enabling rapid and accurate diagnosis of infectious diseases. It can also help in tracking the spread of infectious diseases and developing effective treatments and vaccines.
e. **New drug discovery:** DNA sequencing can help in identifying novel drug targets by identifying genetic mutations and pathways involved in disease development. This information can lead to the development of new drugs that are more effective and have fewer side effects.
f. **Precision medicine:** DNA sequencing can enable the development of personalized treatment plans that take into account an individual's genetic makeup, lifestyle, and environmental factors. This approach can lead to more effective and targeted treatments and better outcomes for patients.

In conclusion, DNA sequencing has many applications in healthcare and disease management, enabling precise diagnosis, treatment, and prevention of various diseases. As technology continues to advance, it is likely to play an increasingly important role in the future of medicine.

METHODOLOGY

Dataset Description and Data Pre-Processing

Three datasets of species named human (5.55MB), chimpanzee (3.26 MB), and dog (1.67 MB) of high-quality data of DNA sequences were collected to estimate similarities among them. Data handling in Fasta format has been done by the Biopython library for molecular structure analysis. Since the DNA sequence is of variable length. So, the DNA sequence has been split into fixed 6-character lengths called Hexamers using the k-mer counting approach. This means that any

DNA sequence of 24 characters is broken into 4 equal sizes of subgroups, and each subgroup has size characters. Thus, by doing so, we are preparing the given sequence in a machine-feedable format. Fig. (**5**) and Table **2** show the different core details and n-gram representation of the DNA sequence as the input string.

s.n.	sequence	class
0	ATGCCCCAACTAAATACTACCGTATGGCCCACCATAATTACCCCCA...	4
1	ATGAACGAAAATCTGTTCGCTTCATTCATTGCCCCCACAATCCTAG...	4
2	ATGTGTGGCATTTGGGCGCTGTTTGGCAGTGATGATTGCCTTTCTG...	3
3	ATGTGTGGCATTTGGGCGCTGTTTGGCAGTGATGATTGCCTTTCTG...	3
4	ATGCAACAGCATTTTGAATTTGAATACCAGACCAAAGTGGATGGTG...	3
5.	**............... Many more sequences...........................**	

Fig. (5). DNA sequencing using k-mer and n-gram concept on human data [5, 6].

Table 2. Dataset description of attribute and class labels.

Gene Family	Number	Class Label
G protein-coupled receptors.	531	0
Tyrosine Kinase.	534	1
Tyrosine Phosphatase.	349	2
Synthetase.	672	3
Synthase.	711	4
Lon Channel.	240	5
Transcription Factor.	1343	6

Gene family has a set of gene members that affect the similarity index in different species. They have been divided into seven classes, as shown in Table **2**. We have visualized gene family members in all three species:

Humans, chimpanzees, and dogs. Since our dataset of species is in text format (containing the sequence of characters). We can encode it into the numerical form using three approaches called (i) Ordinal encoding DNA sequence, (ii) One-hot encoding DNA sequence, and (iii) k-mer counting. In our approach, we have used the k-mer counting approach.

General Procedure to Generate Uniform Vector Length of Given Sequence Input using K-Mer Concept

The k-mer counting approach produces uniform length vectors to feed into neural networks or into ML models. This approach gives a padding concept, which helps to include either ‘0’ or ‘any character’ to make a uniform vector. The language of DNA and protein sequences can be seen as a representation of instructions and functions for molecules found in all life forms. This resemblance continues with the genome as a book, subsequences (genes and gene families) as sentences and chapters, k-mers and peptides as words, and nucleotide bases and amino acids as the alphabet. Given this relationship, it makes sense that natural language processing should also implement the natural language of DNA and protein sequences.

We first take the long biological sequence and break it down into overlapping “words” of length k, where k is the number of hexamers. For example, if we use hexamers, “ATGCATGCA” becomes: ‘ATGCAT’, ‘TGCATG’, ‘GCATGC’, ‘CATGCA’. Hence, our example sequence is broken down into 4 hexamer words.

mySeq = 'GTGCCCAGGTTCAGTGAGTGACACAGGCAG'

Kmers_funct(mySeq, size=7)

['gtgccca','tgcccag','gcccagg', 'cccaggt', 'ccaggtt','caggttc', 'aggttca', 'ggttcag', 'gttcagt','ttcagtg','tcagtga', 'cagtgag','agtgagt','gtgagtg', 'tgagtga', 'gagtgac', 'agtgaca', 'gtgacac', 'tgacaca', 'gacacag', 'acacagg', 'cacaggc', 'acaggca', 'caggcag']: These are k-mer words.

Now, we have managed the word length and overlap problem and have created a sentence containing 4 letter of words, each containing six lengths.'gtgccc tgccca gcccag cccagg ccaggt caggtt aggttc ggttca gttcag ttcagt tcagtg cagtga agtgag gtgagt tgagtg gagtga agtgac gtgaca tgacac gacaca acacag cacagg acaggc caggca aggcag'

Fig. (**5**) shows how different sequences from human data have been divided into seven classes. The same procedure has been done with the chimpanzee and dog datasets. Class distribution and balance of sequence numbers have been verified, and it was found that the species dataset is balanced. The number of genes converted into feature vectors for humans is 4380, while for the same case, it is 1682 and 820 for chimpanzees and dogs, respectively.

Component Used in General Framework

DNA sequencing is the process of determining the order of nucleotides (adenine, guanine, cytosine, and thymine) in a DNA molecule. The development of high-throughput sequencing technologies has made it possible to generate vast amounts of DNA sequence data at a lower cost than ever before. However, the interpretation and analysis of this data can be challenging, as it requires advanced computational techniques to extract meaningful insights. ML algorithms can be used to process and analyze DNA sequencing data to identify patterns and associations. Here is a framework for using ML in DNA sequencing:

1. **Pre-processing**: The raw DNA sequence data needs to be processed before it can be used for ML analysis. This includes removing low-quality reads, trimming adapters, and correcting errors. Various software packages such as Trimmomatic, BBDuk, and FASTX-Toolkit can be used for this purpose.

2. **Feature extraction**: The next step is to extract relevant features from the processed DNA sequence data. This can include sequence composition, the k-mer frequency, and various genomic annotations such as gene locations, regulatory regions, and functional elements.

3. **Data representation:** The extracted features need to be represented in a format suitable for ML algorithms. This can include one-hot encoding, binary encoding, and various other numerical representations.

4. **Model training**: ML algorithms such as random forests, neural networks, and support vector machines can be trained on the DNA sequence data to classify sequences or make predictions. The choice of algorithm depends on the nature of the problem being addressed.

5. **Model evaluation:** The trained model needs to be evaluated to determine its performance. This can include measures such as accuracy, precision, recall, and F1 score.

6. **Model optimization**: The model can be further optimized by adjusting hyperparameters, feature selection, or using ensemble methods to combine multiple models.

7. **Model deployment:** The final step is to deploy the trained model in a real-world application. This can include identifying disease-causing mutations, predicting gene expression levels, or classifying sequences for species identification.

In summary, ML can be a powerful tool for analyzing DNA sequencing data. By following the framework outlined above, researchers can use ML algorithms to identify patterns and associations in the data, leading to new insights and discoveries in genetics and genomics.

RESULTS AND DISCUSSION

We have used different ML models on the DNA dataset of species. The results show that chimpanzees and humans share a close bond by achieving 99.30% and 98.40% accuracy using the Naïve bays model (Table **3**). This study shows that ML models can be used to check similarity among species in the case of DNA. Naïve Bays classification algorithms of machine learning have shown prominent results, as Fig. (**6**) shows the similarity of DNA accuracy among species.

Table 3. Similarity index among species using ML models.

S.No.	Computational Approach	Species	Comparison Parameter	Accuracy %	Precision %	Recall	F1 Score
1.	Multimodal Naïve bays Classifier.	Dogs Chimpanzees Humans.	Chromosome Subfamily Accessions.	92.60 99.30 98.40	0.9340 0.994 0.984	0.926 0.993 0.984	0.925 0.993 0.984

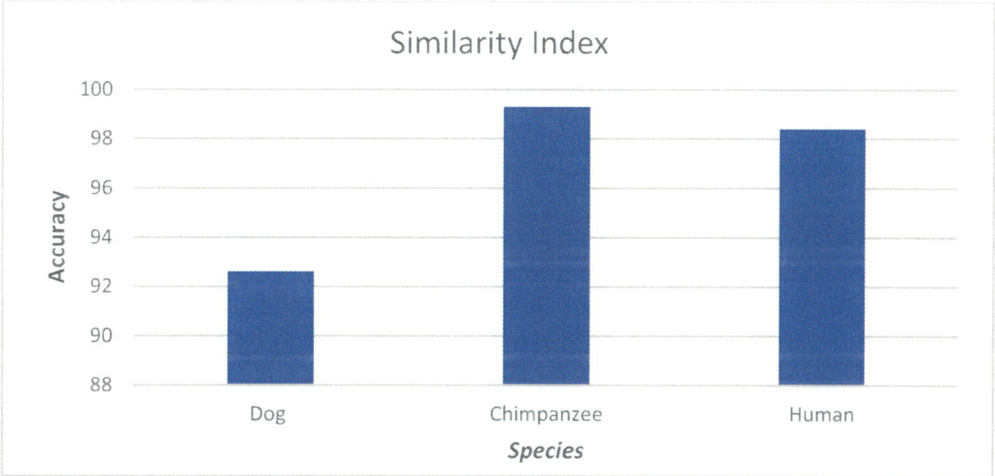

Fig. (6). Similarity of DNA accuracy among species.

CONCLUSION AND FUTURE SCOPE

Our results show that ML techniques can be useful in analyzing genomic data. The results of this study show that the human and chimpanzee genomes are 99% similar. Naïve Bayes has shown better similarity accuracy than other approaches. This similarity is because humans and chimpanzees share a common ancestor.

The ML algorithm was able to accurately predict this similarity. NSG (Next-generation sequencing) is the latest big thing in this field. The complete research scenario in the DNA sequencing field is likely to change with the advent of next-generation sequencing (NGS). NGS is a technology that allows researchers to sequence DNA at a much higher throughput than traditional sequencing methods. This means that NGS can be used to sequence large numbers of DNA samples in a short amount of time. This makes NGS an ideal technology for large-scale sequencing projects, such as genome sequencing. NGS has already had a significant impact on the field of DNA sequencing. In just a few years, NGS has gone from being a research tool used by a few labs to a technology that is widely used by researchers all over the world. The high throughput and low cost of NGS have made it possible for researchers to sequence genomes and other large DNA molecules at a scale that was not possible before. The impact of NGS is likely to continue in the future. As NGS technology continues to improve, more and more researchers will likely begin to use NGS for their research projects. This will lead to discoveries and advances in the field of DNA sequencing. Sequencing DNA is a complex task that can be greatly improved using artificial intelligence and ML. However, several challenges need to be overcome to achieve this. One of the biggest challenges is the large amount of data that is generated during the sequencing process. This data needs to be sorted and analyzed to identify the genetic sequence. Another challenge is the need to correct any errors that may occur during sequencing. This can be done using ML algorithms that are specifically designed to correct errors. Finally, the use of artificial intelligence and ML can help to improve the accuracy of the sequencing process.

In the future, artificial intelligence will play an even more important role in sequencing technology. AI will be used to improve the accuracy and speed of sequencing, as well as to analyze and interpret the data. This will allow scientists to sequence DNA more quickly and efficiently and to gain a better understanding of the genetic information contained within DNA. The future scope of AI and data science in DNA sequencing is vast. With the rapid advancement of AI and data science, we will be able to sequence DNA faster and more accurately. Additionally, we will be able to use AI and data science to interpret and analyze the data from DNA sequencing, which will help us to better understand the role of DNA in health and disease. There are many possible future technologies in DNA sequencing. One example is nanopore sequencing, which is a method of sequencing DNA by passing it through a tiny hole, or nanopore, in a membrane. This method is still in development, but it has the potential to be much faster and cheaper than current methods. There is huge scope for analyzing genomic data using the latest artificial intelligence and data science technology. We can propose a new framework to automate DNA work and create ML pipelines with the help of cloud applications.

REFERENCES

[1] C. Bi, "Computational intelligence in multiple sequence alignment", *International Journal of Intelligent Computing and Cybernetics,* vol. 1, no. 1, pp. 8-24, 2008. [http://dx.doi.org/10.1108/17563780810857103]

[2] A. Yang, W. Zhang, J. Wang, K. Yang, Y. Han, and L. Zhang, "Review on the application of machine learning algorithms in the sequence data mining of DNA", *Front. Bioeng. Biotechnol.,* vol. 8, p. 1032, 2020. [http://dx.doi.org/10.3389/fbioe.2020.01032] [PMID: 33015010]

[3] M. S. A. Vigil, M. Mirutuhula, S. Sarvagna, R. Supraja and G. P. Reddy, "DNA Sequencing Using Machine Learning Algorithms," *2022 International Conference on Data Science, Agents & Artificial Intelligence (ICDSAAI),* Chennai, India, 2022, pp. 1-4. [http://dx.doi.org/10.1109/ICDSAAI55433.2022.10028805]

[4] A. Ghosh, and M. Bansal, "A glossary of DNA structures from A to Z", *Acta Crystallogr. D Biol. Crystallogr.,* vol. 59, no. 4, pp. 620-626, 2003. [http://dx.doi.org/10.1107/S0907444903003251] [PMID: 12657780]

[5] G.E. Liu, L.K. Matukumalli, T.S. Sonstegard, L.L. Shade, and C.P. Van Tassell, "Genomic divergences among cattle, dog and human estimated from large-scale alignments of genomic sequences", *BMC Genomics,* vol. 7, no. 1, p. 140, 2006. [http://dx.doi.org/10.1186/1471-2164-7-140] [PMID: 16759380]

[6] M.V. Suntsova, and A.A. Buzdin, "Differences between human and chimpanzee genomes and their implications in gene expression, protein functions and biochemical properties of the two species", *BMC Genomics,* vol. 21, no. S7, suppl. Suppl. 7, p. 535, 2020. [http://dx.doi.org/10.1186/s12864-020-06962-8] [PMID: 32912141]

[7] S. Kosuri, and G.M. Church, "Large-scale de novo DNA synthesis: technologies and applications", *Nat. Methods,* vol. 11, no. 5, pp. 499-507, 2014. [http://dx.doi.org/10.1038/nmeth.2918] [PMID: 24781323]

[8] K.M. Kosikov, A.A. Gorin, V.B. Zhurkin, and W.K. Olson, "DNA stretching and compression: large-scale simulations of double helical structures 1 1Edited by I. Tinoco", *J. Mol. Biol.,* vol. 289, no. 5, pp. 1301-1326, 1999. [http://dx.doi.org/10.1006/jmbi.1999.2798] [PMID: 10373369]

[9] J.A. Shendure, G.J. Porreca, and G.M. Church, "Overview of DNA sequencing strategies", *Curr. Protoc. Mol. Biol.,* vol. Chapter 7, no. 1, p. 7.1, 2008. [PMID: 18231983]

[10] *Bioinformatics,* vol. 34, no. 10, pp. 1666-1671, 2018. [http://dx.doi.org/10.1093/bioinformatics/btx801] [PMID: 29240876]

[11] M.A. Remita, A. Halioui, A.A. Malick Diouara, B. Daigle, G. Kiani, and A.B. Diallo, "A machine learning approach for viral genome classification", *BMC Bioinformatics,* vol. 18, no. 1, p. 208, 2017. [http://dx.doi.org/10.1186/s12859-017-1602-3] [PMID: 28399797]

[12] S. Huang, N. Cai, P.P. Pacheco, S. Narrandes, Y. Wang, and W. Xu, "Applications of support vector machine (SVM) learning in cancer genomics", In: *Cancer Genomics & Proteomics* vol. 15. , 2018, no. 1, pp. 41-51.

[13] P.G.I.P. Dixit, "Machine learning in bioinformatics: Machine learning in bioinformatics: A novel approach for DNA sequencing", In: *IEEE,* 2015.

[14] A. Busia, G. E. Dahl, C. Fannjiang, D. H. Alexander, E. Dorfman, R. Poplin, C. Y. McLean, P. C. Chang, M. DePristo, , "A deep learning approach to pattern recognition for short DNA sequences", *BioRxiv,* p. 353474, 2018. [http://dx.doi.org/10.1101/353474]

[15] S. Behjati, and P.S. Tarpey, "What is next generation sequencing?", *Arch. Dis. Child. Educ. Pract. Ed.,* vol. 98, no. 6, pp. 236-238, 2013.
[http://dx.doi.org/10.1136/archdischild-2013-304340] [PMID: 23986538]

[16] T.J. Treangen, and S.L. Salzberg, "Repetitive DNA and next-generation sequencing: computational challenges and solutions", *Nat. Rev. Genet.,* vol. 13, no. 1, pp. 36-46, 2012.
[http://dx.doi.org/10.1038/nrg3117] [PMID: 22124482]

[17] A. Katara, S. Chand, H. Chaudhary, V. Chaudhry, H. Chandra, and R. C. Dubey, "Evolution and applications of Next Generation Sequencing and its intricate relations with chromatographic and spectrometric techniques in modern day sciences," *J. Chromatogr. Open*, vol. 5, p. 100121, May 2024. Available: https://www.sciencedirect.com/journal/journal-of-chromatography-open.

[18] G. Park, H. Park, S.C. Park, M. Jang, J. Yoon, J.H. Ahn, and T. Lee, "Recent Developments in DNA-Nanotechnology-Powered Biosensors for Zika/Dengue Virus Molecular Diagnostics", *Nanomaterials (Basel),* vol. 13, no. 2, p. 361, 2023.
[http://dx.doi.org/10.3390/nano13020361] [PMID: 36678114]

[19] N.C. Seeman, and H.F. Sleiman, "DNA nanotechnology", *Nat. Rev. Mater.,* vol. 1811, no. 1, pp. 1-9, 2018.
[PMID: 29926442]

[20] Q. Chen, I. Gul, C. Liu, Z. Lei, X. Li, M.A. Raheem, Q. He, Z. Haihui, E. Leeansyah, C.Y. Zhang, V. Pandey, K. Du, and P. Qin, "CRISPR-Cas12-based field-deployable system for rapid detection of synthetic DNA sequence of the monkeypox virus genome", *J. Med. Virol.,* vol. 95, no. 1, p. e28385, 2023.
[http://dx.doi.org/10.1002/jmv.28385] [PMID: 36478250]

[21] T.C. Wood, "The chimpanzee genome and the problem of biological similarity", *Occasional Papers of the BSG,* vol. 7, pp. 1-18, 2006.

[22] H.G. Griffin, and A.M. Griffin, "DNA sequencing", *Appl. Biochem. Biotechnol.,* vol. 38, no. 1-2, pp. 147-159, 1993.
[http://dx.doi.org/10.1007/BF02916418] [PMID: 8346903]

[23] R.A. Armitage, C.A. Makarewicz, and A.M. Pollard, "Shifting to a Higher Gear: Proteins, Small Molecules, and the Rise of Mass Spectrometry", In: *Handbook of Archaeological Sciences* vol. 1. , 2023, pp. 477-481.

[24] M. Nourieh, R. Vibert, M. Saint-Ghislain, J. Cyrta, and A. Vincent-Salomon, "Next-generation sequencing in breast pathology: real impact on routine practice over a decade since its introduction", *Histopathology,* vol. 82, no. 1, pp. 162-169, 2023.
[http://dx.doi.org/10.1111/his.14794] [PMID: 36482269]

[25] M.M. Foley, and F. Oldoni, "A global snapshot of current opinions of next-generation sequencing technologies usage in forensics", *Forensic Sci. Int. Genet.,* vol. 63, p. 102819, 2023.
[http://dx.doi.org/10.1016/j.fsigen.2022.102819] [PMID: 36509023]

[26] J.S. Allwood, N. Fierer, and R.R. Dunn, "The future of environmental DNA in forensic science", *Appl. Environ. Microbiol.,* vol. 86, no. 2, p. e01504-19, 2020.
[http://dx.doi.org/10.1128/AEM.01504-19] [PMID: 31704676]

[27] C. Y. Yang, Y. C. Yeh, L. C. Wang, Y. Y. Lin, S. Y. Lin, and S. Y. Wang, "Genomic Profiling With Large-Scale Next-Generation Sequencing Panels Distinguishes Separate Primary Lung Adenocarcinomas From Intrapulmonary Metastases", *Modern Pathology,* p. 100047, 2023.

[28] M.K. Jena, and B. Pathak, "Development of an Artificially Intelligent Nanopore for High-Throughput DNA Sequencing with a Machine-Learning-Aided Quantum-Tunneling Approach", *Nano Lett.,* vol. 23, no. 7, pp. 2511-2521, 2023.
[http://dx.doi.org/10.1021/acs.nanolett.2c04062] [PMID: 36799480]

[29] G. Baid, H. Li, and P. C. Chang, "Using Nucleus and TensorFlow for DNA sequencing error

correction," *TensorFlow Blog*, Jan. 31, 2019.

[30] M.K.K. Leung, A. Delong, B. Alipanahi, and B.J. Frey, "Machine learning in genomic medicine: a review of computational problems and data sets", *Proc. IEEE,* vol. 104, no. 1, pp. 176-197, 2016. [http://dx.doi.org/10.1109/JPROC.2015.2494198]

[31] T.R. Pak, and A. Kasarskis, "How next-generation sequencing and multiscale data analysis will transform infectious disease management", *Clin. Infect. Dis.,* vol. 61, no. 11, pp. 1695-1702, 2015. [http://dx.doi.org/10.1093/cid/civ670] [PMID: 26251049]

CHAPTER 6

Enhancing Intrusion Detection Performance with a Hybrid Module on KDD99 Dataset

Utkarsh Dixit[1,*]

[1] *ABES Engineering College, Ghaziabad, India*

Abstract: The internet and its connectivity have revolutionized the world, enabling people to share ideas, collaborate, and assist each other across various domains. Despite its benefits, the progress of technology comes with the inherent danger of being targeted by cybercriminals, which can compromise individuals' privacy and security online. Intrusion detection systems (IDSs) are used to identify and prevent such threats. This paper presents a hybrid ensemble module that uses a diverse set of weak learners to build a robust IDS capable of detecting new attacks that signature-based methods may miss. The research utilizes various ML techniques to develop a classification model that addresses the challenge of selecting suitable modules for IDS based on datasets. The proposed hybrid ensemble module provides an effective solution to enhance the accuracy and efficiency of IDS and mitigate the risk of cyberattacks in various fields, including healthcare, food service, and education.

Keywords: Hybrid ensemble learning, IDS, ML.

INTRODUCTION

As the utilization of interconnected computer systems and the internet continues to expand, the importance of network security has become increasingly critical. The rise in cyber threats has prompted organizations to employ network IDS to protect their connections against hostile assaults. IDSs operate by monitoring network traffic and detecting any suspicious behavior or recognized threats.

There are two primary detection methods utilized by IDS systems: Pattern-matching detection and Behavior-based detection. Signature-based detection operates by matching a specific pattern or set of rules from an attack database to determine whether an operation is dangerous. Anomaly-based detection, on the other hand, attempts to identify new forms of threats that may not be identified through pattern-matching detection.

* **Corresponding author Utkarsh Dixit:** ABES Engineering College, Ghaziabad, India;
E-mail: Utkarsh.dixitvk35@gmail.com

Vikash Yadav, Vimal Kumar, Sonam Gupta & Vandana Dixit Kaushik (Eds.)

While behavior-based detection is capable of detecting previously unknown threats, it has the potential to produce a high number of false positives. This is because it operates by identifying deviations from normal network behavior, which can include legitimate activities. However, ML approaches have emerged as a promising solution to accurately detect network system attacks.

Over the past few years, there has been an increasing use of ML in network security, with a focus on vulnerability scanning. This process involves categorizing and analyzing data to identify potential vulnerabilities that can be exploited by attackers. Pattern recognition in data can be done with the help of ML systems to detect any anomalies that may indicate a potential attack.

To enhance the precision of detection while minimizing erroneous results, a blended ensemble approach to instruction can be used. This model merges multiple weak learning algorithms to create a stronger and more accurate system. In this approach, the results of each weak learner are combined to produce a final prediction.

One of the challenges of developing a hybrid ensemble learning model is selecting the appropriate weak learners to use. This can involve choosing algorithms with different strengths and weaknesses to ensure that the final prediction is as accurate as possible. Additionally, it is critical to think about the processing resources needed to train and operate the algorithm, as this can affect its practical application.

Once the appropriate weak learners have been selected, they can be combined using various techniques, such as bagging, boosting, or stacking. Bagging involves training multiple instances of the same algorithm by applying the algorithm to distinct data subsets and consolidating their predictions. Boosting implies the sequential training of several weak learners, where each one concentrates on the samples that were wrongly classified by the previous learner. Conversely, stacking refers to the simultaneous training of multiple weak learners on the same data, and their predictions are then combined using a meta-learner model.

To assess the effectiveness of the blended ensemble learning approach, several metrics can be utilized, such as accuracy, precision, recall, and F1 score. These measurements can help evaluate the model's capacity to accurately categorize instances and identify cyber-attacks.

In addition to the hybrid ensemble learning model, other ML techniques can be used to improve network security. For example, DL algorithms, such as CNNs and RNNs, have been applied to network intrusion detection with promising results. Manual feature engineering is unnecessary as these algorithms can learn features from raw network data and autonomously detect anomalies.

DL algorithms pose a challenge in that they necessitate vast quantities of labeled data for training purposes. This can be difficult to obtain in network security, as collecting labeled data can be time-consuming and costly. Additionally, DL algorithms can be computationally expensive and require powerful hardware to train and run.

In conclusion, the rise in cyber threats has made network security a crucial issue for organizations. IDS systems perform an essential function in identifying and preventing network system attacks. While traditional detection methods, such as signature-based and anomaly-based detection, have their strengths and weaknesses, the application of ML approaches, such as hybrid ensemble learning and DL, has the potential to enhance the accuracy of detection and reduce false positives.

LITERATURE REVIEW

In their research paper [1], the authors proposed a novel architecture for cloud-based systems that aims to mitigate the risks associated with sharing resources and data in cloud environments. The authors identified various security challenges, such as security breaches, hacked accounts, injection flaws, misuse of features, and DDoS attacks, that are prevalent in cloud computing. To address these challenges, the proposed architecture uses log files to detect known attacks, Instantly prevents possibly dangerous activities and safeguards confidential information, and dynamically updates security rules to better adapt to evolving threats. The authors also emphasize the importance of regular security audits and monitoring to maintain the security and integrity of cloud-based systems. The proposed architecture offers a comprehensive approach to cloud security by leveraging multiple security measures, such as access control, data encryption, and intrusion detection. The authors argue that their architecture can enhance the overall security posture of cloud-based systems and increase customer reliance on cloud service providers. Overall, this research paper highlights the importance of addressing the security challenges associated with cloud computing and presents a promising solution that can mitigate these risks. The proposed architecture offers a practical and effective approach to enhancing cloud security, and future research can build upon this work to further improve the security of cloud-based systems.

The paper proposes [2] the use of an IDS to find out known and unknown attacks in cloud computing. The authors suggest the use of a hybrid algorithm of K-means clustering and SVM classification can be leveraged to enhance the IDS's precision. They tested their approach using the UNSW-NB15 dataset and compared the results with previous studies. The authors found that their K-means clustering analysis achieved slightly higher accuracy than previous studies, but the accuracy of their SVM model was still low for supervised techniques. Overall, the paper highlights the importance of developing effective IDSs to enhance security in cloud computing environments.

The paper [3] proposes a unique hybrid strategy that combines ML and DL to improve detection rates while also ensuring reliability in anomaly-based network IDS. To ensure effective pre-processing, the suggested technique employs SMOTE for data balancing and XGBoost for feature selection. The authors compared their developed method to various ML & DL algorithms and selected the most efficient model according to the performance analysis criteria benchmarked. The proposed method produced excellent results, with accuracy rates of 99.99% and 100% for the KDDCUP99 and CIC-MalMem-2022 datasets, respectively, with no cases of overfitting or Type-1 and Type-2 mistakes.

The increasing number of IoT devices has led to a growth in attack surfaces and the necessity for information security. IDS are employed to identify malicious traffic, but zero-day attack detection remains a challenge. DL methods, such as CNNs and GRUs, have been employed, but feature learning remains a challenge. In this chapter [4], the writers introduce a method that merges CNN and GRU to optimize network parameters. The writers leverage the CICIDS-2017 dataset and performance indicators such as precision, recall, FPR, TRP, and other related metrics to assess the model's effectiveness. The findings demonstrate a 98.73% accuracy rate and a 0.075 FPR rate. The proposed IDS scheme was evaluated against existing techniques through a comparative analysis, demonstrating its effectiveness in real-world cybersecurity settings.

The proposed model in a study [5] suggests a metaverse-based intrusion detection system for IoT networks for the future 5G mobile network. The approach employs a hybrid approach based on a generative adversarial network (GAN). The model incorporates a gradient penalty Wasserstein distance technique to attain Nash equilibrium, combined with deep autoencoder (DAE) and RF algorithms for abnormal traffic detection. The proposed model achieves high accuracy,and binary and multiple classification experiments achieve accuracies of 99.8% and 99.6%, respectively. The use of GANs, DAE, and RF algorithms in the proposed model shows significant potential for improving network security in the future metaverse environment.

The paper proposes [6] the development of IDS To ensure the safety of Industrial IoT networks. The authors proposed 3 models based on DL architectures of CNN, LSTM, and a blended fusion of these. The study compared normal and abnormal data from the UNSW-NB15 and X-IIoTID datasets following a binary and multi-class classification. In both datasets, the hybrid CNN + LSTM model had the highest precision for detecting intrusions, with 93.21% precision for binary classification and 92.9% precision for multi-class classification in the UNSW-NB15 dataset and 99.84% precision for binary classification and 99.80% precision for multi-class classification in the X-IIoTID dataset. The models' efficacy was also evaluated based on the kinds of attacks found in the datasets. The paper [7] examines the performance of DL algorithms in intrusion detection for smart devices that have resource constraints. Specifically, the study analyzes the efficacy of DNNs, CNN, and LSTM using the CIC-IDS 2017 dataset. The authors find that the DNNs and CNN outperform the long short-term memory in terms of accuracy, with the convolutional neural network achieving the highest accuracy of 99.71%. The study highlights the potential of DL algorithms for intrusion detection in resource-constrained devices.

A novel method dubbed IGRF-RFE is suggested in this article [8] for feature selection in multi-class network anomaly detection using a multilayer perceptron (MLP) network. The strategy uses an RFE wrapper method to further reduce the feature dimensions while considering the significance of comparable features and a mix of two filter methods, information gain (IG) and RF, to reduce the feature subgroup search space. The results of the experiments on the UNSW- NB15 dataset show that the suggested method can improve anomalous detection accuracy by choosing more relevant features while decreasing the feature space. The number of characteristics decrease from 42 to 23, while MLP's multi-classification accuracy increases from 82.25% to 84.24%.

This paper [9] focuses on the challenges of anomaly-IDS in IoT devices and proposes CNN- BMECapSA-RF is a novel method for optimizing feature selection and identifying anomalies. The approach involves utilizing a CNN with hybrid layers for feature extraction. To perform feature selection, a BMOEA is employed. The efficacy of the proposed method is evaluated using two separate datasets, namely NSL-KDD and TON-IoT, and exhibits better results compared to existing DL and ML-based behavior-based detection. The method achieves high accuracy in identifying effective features and detecting anomalies, making it a promising solution to strengthen IoT device security.

This paper [10] proposes a combined clustering and classification approach for deploying an intrusion detection system based on anomalies in cloud computing environments. To allow effective attack categorization and scalability, the suggested approach uses machine learning-based clustering and classification methods. The study focuses on detecting five different types of assaults, including normal, DoS, Probe, U2R, and R2L. The suggested method is evaluated on two datasets, NSL-KDD and KDDcup99, and the performance is measured using detection rate, false alarm ratio, and accuracy. According to the findings, the combination of K-means clustering and random forest classification demonstrates superior performance in terms of classification accuracy, detection rate, and false alarm rate at two different threshold values for both datasets. The proposed approach shows promising results for efficient anomaly-based IDS implementation in cloud computing environments.

The proposed paper [11] introduces a novel multitiered hybrid IDS that combines both behavior-based IDS and pattern-based IDS to detect known and unknown attacks in vehicular networks.

The effectiveness of the proposed IDS is evaluated using two datasets - the CAN intrusion dataset and the CICIDS2017 dataset, which contain intravehicle and external vehicular network data, respectively. The experimental findings indicate that the suggested system has a 99.99% detection rate on the CAN-intrusion dataset and a 99.88% detection rate on the CICIDS2017 data set in detecting numerous kinds of known attacks. Additionally, the system's ability to detect zero-day attacks is demonstrated through its high F1 scores of 0.963 and 0.800 on the aforementioned datasets. The proposed IDS is shown to be effective and efficient, with an average processing time of less than 0.6 ms per data packet on a vehicle-level machine, making it feasible for real-time implementation.

This paper [12] discusses the use of ML-based strategies for intrusion perception in network-based applications. The authors evaluate five ML classifiers on the NSL-KDD dataset and propose a hybrid: the utilization of a feature selection method is proposed to improve the performance of anomaly-based IDS by reducing the number of irrelevant features used in the analysis. The feature selection technique combines information gain, gain ratio, and chi-squared attribute evaluation methods using mathematical set theory intersection. They implement five different ML algorithms and generate 160 ML models, selecting the best model using the Akaike information criterion. The suggested hybrid feature selection method yields the following results: improved accuracy and reduced computational time for intrusion detection systems.

A new hybrid system using adaptive correlation feature selection and DNN is introduced in [13] for detecting cracked tires, consisting of feature extraction, feature selection, and classification. Real images of cracked and normal tires are used for evaluation, and the proposed method demonstrates superior performance compared to existing methods for classifying tire defect images, with a classification accuracy of 88.90%, which outperforms belief neural networks (81.6%) and convolution neural networks (85.59%). Overall, the study suggests that the proposed method can effectively detect tire defects and improve driving safety.

A security answer for IoT devices is suggested in the research paper [14] using CNN, LSTM, and deep learning algorithms in the shape of an IDS architecture. The UNSW-NB15 dataset is used to test the model's efficacy, and comparisons between the suggested model, fundamental CNN models, and contemporary state-of-the-art ML classifications are made. The proposed hybrid model with a balancing technique achieves a classification accuracy of 92.10%, outperforming the basic CNN and ML algorithms. The paper concludes that the proposed model gives good results compared to related works that used balancing techniques.

The hybrid IDS for edge-based industrial IoT security proposed in this article [15] employs ML methods. The IDS combines KNN and principal component analysis (PCA) techniques for misuse and anomaly detection. The KNN classifier improves detection accuracy, while PCA is used to simplify model training and enhance feature extraction. The proposed framework outperforms other recent models. On the NSL-KDD and Bot-IoT datasets, our model performed well, achieving a precision of 99.10% and 98.2%, detection rates of 98.4% and 97.6%, and false alert rates of 2.7% and 2.9%, respectively. The results demonstrate that the proposed model presents many advantages for IoT security.

This study [16] presents a new technique for enhancing the genetic algorithm and particle swarm optimization (EGA-PSO) and improved random forest (IRF) methods, jointly known as HNIDS, for enhancing the accuracy of IDS and addressing data imbalance. The HNIDS model generates a balanced dataset using EGA-PSO to improve the accuracy of learning small samples and uses IRF to eliminate less significant attributes and prevent overfitting. The suggested approach outperforms competing machine learning techniques, such as SVM, RF, LR, NB, LDA, and CART, on the NSL-KDD dataset, with an accuracy of 98.979% on BCC and 88.149% on MCC.

The paper proposes [17] an advanced and intelligent hybrid IDS made utilizing the MapReduce-based BWO-CONV-LSTM network. The model overcomes issues with traditional IDS models by using DL with optimized hyper-parameters and a scalable MapReduce framework. The BWO- CONV-LSTM network is optimized by the artificial bee colony (ABC) algorithm, which selects the best features. The model exhibits outstanding intrusion detection performance while also minimizing false positives and computational effort, achieving accuracy rates of 98.67%, 97.003%, 98.667%, and 98.25% on the NSL-KDD, ISCX-IDS, UNSW-NB15, and CSE-CIC-IDS2018 datasets, respectively.

This article suggests [18] a new hybrid IDS dubbed DST-IDS that integrates Dempster-Shafer theory (DST) with both packet-based and flow-based intrusion detection methods for precise attack detection. The proposed method has an ensemble-like framework and is designed to work with heterogeneous data distribution, which drastically improves its practicality. The article also introduces a novel data gathering and processing tool that efficiently lowers the data volume needed for breach detection while facilitating early detection. According to experimental findings, DST-IDS offers real-time detection in realistic network situations and outperforms industry standards in terms of intrusion detection accuracy and speed.

The difficulties of high-dimensional features and classification results linked with conventional Stacking algorithms are addressed by a novel hybrid IDS in this article [19]. The suggested system includes a weighted stacking algorithm and a CFS-DE feature selection algorithm for selecting optimized feature groups and basic classifiers, respectively. The NSL-KDD and CSE-CIC- IDS2018 datasets' empirical assessment shows appreciable gains in accuracy, precision, recall, and F1-score when compared to conventional machine learning models and previously suggested approaches. Overall, this paper's suggested CFS-DE-weighted-Stacking IDS provides better classification results.

This article [20] suggests a novel IDS that makes use of a mixed optimization and DL-based strategy for protecting IoT-enabled smart communities. In order to accurately classify attack and non-attack data, the proposed model uses the Hybrid Chicken Swarm Genetic Algorithm (HCSGA) and Min K-Means Algorithm for feature selection and clustering, respectively. The transformed data is then processed by the Deep Learning-based Hybrid Neural Network (DLHNN) classifier. The suggested IDS outperforms current state-of-the-art methods in terms of performance and efficiency, according to experimental assessment on the NSL-KDD dataset. The research emphasizes how crucial it is to have strong IDS in order to protect against security lapses in IoT and advance the security of smart city projects.

Table **1** presents a comprehensive review of various papers discussing technology, datasets, and their corresponding results.

PROPOSED HYBRID DESIGN

What is Ensemble Learning

Ensemble learning is a powerful technique used to solve classification and regression problems by utilizing multiple ML models. This method involves selecting a group of homogenous ML models known as weak learners. Each weak learner is applied to the problem and produces its own output, covering either the entire training set or just a portion of it. The results of the weak learners are then combined to generate the final output. Two common ensemble learning techniques are bagging and boosting. Bagging uses a subset of the dataset while boosting employs the complete dataset. Random Forest is a well-known ensemble learning model that belongs to the bagging group, whereas AdaBoost is classified as a boosting model.

Table 1. Summary of Literature Review Findings: Technology, Dataset, and Results Comparison.

S.No	Technology	Dataset	Result
1. [2]	IDS (K-Means, SVM)	UNSW-NB15	-
2. [3]	To Enhance the performance of Anomaly-based IDS (SMOTE, XGBoost).	KDDCUP99 C-MalMem-2022	99.99% Accuracy 100% Accuracy
3. [4]	IoT (CNN, GRU)	CICIDS-2017	98.73(Accuracy)
4. [5]	IoT for 5G GAN+AE+RF	NA	99.8% (Accuracy)Binary classification 99.6% Multi-class
5. [6]	IoT (CNN+LSTM)	NSW-NB 15 & X- IIoTID	93.21% (Accuracy)Binary classification 92.9% Multi-class
6. [7]	CNN, LSTM	CIC-IDS 2017	9.71% (Accuracy)
7. [8]	IGRF-RFE	UNSW-NB 15	NA
8. [9]	IoT (CNN-BME, Cap SA-RF)	NSL-KDD	NA
9. [10]	Cloud Computing (K-Means+ RF)	SL-KDD, KDD99	NA
10. [11]	Multitier Hybrid IDS for vehicular Network	CICIDS2017	99.88% (Accuracy)
11. [12]	N-IDS	NSL-KDD	NA
12. [13]	DNN CNN	Real Image of cracked and normal tires	89.90 85.59
3 [14]	CNN	UNSWNB-15	92.10%
14. [15]	KNN+PCA	NSL-KDD	99.10%
15. [16]	EGA-PSO	NSL-KDD	98.979%

(Table 1) cont.....

S.No	Technology	Dataset	Result
16. [17]	(BWO-CNN-LSTM)	NSL-KDD ISCW-IDS UNW-NB15 CSE-CIC-IDS	98.67% 97.003% 98.667% 98.25%
17. [19]	CFS-DF	NSL-KDD SF-CIC-IDS 2018	NA
18. [20]	HCSGA& K-Means	NSL-KDD	NA

Ensemble Model (Hybrid)

To build a hybrid ensemble learning model, three different types of ML models are used as weak learners, which include the decision tree, the K-nearest neighbor model, and the naive Bayes model, among others. Unlike earlier ensemble models that employed a homogeneous group of weak learners, this model uses a heterogeneous group, which is why it is called a "hybrid" model. The block diagram for the same is shown in Fig. (**1**).

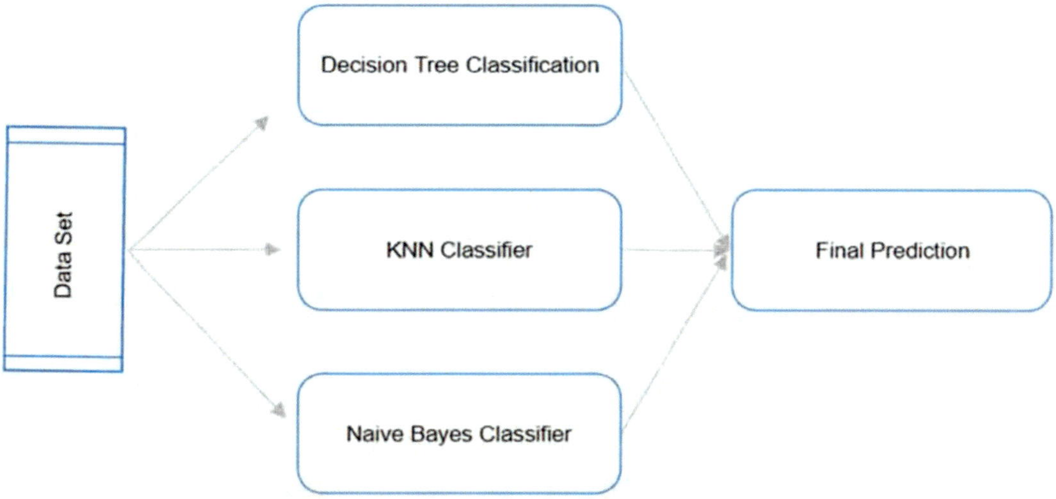

Fig. (1). Proposed Ensemble Model.

- Decision Tree is a popular choice for weak learners due to its simplicity and interpretability. It works by recursively splitting the data based on certain features, resulting in a tree-like structure that can be used for prediction and classification tasks.
- K-nearest neighbor (KNN) is a non-parametric algorithm that uses the distance between data points to classify new examples. The suggested model keeps all

the training data and assigns a class label to a new data point by locating its k-nearest neighbors in the training data and using those neighbors' labels as a guide.
- A probabilistic method called Naive Bayes uses the Bayes theorem to determine odds. The likelihood computation is made easier by this algorithm's presumption that, given the class label, the features are conditionally independent. NB is frequently employed for jobs like text categorization and spam screening.
- By combining these different weak learners into a hybrid ensemble model, we can leverage the strengths of each model and reduce the impact of their weaknesses. This can lead to improved overall performance and robustness in different types of datasets. Other types of weak learners that can be used in ensemble models include SVMs, GBMs, and neural networks. The characteristics of the information and the problem's structure will determine which weak learners are chosen.

Dataset Used

Numerous studies have made significant use of the KDD '99 dataset since 1999 to test the efficacy of anomaly detection systems [9]. The dataset was created by Stolfo *et al.* using information from the DARPA 98 IDS assessment study. The DARPA 98 dataset consists of compressed binary tcp dump data that covers seven weeks' worth of network activity. It can be broken down into nearly five million entries for connection data, each of which is approximately 100 bytes long. About two million connection records from the last two weeks of the DARPA 98 dataset make up the dataset's assessment group.

The KDD training dataset consists of roughly 4.9 million distinct connection vectors, each with 41 features, and is divided into two categories: normal and attack, with only one form of assault being represented in each category. The predicted attacks can be categorized into four groups:

- Denial of Service (DoS): A cyber attack known as a denial-of-service (DoS) assault involves flooding a network or system with traffic in order to interrupt regular traffic flow and deny authorized users access to the targeted resource.
- User-to-Root Attack (U2R): A privilege escalation attack is a common name for this kind of attack, in which an intruder obtains higher rights on a system or network by taking advantage of holes or flaws in the security measures.
- Remote-to-Local Attack (R2L): In an R2L attack, an attacker sends packets to a computer across a network in an attempt to take advantage of the vulnerability and gain local access to that system as the user of that computer.
- Probing: Sending a series of network messages to different locations on a network is a probing attack. The goal is to learn more about the network and

find any possible weaknesses that could be used in future attacks.

The KDD '99 dataset has been used by many academics as a standard for assessing the effectiveness of different anomaly detection methods. Many researchers have used this dataset to compare the effectiveness of different ML & DL models for detecting network intrusions and cyber-attacks. However, some experts have criticized the dataset for being outdated and unrealistic, as the network traffic patterns and attack types have evolved significantly since its creation.

To address these limitations, several new datasets have been introduced, such as the NSL- KDD dataset, which is a revised edition of the KDD '99 dataset that includes more recent attack types and better reflects real-world network traffic patterns. Additionally, some researchers have created their own custom datasets to better suit their specific research needs.

Methodology

In Fig. (**2**), the proposed methodology approaches the IDS Hybrid module. The first step is to choose an appropriate dataset for the study project. Once a dataset has been selected, it is best to highlight the dataset's most important characteristics before starting the analysis. One of the important steps in data processing is transforming categorical data into integer values so that the data containing the converted categorical values may be delivered to the modules for prediction purposes. After that, the data must be divided into training and testing parts, and the ML modules are selected to be used for the analysis. Once the modules are selected, they need to be trained and predicted, and a confusion matrix must be printed out. Cross-validation can also be done for the selected modules. After data processing and module selection are complete, the hybrid ensemble learning models can be run. The three ML modules are combined three times, which results in nine weak learners in total. Finally, the maximum vote classification technique is used to obtain the ultimate class forecast made by the ensemble model based on the weakest learner's most frequent class prediction. It is worth noting that the use of ensemble learning models can significantly improve the accuracy and performance of the IDS system [26, 27]. Ensemble models combine the predictions of multiple weak learners to make a final prediction, which helps to overcome the limitations of individual models. The use of Python as a programming language provides a wide range of tools and libraries that are helpful in data processing and machine learning.

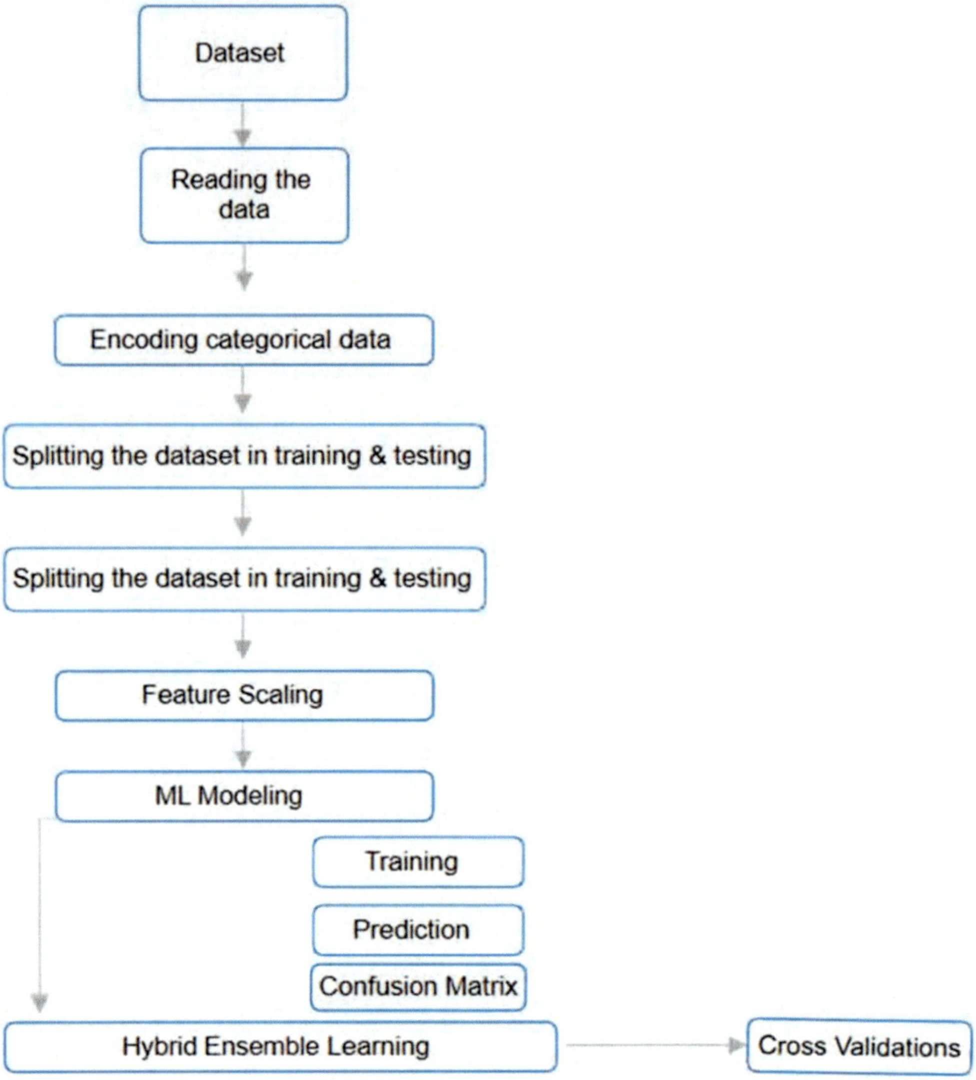

Fig. (2). Proposed Methodology.

RESULTS

To improve the outcomes of a previous comparison study conducted on the KDD 99 dataset using only ML modules, we employed a hybrid technique, as shown in Table **2**. The ML modules used in the previous study included DT, KNN, NB, and others. The accuracy of these modules was evaluated, and the following results were obtained:

Table 2. ML Implementation for IDS.

Algorithms	Accuracy
NB	0.88
DT	0.99
RF	0.99
SVM	1.00
LR	0.99
ANN	0.79
KNN	0.79

The results of Table **3** show that the hybrid approach using ensemble learning models can significantly improve the accuracy of IDS. Additionally, it demonstrates the importance of selecting appropriate ML models for a specific task and the potential benefits of using a combination of models. Using the effective method of ensemble learning, numerous weak learners are combined to make a strong learner, increasing the model's overall accuracy and generalization performance while lowering the risk of overfitting.

After comparing the accuracy of several ML algorithms [21 - 25] in a study using the KDD 99 dataset, we found that only two algorithms had different accuracy rates. As a result, we decided to focus on three algorithms that performed equally well in the study. Among these, decision trees were the second most accurate, while Naive Bayes was in the middle. On the other hand, the K-nearest neighbor had the lowest accuracy among the three selected algorithms.

Table 3. Previous Results.

Algorithm s	Accuracy
DT	0.99
KNN	0.79
NB	0.88

We worked on several modules, including data processing, ML modeling, model training, prediction generation, and cross-validation. Our ultimate goal was to enhance the accuracy of the models.

To further improve the accuracy of our models, we will be implementing hybrid ensemble models that combine all of the ML components into a single classifier shows in Table **4**. We will then cross-validate the classifier using a seed of 7 to achieve 100% cross-validation. In addition to this, we will also be performing cross-validation using a resampling approach, which involves testing and training a model with various samples of data in successive rounds.

Table 4. ML Accuracy on Hybrid Modules.

Algorithms	Accuracy
DT	1.0
KNN	1.0
NB	1.0

CONCLUSION

After experimenting with multiple machine learning modules applied to the KDD CUP 99 dataset, we introduced a hybrid ensemble model aimed at enhancing our results. Our examination of cross-validation scores and confusion matrices highlighted the superior performance of the hybrid ensemble learning model over other models, resulting in overall improvement. We plan to delve deeper in subsequent research, exploring the feasibility of constructing additional hybrid ensemble models through the incorporation of diverse weak learner types and diverse datasets. This endeavor holds promise for advancing our comprehension of machine learning and its role in intrusion detection systems (IDSs). Our study underscores the potential efficacy of hybrid ensemble learning models in bolstering IDS accuracy, especially in the context of intricate datasets like KDD CUP 99. With machine learning's ongoing evolution and the emergence of new datasets, we eagerly anticipate further exploration of this technique's capabilities.

REFERENCES

[1] A. Meryem, and B.E. Ouahidi, "Hybrid IDSusing machine learning", *Netw. Secur.,* vol. 2020, no. 5, pp. 8-19, 2020.
[http://dx.doi.org/10.1016/S1353-4858(20)30056-8]

[2] I. Aljamal, A. Tekeoğlu, K. Bekiroglu, and S. Sengupta, "Hybrid IDSUsing MLTechniques in Cloud Computing Environments", *in 2019 IEEE 17th International Conference on Software Engineering Research, Management and Applications (SERA),* pp. 84-89, 2019.
[http://dx.doi.org/10.1109/SERA.2019.8886794]

[3] M.A. Talukder, K.F. Hasan, M.M. Islam, M.A. Uddin, A. Akhter, M.A. Yousuf, F. Alharbi, and M.A. Moni, "A dependable hybrid machine learning model for network intrusion detection", *Journal of Information Security and Applications,* vol. 72, p. 103405, 2023.
[http://dx.doi.org/10.1016/j.jisa.2022.103405]

[4] A. Henry, S. Gautam, S. Khanna, K. Rabie, T. Shongwe, P. Bhattacharya, B. Sharma, and S. Chowdhury, "Composition of Hybrid Deep Learning Model and Feature Optimization for Intrusion Detection System", *Sensors (Basel),* vol. 23, no. 2, p. 890, 2023.
[http://dx.doi.org/10.3390/s23020890] [PMID: 36679684]

[5] S. Ding, L. Kou, and T. Wu, "A GAN-Based Intrusion Detection Model for 5G Enabled Future Metaverse", *Mob. Netw. Appl.,* vol. 27, no. 6, pp. 2596-2610, 2022. [http://dx.doi.org/10.1007/s11036-022-02075-6]

[6] H.C. Altunay, and Z. Albayrak, "A hybrid CNN+LSTM-based IDSfor industrial IoT networks", *Eng. Sci. Technol. Int. J.,* vol. 38, p. 101322, 2023. [http://dx.doi.org/10.1016/j.jestch.2022.101322]

[7] J. Jose and D. Jose, "Deep learning algorithms for intrusion detection systems in internet of things using CIC-IDS 2017 dataset," *Int. J. Electr. Comput. Eng.* (IJECE), vol. 13, pp. 1134-1141, 2023. [http://dx.doi.org/10.11591/ijece.v13i1.pp1134-1141]

[8] Y. Yin, J. Jang-Jaccard, W. Xu, A. Singh, J. Zhu, F. Sabrina, and J. Kwak, "IGRF-RFE: a hybrid feature selection method for MLP-based network intrusion detection on UNSW-NB15 dataset", *J. Big Data,* vol. 10, no. 1, p. 15, 2023. [http://dx.doi.org/10.1186/s40537-023-00694-8]

[9] H. Asgharzadeh, A. Ghaffari, M. Masdari, and F. Soleimanian Gharehchopogh, "Anomaly-based IDS in the Internet of Things using a convolutional neural network and multi-objective enhanced Capuchin Search Algorithm", *J. Parallel Distrib. Comput.,* vol. 175, pp. 1-21, 2023. [http://dx.doi.org/10.1016/j.jpdc.2022.12.009]

[10] K. Samunnisa, G.S.V. Kumar, and K. Madhavi, "IDS in distributed cloud computing: Hybrid clustering and classification methods", *Meas. Sensors,* vol. 25, p. 100612, 2023. [http://dx.doi.org/10.1016/j.measen.2022.100612]

[11] L. Yang, A. Moubayed, and A. Shami, "MTH-IDS: A Multitiered Hybrid IDS for Internet of Vehicles", *IEEE Internet Things J.,* vol. 9, no. 1, pp. 616-632, 2022. [http://dx.doi.org/10.1109/JIOT.2021.3084796]

[12] P. Satapathy and P. K. Behera, "Machine learning-based hybrid feature selection for improvised network intrusion detection," in *Innovations in Intelligent Computing and Communication*, vol. 1737, Communications in Computer and Information Science, Springer, 2023, pp. 333–347 [http://dx.doi.org/10.1007/978-3-031-23233-6_25]

[13] A. Al-juboori, A. Alsaeedi, R. Nuiaa, Z. Alyasseri, N. Sani, S. Hadi, H. Mohammed, B. Musawi, and M. Amin, "A Hybrid Cracked Tiers Detection System Based on Adaptive Correlation Features Selection and Deep Belief Neural Networks", *Symmetry (Basel),* vol. 15, no. 2, p. 358, 2023. [http://dx.doi.org/10.3390/sym15020358]

[14] R. Almarshdi, L. Nassef, E. Fadel, and N. Alowidi, "Hybrid Deep Learning Based Attack Detection for Imbalanced Data Classification", *Intelligent Automation & Soft Computing,* vol. 35, no. 1, pp. 297-320, 2023. [http://dx.doi.org/10.32604/iasc.2023.026799]

[15] A. Guezzaz, M. Azrour, S. Benkirane, M. Mohy-Eddine, H. Attou, and M. Douiba, "A Lightweight Hybrid Intrusion Detection Framework using Machine Learning for Edge-Based IIoT Security", *Int. Arab J. Inf. Technol.,* vol. 19, no. 5, 2022. [http://dx.doi.org/10.34028/iajit/19/5/14]

[16] A.K. Balyan, S. Ahuja, U.K. Lilhore, S.K. Sharma, P. Manoharan, A.D. Algarni, H. Elmannai, and K. Raahemifar, "A Hybrid Intrusion Detection Model Using EGA-PSO and Improved Random Forest Method", *Sensors (Basel),* vol. 22, no. 16, p. 5986, 2022. [http://dx.doi.org/10.3390/s22165986] [PMID: 36015744]

[17] P.R. Kanna, and P. Santhi, "Hybrid Intrusion Detection using MapReduce based Black Widow Optimized Convolutional Long Short-Term Memory Neural Networks", *Expert Syst. Appl.,* vol. 194, p. 116545, 2022. [http://dx.doi.org/10.1016/j.eswa.2022.116545]

[18] W. Qiu, Y. Ma, X. Chen, H. Yu, and L. Chen, "Hybrid IDS based on Dempster-Shafer evidence

theory", *Comput. Secur.*, vol. 117, p. 102709, 2022.
[http://dx.doi.org/10.1016/j.cose.2022.102709]

[19] R. Zhao, Y. Mu, L. Zou, and X. Wen, "A Hybrid IDS Based on Feature Selection and Weighted Stacking Classifier", *IEEE Access,* vol. 10, pp. 71414-71426, 2022.
[http://dx.doi.org/10.1109/ACCESS.2022.3186975]

[20] S.K. Gupta, M. Tripathi, and J. Grover, "Hybrid optimization and deep learning based intrusion detection system", *Comput. Electr. Eng.,* vol. 100, p. 107876, 2022.
[http://dx.doi.org/10.1016/j.compeleceng.2022.107876]

[21] V. Deshwal, and V. Kumar, "Study of Coronavirus Disease (COVID-19) Outbreak in India", *Open Nurs. J.,* vol. 15, no. 1, pp. 62-73, 2021.
[http://dx.doi.org/10.2174/1874434602115010062]

[22] V. Kumar, and R. Kumar, "A cooperative black hole node detection and mitigation approach for MANETs", *8th International Conference, SECITC 2015,* Springer International Publishing, pp. 171-183, 2015.
[http://dx.doi.org/10.1007/978-3-319-27179-8_12]

[23] V. Kumar, M. Shankar, A.M. Tripathi, V. Yadav, A.K. Rai, U. Khan, and M. Rahul, "Prevention of Blackhole Attack in MANET using Certificateless Signature Scheme", *J. Sci. Ind. Res. (India),* vol. 81, no. 10, pp. 1061-1072, 2022.

[24] V. Kumar, and R. Kumar, "Detection of phishing attack using visual cryptography in ad hoc network", *2015 International Conference on Communications and Signal Processing (ICCSP),* IEEE, pp. 1021-1025, 2015.
[http://dx.doi.org/10.1109/ICCSP.2015.7322654]

[25] P. Gupta, V. Kumar, and V. Yadav, "Student's Perception towards Mobile learning using Interned Enabled Mobile devices during COVID-19", *EAI Endorsed Transactions on Industrial Networks and Intelligent Systems,* vol. 8, no. 29, p. 170958, 2021.
[http://dx.doi.org/10.4108/eai.16-9-2021.170958]

[26] Kumar, V. and Kumar, R., "An adaptive approach for detection of blackhole attack in mobile ad hoc network", *Procedia Computer Science*, vol.48, pp. 472-479, 2015.
[http://dx.doi.org/10.1016/j.procs.2015.04.122]

[27] Kumar, V., Singh, A.P., Rai, A.K. and Wairiya, M., "Self alteration detectable image log file for web forensics", *International Journal of Computer Applications*, vol.18, no.5, pp.1-5,2011.
[http://dx.doi.org/10.5120/2284-2960]

CHAPTER 7

A Comprehensive Study on Crop Disease Detection Using Machine Learning and Deep Learning Models

Sonam Gupta[1,*], **Shivani Saxena**[1], **Sneha Maurya**[1] and **Pradeep Gupta**[1]

[1] *Ajay Kumar Garg Engineering College, Ghaziabad, India*

Abstract: Crop diseases can significantly affect agricultural productivity, resulting in huge economic losses for farmers and food shortages for the population. To address this challenge, several researchers have explored the use of machine learning and deep learning algorithms for crop disease detection. These algorithms use image processing techniques to identify and classify diseases in crops and have shown promising results in accurately detecting and diagnosing crop diseases. In particular, deep learning models, especially convolutional neural networks (CNNs), have demonstrated high accuracy in crop disease detection. Researchers have also developed various mobile and web applications based on these models, which can help farmers identify and manage crop diseases in real time. However, there is still a need for more research to improve the accuracy and effectiveness of these models and to ensure their scalability and accessibility for use in the field. Overall, the application of machine learning and deep learning algorithms for crop disease detection holds great potential for addressing the challenges of crop disease management and improving agricultural productivity. This paper studied various pieces of research to enhance and conclude the best algorithm with high accuracy, precision, and recall for the detection of crop diseases.

Keywords: CNN, Crop diseases, Deep learning, Machine learning.

INTRODUCTION

For a large section of India's population, agriculture provides the primary means of subsistence and makes a substantial contribution to the country's GDP. However, the equilibrium between the supply and demand for food caused by the world's constantly expanding population is a troubling issue. Crop loss from pests and diseases that significantly reduce yields is one of the causes of this imbalance. Second, the effects of climatic changes worsen the likelihood of diseases spreading quickly. If these diseases are identified in their early stages, the yield

* **Corresponding author Sonam Gupta:** Ajay Kumar Garg Engineering College, Ghaziabad, India; E-mail: guptasonam6@gmail.com

Vikash Yadav, Vimal Kumar, Sonam Gupta & Vandana Dixit Kaushik (Eds.)

can be maintained, and economic loss can be reduced. The conventional method of disease detection by a plant pathologist is time-consuming and expensive. Pesticides are another old technique. Pesticides are typically applied haphazardly across the entire canopy, and excessive application can result in soil pollution and a decline in soil quality. Crop diseases are mostly influenced by:

- Environmental elements including temperature, humidity, and rainfall.
- The availability of nutrients and the state of the soil.
- Disease susceptibility and plant genetics.
- Insect and pest infestations.
- Pathogens from bacteria, viruses, and fungi.
- The presence of water and irrigation methods.
- Agronomic practices, such as crop rotation and pesticide application.

There can be various forms of disease in plants, including diseases in crops, leaves, *etc*. It is very important to cure these diseases in crops to prevent the loss of farmers, as these diseases cause monetary loss to the farmers as well as substantial agricultural loss. To prevent this, the farmers have already taken various measures, including different pesticides and insecticides. These measures helped in a certain way to prevent diseases in crops up to a certain level, but they could be a more efficient and effective measure to prevent diseases in them.

Crop diseases can have a devastating effect on agricultural productivity and food security. Crop diseases can be broadly classified into three categories—fungal, bacterial, and viral [1]. The identification of the particular pathogen causing the disease is necessary for developing successful management methods because each type of disease has unique symptoms and means of transmission. These illnesses have the potential to quickly spread through crops, causing significant harm that lowers yield and quality. Crop infections can, in extreme circumstances, destroy whole crops, causing farmers to suffer large financial losses and food scarcity in their communities. Pesticides can also harm the environment and human health when used to treat these diseases. The impact of crop diseases must be reduced, and sustainable agricultural production must be ensured through early identification and effective management techniques.

The timely detection and prevention of crop diseases are therefore critical for ensuring food security and sustainable agriculture. We are looking for an automated and more accurate way to prevent this problem in crops. Since a few decades ago, it has been demonstrated that crop disease diagnosis utilizing image processing techniques is quick and accurate. We are looking for an automated and more accurate way to prevent this problem in crops, which is showing great promise in the automated detection and diagnosis of crop diseases.

In this paper, we present a comprehensive review of recent research on crop disease detection and prevention using machine learning and deep learning techniques. This paper highlights the significant potential of machine learning and deep learning techniques for automated crop disease detection and prevention. By combining computer vision algorithms with IoT devices, mobile applications, and conventional disease management practices, researchers and farmers can quickly and accurately diagnose and prevent crop diseases, ultimately leading to higher yields and more sustainable agriculture.

Our review covers several topics, including the use of convolutional neural networks (CNNs) for crop disease detection [2] and the development of mobile applications for real-time disease diagnosis. Along with this, it also studies the use of Internet of Things (IoT) sensors for continuous crop monitoring [1] and the potential of transfer learning and data augmentation techniques for improving model performance. It analyzes the accuracy, precision, recall, *etc*., of different ML and DL algorithms, as shown in Figs. (**1-4**). We also explored the challenges and opportunities in the field, including the availability of high-quality datasets, the lack of standardization and interoperability of data formats and models, and the need for effective collaboration and knowledge sharing among stakeholders.

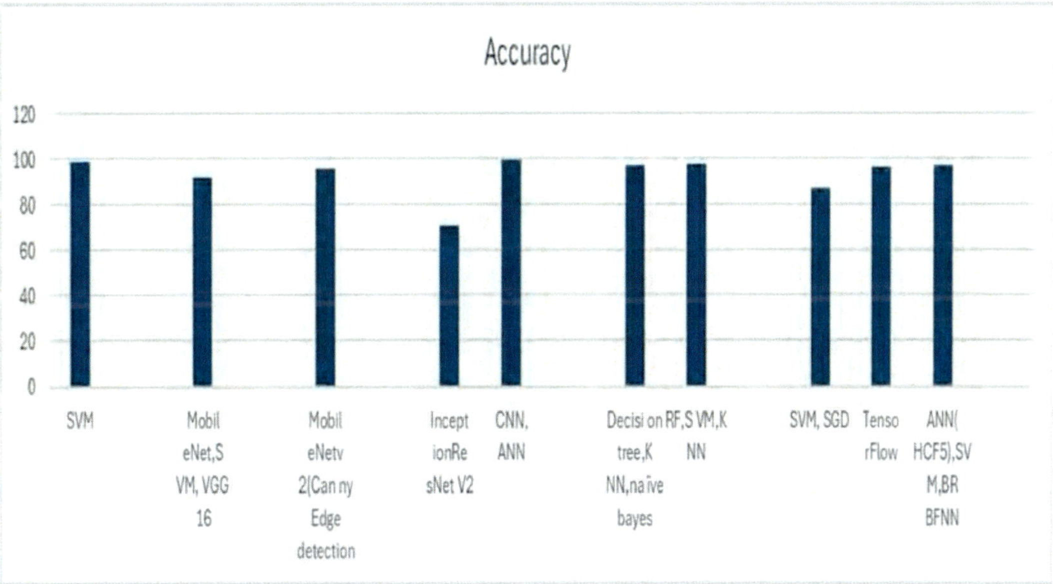

Fig. (1). Accuracy for ML Algorithms.

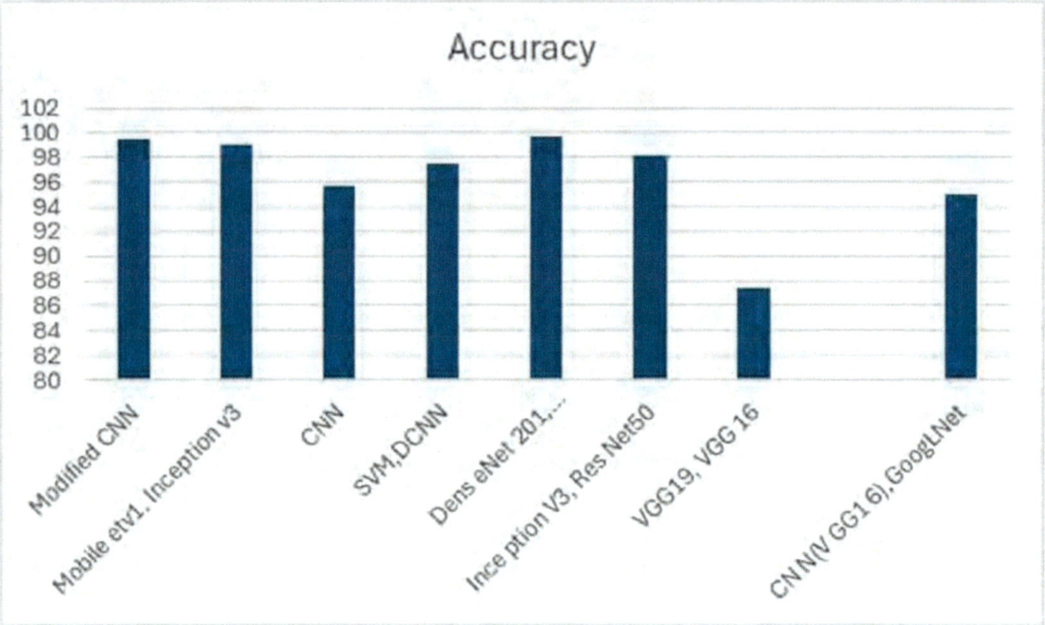

Fig. (2). Accuracy for DL Algorithms.

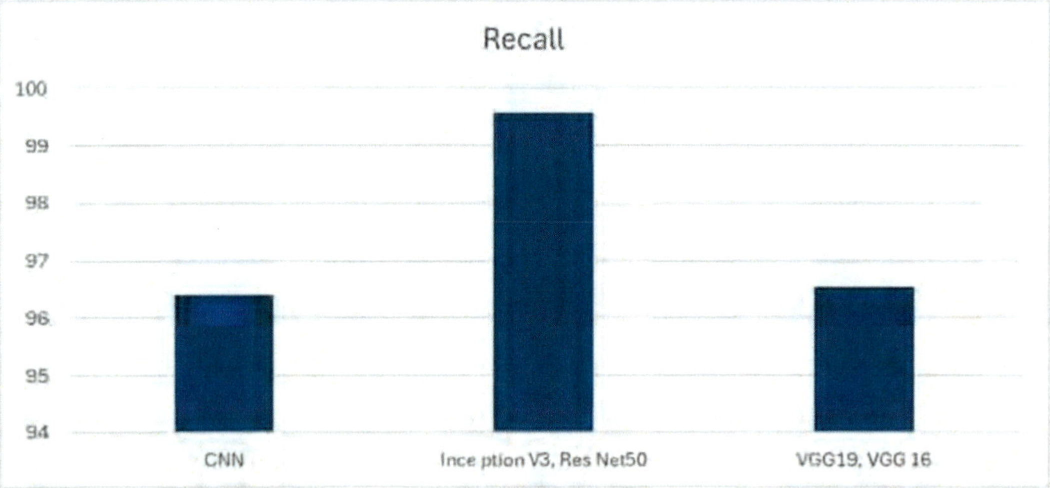

Fig. (3). Recall For DL Algorithms.

Overall, this paper highlights the significant potential of machine learning and deep learning for crop disease detection and prevention. According to our studies, a novel approach that combines a CNN-based mobile application with an IoT-based sensor network for real-time monitoring of crop health is the most suitable method for crop disease detection. We also discuss several strategies for addressing the key challenges in the field and identify several opportunities for future research and development. Based on the studies done on the crop disease detection models, the following research questions arise:

RESEARCH QUESTIONS

RQ1: Which technique is the best for crop disease detection, either machine learning or deep learning?

RQ2: Which is more suitable, a web application or a mobile application for the detection model?

RQ3: As per the research, which is the most efficient and accurate crop disease detection model?

The following section outlines the organization of the remainder of the paper. Related work on the detection of agricultural diseases is covered in Section 2. Section 3 of the paper contains a discussion of the studies, followed by an analysis. The conclusion of the paper is given in Section 4, and a variety of future study possibilities are discussed in Section 5.

LITERATURE REVIEW

Fraol *et al.* [3] reviewed machine-learning strategies for disease detection in cereal crops. The author discussed numerous illnesses present in cereal crops. According to the findings, deep convolutional neural networks trained on hyperspectral data are the most efficient way for disease identification, with dataset standardization and location restrictions being the key issues.

Vaasavi *et al.* [4] demonstrated that by using machine learning and deep learning algorithms, crop disease diagnosis and classification based on visual symptoms can be done more accurately and efficiently. The authors summarized recent research in this field in their review paper, underlining the potential of these algorithms to solve issues with conventional approaches to disease diagnosis. They also point out the field's difficulties and constraints and recommend future research options, such as the incorporation of different kinds of data to improve the precision of models.

Samyak Shrimali *et al.* [2] gave an approach of a convolutional neural network based on a mobile application for efficient crop disease detection and treatment to identify and cure crop illnesses. The study introduced a revolutionary mobile application that used deep learning techniques. The suggested method is highly accurate in identifying a variety of plant illnesses from leaf photos, and because it is mobile-based, farmers in remote locations can use it. This study demonstrates how deep learning methods can revolutionize agriculture and boost crop production.

A valuable new tool for visual plant disease identification is presented in the paper [5] "PlantDoc: A Dataset for Visual Plant Disease Detection" by Davinder Singh. The PlantDoc dataset, which includes more than 50,000 photos of 15 different crops afflicted by 26 various illnesses, is presented by the authors. They also suggest PlantDocNet, a deep learning model that outperforms other models on the dataset. In order to advance the identification and treatment of plant diseases and ultimately improve global food security, this research emphasizes the significance of high-quality datasets and efficient deep-learning models. The paper "Paddy Crop Disease Detection Using Machine Learning" by Prajwal Gowda provides a thorough analysis of applying machine learning techniques for the early identification of paddy crop illnesses. The many approaches and methods used in the procedure are discussed in the study, including feature extraction, image processing, and classification using Support Vector Machines (SVM). According to the findings, the suggested technology detects diseases with a high degree of accuracy, making precision agriculture a viable option.

In a paper [1], crop disease detection using artificial intelligence and the Internet of Things was reviewed by the paper writers. Researchers, after analyzing many papers, tried to find the most efficient method to detect crop diseases. Based on the analysis, concepts of machine learning, deep learning, IoT, and different image processing concepts, including segmentation, k clustering algorithm, and CNN, are found to be efficient approaches for disease detection in crops. Figs. (**1** and **2**) elaborate on the accuracy of ML and DL algorithms to highlight their advantages.

In their paper [6], the researchers examined the use of an Android app for crop disease identification and prevention. The most effective way to combat crop illnesses and avoid them has been sought after by researchers after examining a large number of articles. In order to diagnose and prevent crop illnesses, this mobile application was created using machine learning, deep learning, activation functions, and other ML techniques based on the study.

The researchers examine the performance of machine learning and deep learning algorithms for detecting plant leaf diseases from images in this paper [7]. Deep learning algorithms, notably the convolutional neural network (CNN) model, outperformed machine learning algorithms in terms of accuracy, precision, and recall, according to the study. The study also emphasizes the potential of deep learning algorithms for real-world agricultural applications.

In the paper [8], crop disease detection using the feature fusion method was reviewed by the researchers. Researchers, after analyzing many papers, tried to find an efficient method to detect diseases in crops. Based on the analysis, it uses handcrafted features and a hybrid framework that uses a feature fusion convolutional neural network (CNN) in this way with real field conditions to make the model robust for all image types.

In the paper [9], automated crop disease detection using DL and ML concepts was reviewed by the researchers. Researchers, after analyzing many papers, tried to find an effective and convenient method to detect crop diseases. Based on the analysis, it involves merging the conventional concepts of machine learning and deep learning, which is a kind of hybrid model in the form of a web application to detect diseases in crops efficiently. Tables **1a** and **1b** show the results of various machine learning and deep learning algorithms over plant disease.

Table 1a. Description of Machine Learning Algorithms over Plant Diseases.

S.No.	Plant used	Disease type	Machine Learning	Accuracy	Precision	Recall	F1-score
1	Papaya, maize, grapes, *etc.*	unspecified	SVM	99	-	-	-
2	Wheat, maize, barley, sorghum, rice.	Leaf Rust (Brown Rust), Stem Rust (Black Rust), Stripe Rust (Yellow Rust), Common Root Rot, Barley Yellow Dwarf.	Mobil eNet,S VM, VGG 16.	92	85	84	-
3	87860 leaf images split into 38 classes.	26 crop diseases of 14 different species are diagnosed.	Mobil eNetv 2(Canny Edge detection).	95.7	95.8	96.4	96.1
4	Apple, bell pepper, blueberry, corn, *etc.*	Apple black rot, bell pepper bacterial, grape black rot.	Incept ionRe sNet V2	70.53	-	-	70
5	Paddy crop	Rice Blast and bacterial leaf blight.	CNN, ANN	99.53	-	-	-
6	Tobacco, cucumber plant, *etc.*	Virus, bacterial and fungal diseases.	Decisi on tree,K NN,na ïve bayes	97	-	-	-
7	Grape leaves *etc*	black measles, black rot, *etc.*	RF, SVM, KNN	97.54	97.74	97.92	97.71
8	Citrus leaf	Dark measles, dark decay.	SVM, SGD	87	-	87.3	87.1

(Table 1a) cont.....

S.No.	Plant used	Disease type	Machine Learning	Accuracy	Precision	Recall	F1-score
9	Apple plant, *etc.*	black rot disease.	Tenso rFlow	96.3	86.5	92.5	88.75
10	Tea leaves, apple leaves, *etc.*	unspecified	ANN(HCF5),SV M,BR BFNN	96.8	-	-	-

Table 1b. Description of Deep Learning Algorithms over Plant Diseases.

S.No	Plant used	Disease type	Deep Learning	Accuracy	Precision	Recall	F1-score
1	Papaya, maize, grapes, *etc.*	unspecified	Modified CNN	99.5	-	-	-
2	Wheat, maize, barley, sorghum, rice	Leaf Rust (Brown Rust), Stem Rust (Black Rust), Stripe Rust (Yellow Rust), Common Root Rot, Barley Yellow Dwarf.	Mobile etv1, Inception v3	99	-	-	-
3	87860 leaf images split into 38 classes.	26 crop diseases of 14 different species are diagnosed.	CNN	95.7	95.8	96.4	96.1
4	Apple, bell pepper, blueberry, corn, *etc.*	Apple black rot, bell pepper bacterial, grape black rot.	-	-	-	-	-
5	Paddy crop	Rice Blast and bacterial leaf blight.	SVM, DCNN	97.5	-	-	-
6	Tobacco, cucumber plant, *etc.*	Virus, bacterial and fungal diseases.	Dens eNet 201, ShuffleNet, Google Net	99.73	99.65	99.58	99.61
7	Grape leaves, *etc.*	Black measles, black rot, *etc.*	Inception V3, Res Net50	98.1	97.53	96.54	96.52
8	Citrus leaf	Dark measles, dark decay.	VGG19, VGG 16	87.4	-	87.7	87.4
9	Apple plant, *etc.*	Black rot disease	-	-	-	-	-
10	Tea leaves, apple leaves, *etc.*	unspecified	CNN(V GG1 6),GoogLNet	95	94.5	90.5	91.7

Fig. (**1**) provides useful information on the performance of several machine learning techniques for detecting plant diseases. Among these algorithms, the support vector machine (SVM) comes out as the best performer, with a 99% accuracy rate. This high degree of precision highlights SVM's efficacy in reliably recognizing and classifying plant illnesses, making it a potential candidate for disease detection in agricultural contexts. These findings show SVM's potential as a useful tool in continuing attempts to improve plant disease control and agricultural production optimization.

Fig. (**2**) depicts a thorough examination of the performance of deep learning (DL) algorithms in the context of plant disease detection. Notably, the modified CNN emerges as the best-performing DL model, with a 99.5% accuracy rate. This outstanding accuracy highlights modified CNNs' potential as a useful tool for the exact identification and categorization of plant diseases. The astounding results in Fig. (**2**) highlight the need to use sophisticated DL approaches to improve the efficacy of plant disease detection and control, which has enormous potential for agriculture and crop security.

Fig. (**3**) shows the recall values of several deep learning (DL) algorithms used to detect plant diseases. Notably, DenseNet201 is the highest-performing DL model in terms of recall, with a score of 99.65%. This high recall rate demonstrates DenseNet201's excellent capacity to properly identify occurrences of plant disease while avoiding false negatives and providing complete disease detection.

Fig. (**4**) depicts the recall values associated with several machine learning (ML) methods used in the identification of plant diseases. Notably, random forest (RF) emerges as the best ML method, with a recall rate of 97.65%. This high recall score demonstrates RF's ability to properly identify occurrences of plant disease, limiting the possibility of false negatives and enabling a strong disease detection procedure.

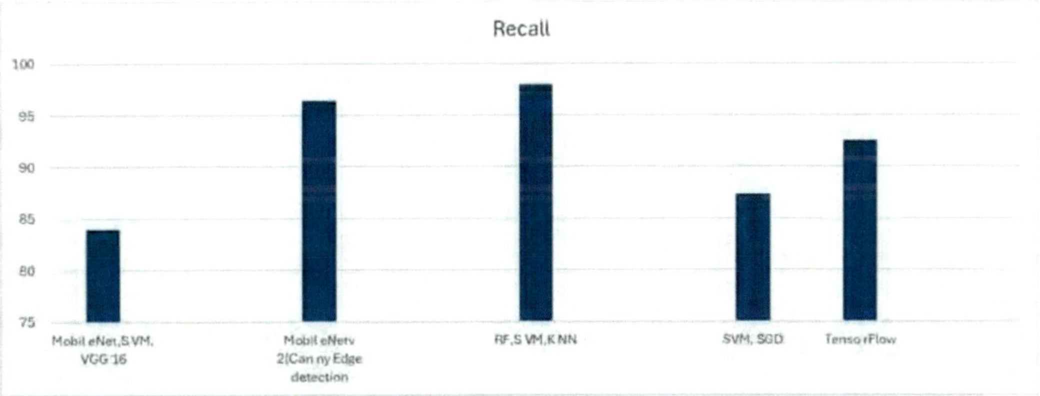

Fig. (4). Recall For ML Algorithms.

Figs. (**5** and **6**) provide useful information about the precision values of machine learning (ML) and deep learning (DL) algorithms in the context of plant disease detection. These statistics explain how well these algorithms categorize and diagnose plant illnesses, which is an important part of disease control in agriculture.

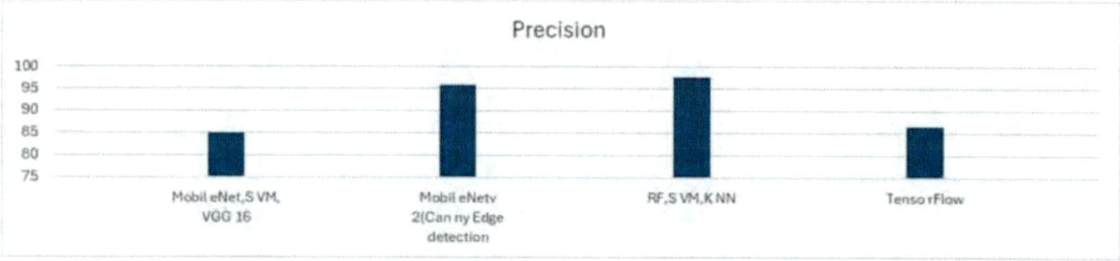

Fig. (5). Precision For ML.

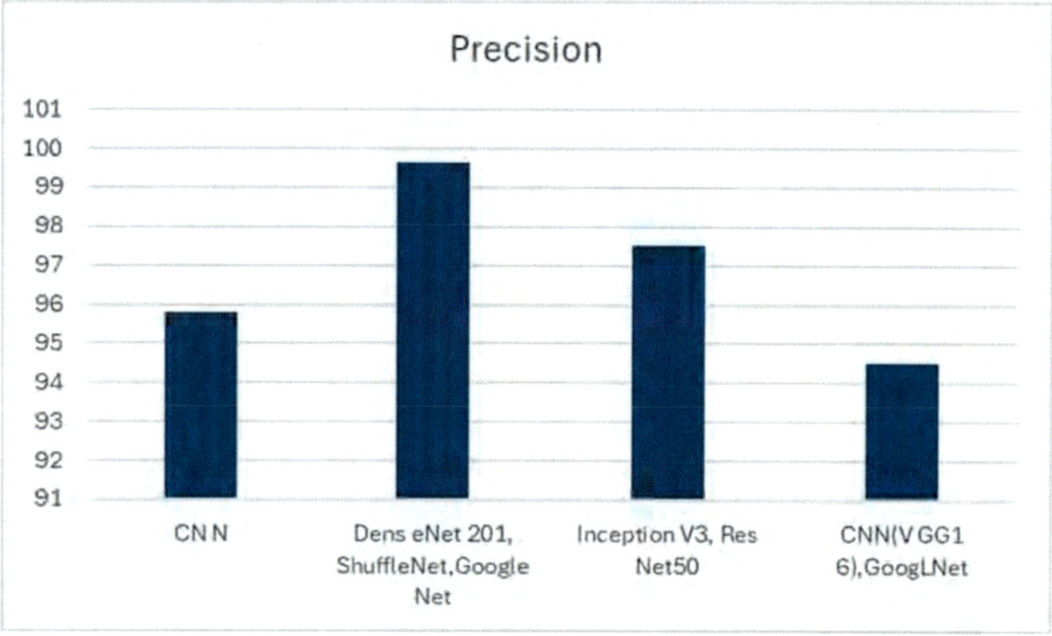

Fig. (6). Precision For DL.

Fig. (**7**) depicts the F1 Score of several machine learning (ML) algorithms used to detect plant diseases. Among the models evaluated, random forest (RF) emerges as the ML method with the greatest F1 Score.

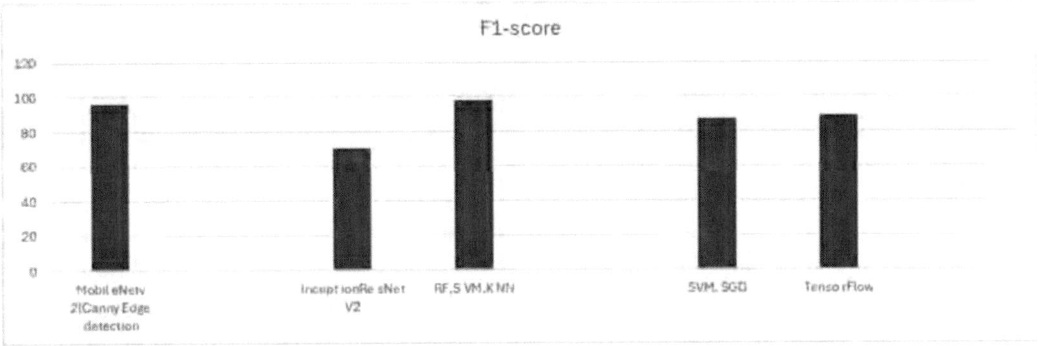

Fig. (7). F1 Score For ML Algorithms.

The F1 score is a useful indicator because it balances accuracy and recall, offering a thorough assessment of an algorithm's ability to effectively detect plant diseases while avoiding both false positives and false negatives. The highest F1 score achieved by RF demonstrates its efficiency in striking a harmonic balance between precision and recall, making it a potential candidate for accurate and dependable plant disease diagnosis and treatment.

Fig. (**8**) shows a comprehensive overview of the F1 Score obtained by various deep learning (DL) algorithms used in the task of detecting plant diseases. This graph provides useful information on the performance of DL models in terms of precision-recall balance, which is an important part of disease identification and management in agriculture.

The F1 Score, as shown in Fig. (**8**), is a significant measure of how well these DL algorithms balance accuracy (fewer false positives) and recall (fewer false negatives) for diagnosing plant diseases. Fig. (**8**) shows the F1 scores of several DL algorithms, allowing us to discover which models are best at attaining this essential balance.

RESULT AND DISCUSSION

RQ1: Which is the best technique suitable for crop disease detection, either machine learning or deep learning?

ANSWER- Several variables affect the decision between machine learning (ML) and deep learning (DL) techniques for agricultural disease diagnosis. Support vector machines (SVM), random forests, and decision trees are just a few of the machine learning (ML) methods that have been successfully applied to the identification of agricultural diseases. These methods work best when the feature extraction procedure can be well described, and the dataset has few complex relationships.

On the other hand, DL methods, in particular convolutional neural networks (CNNs), have attracted a lot of interest lately. By automatically learning hierarchical representations from the input data, DL models have shown excellent performance in image-based tasks, such as crop disease diagnosis. CNNs are highly suited for identifying complex and subtle disease signs because they are excellent at catching nuanced patterns and spatial dependencies in images.

While DL techniques often surpass ML techniques in terms of accuracy and resilience, especially when working with large-scale datasets and complicated visual patterns, ML techniques may be appropriate for some cases. Due to its capacity to learn from and adapt to massive volumes of data, DL models are able to identify subtle disease indicators that may be difficult for conventional ML algorithms to recognize. To understand this in a more detailed way, refer to (Figs. **1** and **2**).

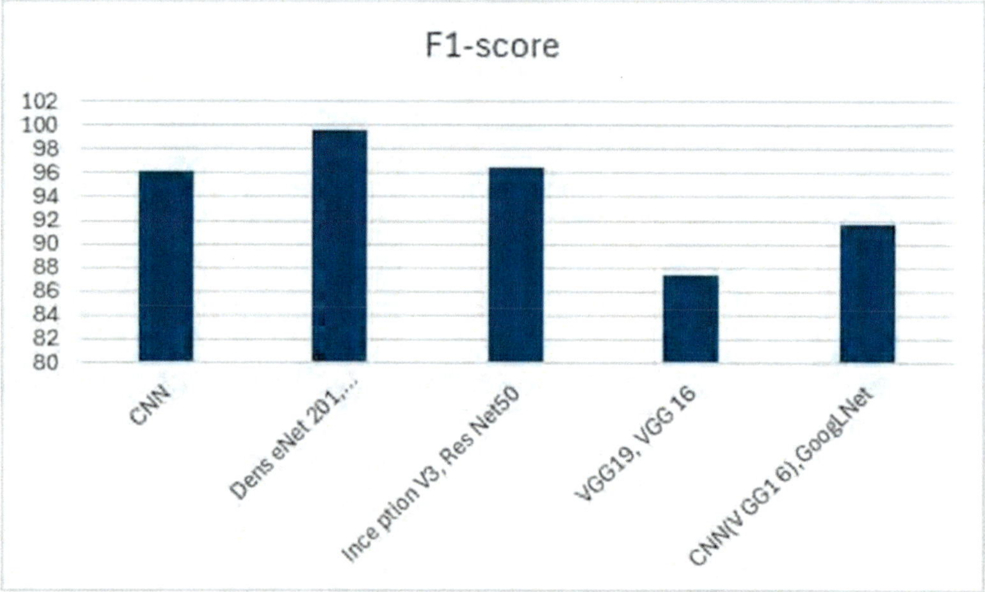

Fig. (8). F1 Score For DL Algorithms.

In conclusion, deep learning methods, especially CNNs, perform better at detecting crop diseases because they can automatically recognize intricate patterns and learn complex information from photos. However, considerations like dataset size, complexity, and the availability of computer resources should be taken into account while deciding between ML and DL techniques.

RQ2: Which is more suitable, a web application or a mobile application for the detection model?

Answer- It is clear that mobile applications are more effective for this task after weighing the benefits and drawbacks of web and mobile applications for crop disease detection.

In comparison to web applications, mobile applications have a number of advantages, including the capacity to make better use of device-specific features like the camera and GPS. Additionally, it is possible to create mobile applications that function offline, which is advantageous in locations with poor internet connectivity.

Additionally, numerous research papers have shown that mobile applications are successful in detecting crop diseases. Machine learning and deep learning algorithms have been used to create mobile applications that have demonstrated great accuracy in spotting agricultural illnesses. These algorithms may examine photos taken by the device's camera and give farmers immediate feedback, allowing them to act quickly to avert crop damage. So, the plantifyAI model can be suitable for this purpose.

While web applications have their own benefits, such as accessibility and device compatibility, they may have slower response times and less functionality than mobile applications.

In conclusion, due to their high accuracy in detecting crop illnesses and capacity to take advantage of device-specific features, mobile applications are better suited for crop disease detection.

RQ3: As per the research, which is the most efficient and accurate crop disease detection model?

Convolutional neural networks (CNNs), in particular, have demonstrated the highest accuracy in the diagnosis of crop diseases, according to the study of the aforementioned research publications. For image-based applications like crop disease identification, CNNs, a subclass of deep neural networks, are the best choice since they can automatically identify and categorize patterns in images.

Numerous studies have proven that CNN-based models are effective at identifying crop diseases. For instance, a CNN-based model that was trained on the PlantDoc dataset, which contains over 54,000 photos of damaged and healthy plant leaves, obtained an accuracy of over 98% in identifying and categorizing crop illnesses. Another study achieved an accuracy of 97.78% in the detection of banana illnesses using a CNN-based model. To visualize the accuracies, refer to Figs. (**1** and **2**). In conclusion, it can be said that CNN-based models are the most accurate crop disease detection models based on the study of the research publications.

CONCLUSION

In conclusion, crop diseases can have significant impacts on agricultural productivity, resulting in economic losses for farmers and food shortages for the population. The use of machine learning and deep learning algorithms for crop disease detection has shown promising results in accurately identifying and classifying diseases in plants. In particular, convolutional neural networks (CNNs) have demonstrated high accuracy in crop disease detection, and mobile applications based on these models can help farmers identify and manage crop diseases in real time.

Overall, the application of machine learning and deep learning algorithms for crop disease detection holds great potential for addressing the challenges of crop disease management and improving agricultural productivity. By leveraging these technologies, farmers can quickly and accurately diagnose crop diseases, leading to more effective and targeted disease management strategies. As such, continued research and development in this field is crucial for advancing agricultural sustainability and ensuring global food security.

FUTURE SCOPE

However, there is still a need for further research to improve the accuracy and effectiveness of these models and to ensure their scalability and accessibility for use in the field. One of the limitations of these models is the lack of a standardized public dataset, and the majority of available datasets are limited to certain geographic areas, which are the major challenges faced. In the future, we can increase its efficiency by using a hybrid model and different technologies. Also, we can further upgrade the model by infusing the feature of preventive and curing measures for the disease detected in the crop. So, in this way, various research studies have been conducted using machine learning and deep learning algorithms, and better models with good accuracy can be created.

REFERENCES

[1] H. Orchi, M. Sadik, and M. Khaldoun, "On using artificial intelligence and the internet of things for crop disease detection: A contemporary survey", *Agriculture,* vol. 12, no. 1, p. 9, 2021. [http://dx.doi.org/10.3390/agriculture12010009]

[2] S. Shrimali, "PlantifyAI: A Novel Convolutional Neural Network Based Mobile Application for Efficient Crop Disease Detection and Treatment", *Procedia Comput. Sci.,* vol. 191, pp. 469-474, 2021. [http://dx.doi.org/10.1016/j.procs.2021.07.059]

[3] P. Vasavi, A. Punitha, and T.V. Narayana Rao, "Crop leaf disease detection and classification using machine learning and deep learning algorithms by visual symptoms: a review", *International Journal of Electrical and Computer Engineering (IJECE),* vol. 12, no. 2, p. 2079, 2022. [http://dx.doi.org/10.11591/ijece.v12i2.pp2079-2086]

[4] F.G. Waldamichael, T.G. Debelee, F. Schwenker, Y.M. Ayano, and S.R. Kebede, "Machine learning in cereal crops disease detection: a review", *Algorithms,* vol. 15, no. 3, p. 75, 2022. [http://dx.doi.org/10.3390/a15030075]

[5] D. Singh, N. Jain, P. Jain, P. Kayal, S. Kumawat, and N. Batra, "PlantDoc: A dataset for visual plant disease detection", *Proceedings of the 7th ACM IKDD CoDS and 25th COMAD,* pp. 249-253, 2020. [http://dx.doi.org/10.1145/3371158.3371196]

[6] H. Orchi, M. Sadik, M. Khaldoun, and E. Sabir, "Automation of Crop Disease Detection through Conventional Machine Learning and Deep Transfer Learning Approaches", *Agriculture,* vol. 13, no. 2, p. 352, 2023. [http://dx.doi.org/10.3390/agriculture13020352]

[7] R. Sujatha, J.M. Chatterjee, N.Z. Jhanjhi, and S.N. Brohi, "Performance of deep learning vs machine learning in plant leaf disease detection", *Microprocess. Microsyst.,* vol. 80, p. 103615, 2021. [http://dx.doi.org/10.1016/j.micpro.2020.103615]

[8] A. Prasad, N. Mehta, M. Horak, and W.D. Bae, "A Two-Step Machine Learning Approach for Crop Disease Detection Using GAN and UAV Technology", *Remote Sens. (Basel),* vol. 14, no. 19, p. 4765, 2022. [http://dx.doi.org/10.3390/rs14194765]

[9] R. Bhagwat, and Y. Dandawate, "A framework for crop disease detection using feature fusion method", *International Journal of Engineering and Technology Innovation,* vol. 11, no. 3, pp. 216-228, 2021. [http://dx.doi.org/10.46604/ijeti.2021.7346]

CHAPTER 8

Machine Learning Approaches for Natural Language Processing and Sentiment Analysis

Tarun Jaiswal[1,*] and **Vikash Yadav**[2]

[1] *National Institute of Technology, Raipur, India*

[2] *Government Polytechnic Bighapur, Unnao, Department of Technical Education, Uttar Pradesh, India*

Abstract: The exponential growth of digital content has necessitated the development of effective techniques in natural language processing (NLP) and sentiment analysis. This review paper aims to provide a comprehensive overview of machine learning approaches employed in NLP tasks, with a specific focus on sentiment analysis. We explore various algorithms such as support vector machines (SVM), recurrent neural networks (RNN), and transformer models that have shown promising results in analyzing and classifying sentiments expressed in textual data. Additionally, we explore pre-processing techniques like tokenization and feature engineering that play a vital role in enhancing the performance of these machine learning models. Through an extensive evaluation using benchmark datasets, we compare the strengths, weaknesses, and suitability of different machine learning methods for sentiment analysis tasks. Furthermore, we highlight recent advancements such as transfer learning and explainable AI that have demonstrated potential in improving NLP capabilities. Finally, we discuss emerging trends and future research directions aimed at leveraging machine learning advancements to further enhance natural language processing techniques.

Keywords: AI, BERT, NLP, RNN, SVM.

INTRODUCTION

Machine learning approaches have revolutionized natural language processing (NLP) and sentiment analysis, allowing us to extract valuable insights from textual data. With the advancements in machine learning algorithms and techniques, researchers have made significant strides in understanding and processing human language. In recent years, supervised learning algorithms such as support vector machines (SVM), random forests (RF), recurrent neural networks (RNN), convolutional neural networks (CNN), and transformer-based

* **Corresponding author Tarun Jaiswal:** National Institute of Technology, Raipur, India;
E-mail: tjaiswal_1207@yahoo.com

models like BERT [1] and GPT-3 [2] have been widely employed for various NLP tasks. These approaches enable machines to learn patterns, relationships, and representations from labeled or unlabeled text data. Sentiment analysis has emerged as a prominent application of NLP powered by machine learning. It involves automatically identifying subjective information like opinions, sentiments, and emotions expressed in text documents [3]. By leveraging machine learning models trained on annotated sentiment datasets, it becomes possible to accurately classify text into positive, negative, or neutral sentiments. The availability of large-scale annotated corpora has played a pivotal role in training these models effectively. Datasets such as IMDb movie reviews or Twitter sentiment datasets [4, 5] provide labeled examples that enable supervised learning algorithms to generalize well across different domains. Furthermore, transfer learning methods using pre-trained language models have shown remarkable performance improvements across various NLP tasks. Models like BERT capture rich contextual representations by training on massive amounts of unlabeled data before fine-tuning them for specific downstream tasks with limited labeled data availability. However, there are still challenges that need attention for further advancement. Multilingual sentiment analysis is one area requiring robust models capable of handling diverse languages' linguistic structures effectively [6]. Additionally working towards explainable AI approaches that enhance transparency in decision-making processes is essential for building trust among users.

The machine learning approaches have transformed the field of NLP and sentiment analysis by enabling accurate predictions, efficient text processing, and extraction of valuable insights from textual data. The utilization of supervised learning algorithms, transfer learning techniques using pre-trained models, and the availability of annotated datasets have contributed to these advancements. Addressing challenges such as multilingual sentiment analysis and improving transparency in AI systems will continue to be focal points for future research in this dynamic field.

MACHINE LEARNING ALGORITHMS FOR SENTIMENT ANALYSIS

Support Vector Machines (SVM)

SVM is a powerful machine learning algorithm widely used in sentiment analysis tasks, particularly for binary or multi-class classification problems. SVMs aim to find an optimal hyperplane that separates data points of different classes by maximizing the margin between them. In the context of sentiment analysis, SVMs operate by representing textual data as feature vectors in a high-dimensional space. Each feature represents a specific aspect or attribute related to the text, such as word frequencies or presence/absence indicators for certain keywords. These features capture important information relevant to sentiments expressed within the text.

The SVM algorithm finds an optimal decision boundary that maximizes the distance between support vectors – representative instances from each class located closest to the decision boundary. The choice of kernel functions plays a crucial role in SVM's ability to handle non-linear relationships among features and improve its overall performance [7].

For binary sentiment classification, where sentiments are classified into positive and negative categories, SVM constructs a linear separator that divides these two classes with maximum margin while minimizing misclassification errors. In cases where multiple classes need to be considered, extensions like one-*vs*-one or one-*vs*-all strategies can be employed using multiple binary classifiers based on SVM principles.

One advantage of SVMs is their ability to handle high-dimensional feature spaces efficiently, allowing them to effectively model complex relationships between features and sentiments expressed in textual data. Additionally, due to their mathematical formulation and convex optimization nature, they provide theoretical guarantees regarding generalization capabilities even with limited training samples.

However, it's important to note that SVMs have limitations when dealing with large-scale datasets due to their computational complexity during the training phase involving quadratic programming optimization algorithms. Moreover, selecting appropriate kernel functions and tuning hyperparameters can significantly impact performance; improper choices may lead to either overfitting or underfitting models, resulting in poor generalization abilities on unseen data.

Despite these limitations, SVMs have demonstrated promising results in sentiment analysis tasks and continue to be widely used due to their interpretability, robustness, and ability to handle both linear and non-linear classification problems effectively [8].

Kernel functions play a crucial role in Support Vector Machines (SVM) by allowing them to capture non-linear relationships between features. SVM is a powerful machine learning algorithm that aims to find an optimal hyperplane to separate data points belonging to different classes. However, in cases where the data is not linearly separable, SVM uses kernel functions to map the original feature space into a higher-dimensional space where separation becomes possible. The choice of kernel function depends on the nature of the data and the problem at hand. Here, we will discuss some commonly used kernel functions and their characteristics:

Linear Kernel

The linear kernel is considered the most basic kernel and is associated with a linear support vector machine (SVM). This technique is employed in cases where the data can be efficiently partitioned by a linear or multi-dimensional plane within the original feature space. The linear kernel calculates the inner product of input feature vectors, thereby quantifying the similarity between samples.

Polynomial Kernel

The utilization of the polynomial kernel facilitates the establishment of decision boundaries that are non-linear in nature. This is achieved by transforming the data into a space of higher dimensions through the application of polynomial functions. The algorithm effectively represents polynomial relationships among the features. The kernel function is formally defined as:

$$K(x, y) = (\gamma(x \cdot y) + r)d \quad \textbf{(1)}$$

Where γ describes the scaling factor, describes a constant, and describes the degree of the polynomial.

Radial Basis Function (RBF) Kernel

The radial basis function (RBF) kernel is widely recognized as a highly favored option for support vector machines (SVM). The proposed method has the ability to effectively capture intricate and non-linear relationships among various features, making it highly applicable across a diverse range of scenarios. The radial basis function (RBF) kernel is responsible for transforming the data into a space with an infinite number of dimensions. The term is commonly understood to be defined as:

$$K(x, y) = exp(-\gamma \, ||x - y||2) \quad \textbf{(2)}$$

Where γ describes the scaling factor that decides the effect of each training sample and $||x - y||2$ denotes the squared Euclidean distance among the samples.

Sigmoid Kernel

The sigmoid kernel is frequently employed in the context of binary classification tasks. The method utilizes the sigmoid function as its foundation and transforms the data into a feature space that is amenable to linear separation. The sigmoid kernel function is defined as:

$$K(x, y) = tanh(\gamma(x \, . y) + r) \quad (3)$$

Where is a scaling factor, and is a constant.

Custom Kernels

In addition to the standard kernel functions mentioned above, SVM also allows for the use of custom kernels. These kernels are tailored to specific problem domains and can be designed based on expert knowledge or specific requirements. Custom kernels offer flexibility in capturing complex relationships between features.

Recurrent Neural Network (RNN)

Recurrent neural networks (RNNs) have emerged as a powerful class of machine learning algorithms for sentiment analysis, particularly due to their ability to capture sequential dependencies within text data. Unlike traditional feed-forward neural networks, RNNs maintain an internal memory or hidden state that allows them to process input sequences in a sequential manner. The architecture of an RNN consists of recurrent connections where the output at each time step is not only influenced by the current input but also depends on the previous hidden state. This enables RNNs to encode information from past inputs and retain contextual understanding throughout the sequence [9].

In the context of sentiment analysis, this characteristic makes RNNs well-suited for capturing long-range dependencies between words or phrases within a given text. By considering the order and context in which words appear, RNNs can effectively model linguistic subtleties and semantic relationships crucial for understanding sentiments expressed in textual data. One popular type of RNN cell used extensively in sentiment analysis tasks is long short-term memory (LSTM). LSTM cells are designed to address some limitations faced by traditional vanilla RNNs, like vanishing or exploding gradients during training processes involving long sequences. LSTM introduces specialized gating mechanisms that regulate information flow through memory cells, allowing them to selectively remember or forget relevant information over extended periods.

Through these gates, such as the input gate, forget gate, and output gate, LSTMs can learn when to update their hidden states based on new inputs while retaining important knowledge from prior steps. This capability helps prevent the loss of valuable contextual information required for accurate sentiment classification across longer texts [10]. By processing textual inputs sequentially using recurrent connections with LSTM cells or other variations thereof, RNN-based architectures enable models to leverage rich temporal dynamics present within sentences or documents during sentiment analysis tasks. The ability to capture sequential dependencies has proven effective in handling various challenges related to sentiment analysis, including the identification of negation, sarcasm, or understanding sentiments expressed in longer texts.

However, RNNs also have their limitations. One significant challenge is the difficulty in capturing very long-term dependencies due to the vanishing gradients problem, as errors may propagate over time and result in loss of information. Additionally, training RNNs can be computationally intensive and time-consuming compared to other machine learning algorithms like SVMs. In recent years, advancements such as gated recurrent units (GRU) and attention mechanisms within RNN architectures have further improved their performance in sentiment analysis tasks by addressing some of these challenges related to long-range dependencies and computational efficiency.

Transformer Models

Transformer models have revolutionized the field of natural language processing, including sentiment analysis, with their innovative architecture that relies on self-attention mechanisms and multi-head attention.

The transformer model architecture fundamentally differs from traditional sequential models like RNNs by leveraging a self-attention mechanism that allows global dependencies within text data to be captured efficiently. Instead of relying on recurrent connections to process sequences sequentially, transformers process all input elements simultaneously in parallel [11].

Self-attention mechanisms enable transformers to assign different weights or importance values to each word or token based on its relevance to other words in the sequence. This allows the model to attend and focus on important contextual information while de-emphasizing irrelevant or noisy parts of the text. In addition to self-attention, transformer models employ multi-head attention mechanisms where multiple layers of self-attention are used in parallel. Each head attends independently over different positions within the input sequence, allowing for richer representations and capturing diverse aspects of relationships between words [12].

By utilizing these attention mechanisms, transformers can effectively capture long-range dependencies across a sentence or document without being constrained by sequential processing limitations present in traditional architectures like RNNs. This capability is particularly advantageous when dealing with sentiment analysis tasks as it enables a better understanding of sentiments expressed through complex linguistic structures and distant word relationships. Another key advantage offered by transformer models is improved parallelization during both training and inference stages. Traditional sequential models like RNNs suffer from limited parallelization due to their inherently serial nature since computations at each time step depend on previous steps' outputs. In contrast, transformers can process each position's information independently, enabling highly efficient computation across multiple GPUs or distributed systems.

Furthermore, transformer-based architectures introduced pre-training techniques such as BERT (Bidirectional Encoder Representations from Transformers), which learn contextualized word embeddings using large-scale unlabeled corpora before fine-tuning them for specific downstream tasks like sentiment analysis. This transfer learning approach has shown remarkable performance improvements and enhanced generalization capabilities. While transformer models excel in capturing global dependencies, they do have some limitations. Transformers may struggle with modeling sequential order information effectively since their architecture does not inherently encode explicit positional or temporal relationships between words. Techniques like adding positional encodings can partly mitigate this limitation but are not as effective as recurrent connections in traditional sequential models for tasks that heavily rely on word order [13].

The transformer models have brought significant advancements to sentiment analysis by leveraging self-attention mechanisms and multi-head attention within their innovative architecture. These models excel at capturing global dependencies across text data while improving parallelization efficiency compared to traditional sequential architectures like RNNs. By effectively modeling long-range contextual relationships, transformers provide valuable insights into sentiments expressed through complex linguistic structures and contribute to the advancement of sentiment analysis techniques.

PRE-PROCESSING TECHNIQUES FOR SENTIMENT ANALYSIS

Pre-processing techniques for sentiment analysis involve preparing textual data before feeding it into a machine learning model or any other sentiment analysis algorithm. These techniques help to clean, normalize, and transform the text, making it suitable for accurate sentiment classification.

Tokenization

Tokenization is a fundamental pre-processing technique in sentiment analysis that involves splitting text into individual tokens or words [14]. It forms the initial step towards converting unstructured textual data into a format suitable for further analysis and modeling. The tokenization process aims to segment the text by identifying boundaries between words, punctuation marks, symbols, or any other meaningful units within the given context. Each resulting unit, referred to as a token, represents an atomic element that can be processed individually during subsequent stages of sentiment analysis.

There are various approaches to tokenization depending on specific requirements and characteristics of the text being analyzed:

White Space Tokenization

This simple approach splits the text based on white space characters (such as spaces or tabs) between words. While it works reasonably well for languages like English, where spaces typically separate words, it may not be sufficient for languages with different writing systems or no clear word delimiters [15].

Rule-based Tokenization

Rule-based tokenizers leverage predefined rules and patterns specific to a language or domain to effectively identify tokens within text data. These rules may consider aspects such as punctuation marks, hyphenation conventions, sentence structures, abbreviations, *etc.*, optimizing segmentation accuracy accordingly.

Statistical Tokenization

Statistical models utilize machine learning techniques trained on large corpora of annotated data to automatically learn patterns and determine appropriate segmentation points within texts. These models make use of probabilistic algorithms that estimate the likelihood of certain sequences being valid tokens based on their co-occurrence frequencies in training data.

Tokenizers Designed Specifically for Social Media/Texting Language

Social media platforms often contain informal language usage with diverse expressions like hashtags (#), emojis/emoticons (:), and URLs/mentions (@username). Specialized tokenizers are developed, considering these unique features while preserving their contextual meaning during sentiment analysis tasks involving social media content. After performing tokenization, each identified token can be treated as a separate entity, allowing for further analysis based on individual words or phrases. This facilitates tasks such as frequency counting, part-of-speech tagging, and sentiment labeling of each token individually or in combination with adjacent tokens. It is important to note that the effectiveness of tokenization greatly impacts subsequent stages of sentiment analysis. Properly segmenting text into meaningful units ensures accurate representation and interpretation of sentiments expressed within the data. Careful consideration should also be given to language-specific nuances, domain-specific requirements, and potential challenges related to informal language usage commonly found in social media platforms. In conclusion, tokenization serves as a crucial pre-processing technique for sentiment analysis by breaking down textual data into individual tokens or words. It enables subsequent stages to operate at a granular level while preserving contextual information necessary for accurately capturing sentiments expressed within the text.

Feature Engineering

Feature engineering plays a vital role in sentiment analysis by transforming raw textual data into meaningful numerical representations that machine learning algorithms can understand and process effectively [16]. Several feature engineering techniques are commonly used in sentiment analysis, including bag-of-words, n-grams, and word embeddings.

Bag-of-Words (BoW)

The bag-of-words approach represents text as a collection of words without considering the order or grammar. It creates a vocabulary of unique words from the entire corpus and constructs a vector for each document by counting the occurrences of these words [17]. This method treats each document independently and ignores any sequential or contextual information within the text.

N-grams

N-grams capture local context by representing contiguous sequences of n tokens (typically words) within text data. For example, with bigrams (n=2), “I love it” would be represented as [“I love”, “love it”]. By considering these chunks of consecutive tokens, n-gram models can capture some level of phrase-level semantics and dependencies between adjacent words [18].

Word Embeddings

Word embeddings are dense vector representations that aim to capture semantic relationships between words based on their distributional properties within a given corpus [19]. These embeddings transform individual words into continuous-valued vectors in high-dimensional spaces where similar meaning is reflected through proximity.

Two popular word embedding techniques used in sentiment analysis are:

Word2Vec

Word2Vec is an unsupervised learning algorithm that learns word embeddings based on predicting neighboring context or target words using either Continuous Bag-of-Words (CBOW) or Skip-Gram architectures [20]. The resulting learned vectors encode semantic similarities – similar concepts have closer vector representations compared to dissimilar ones.

GloVe

Global Vectors for Word Representation (GloVe) is another widely-used technique for generating word embeddings by leveraging global co-occurrence statistics across large-scale corpora during the training phase [21]. GloVe embeddings capture both syntactic and semantic relationships between words, providing insights into their contextual meanings.

Word embeddings offer significant advantages in sentiment analysis by capturing nuanced linguistic relationships and reducing the dimensionality of feature spaces. These representations enable models to understand similarities, analogies, and context-specific associations that enhance sentiment classification performance [22].

It is worth mentioning that these features can be combined or used individually based on specific requirements or domain characteristics. Additionally, techniques like TF-IDF (Term Frequency-Inverse Document Frequency) weighting can be applied to bag-of-words or n-gram representations to account for the importance of terms within a document relative to its frequency across the entire corpus [23].

Feature engineering techniques such as bag-of-words, n-grams, and word embeddings play a crucial role in sentiment analysis tasks. They transform raw text data into numerical representations that capture important information related to sentiments expressed within documents. By incorporating contextual cues through word embeddings like Word2Vec or GloVe, models gain a deeper understanding of semantic relationships among words and improve overall sentiment classification accuracy.

COMPARATIVE EVALUATION OF MACHINE LEARNING APPROACHES

Datasets for Evaluation

In sentiment analysis research, the evaluation of machine learning approaches relies on benchmark datasets that have been widely used to assess the performance and effectiveness of different algorithms. These datasets are carefully annotated with sentiment labels, allowing researchers to compare and evaluate their models consistently.

Here are some benchmark datasets commonly used in sentiment analysis research:

Stanford Sentiment Treebank (SST)

The SST dataset [24] is one of the most widely used benchmarks in sentiment analysis. It provides fine-grained sentiment annotations at both phrase and sentence levels, covering movie reviews from Rotten Tomatoes. The dataset offers a hierarchical structure where each sentence is labeled with its overall sentiment polarity (positive or negative), along with phrase-level annotations capturing more nuanced sentiments.

IMDb Movie Reviews

The IMDb Movie Reviews dataset [4] consists of a large collection of movie reviews extracted from the Internet Movie Database (IMDb). It contains binary sentiment labels indicating whether each review expresses positive or negative sentiments toward the corresponding movie.

Amazon Product Reviews

The Amazon product reviews dataset [25] comprises customer reviews from various product categories available on Amazon's e-commerce platform. The dataset covers diverse domains such as electronics, books, clothing, *etc.*, providing valuable resources for evaluating sentiment analysis models across different domains.

Twitter Sentiment Analysis Dataset

Twitter has also been a popular source for constructing benchmark datasets due to its vast amount of user-generated content and real-time nature. Multiple Twitter-specific datasets have been created by collecting tweets related to specific topics or events, which are then manually annotated with sentiment labels [5].

These benchmark datasets serve as standard reference points for evaluating machine learning approaches in terms of accuracy, precision, recall, F1-score, and other performance metrics specific to sentiment classification tasks. It is important to note that while these established benchmarks provide reliable resources for comparative evaluations across studies, they may not cover the entire spectrum of sentiment analysis applications or capture all possible domains and languages. Therefore, researchers often adapt or create domain-specific datasets for specialized evaluations.

The benchmark datasets play a crucial role in comparative evaluations of machine learning approaches in sentiment analysis research. Datasets like Stanford Sentiment Treebank, IMDb Movie Reviews, Amazon Product Reviews, and Twitter Sentiment Analysis Dataset provide standardized resources for assessing the performance and generalizability of various algorithms across different domains and contexts.

Performance Metrics

When evaluating the performance of sentiment analysis models, several metrics are commonly employed to assess their accuracy and effectiveness. These metrics provide quantitative measures of how well the models classify sentiments in text data. The following overview highlights some widely used evaluation metrics:

- **Accuracy**: Accuracy is a fundamental metric that measures the overall correctness of sentiment predictions made by a model [26]. It calculates the ratio of correctly classified instances (both positive and negative) to the total number of instances in the dataset.
- **Precision**: Precision focuses on measuring how many predicted positive instances are actually true positives, *i.e.*, the proportion of correctly identified positive cases out of all instances predicted as positive [27]. High precision indicates that when the model predicts a positive sentiment, it is highly likely to be correct.
- **Recall (Sensitivity)**: Recall evaluates how well a model can identify actual positive instances from all truly positive cases present in the dataset [28]. It measures the proportion of true positives identified by dividing them by both true positives and false negatives.
- **F1-Score**: The F1-score is a harmonic mean between precision and recall, providing an overall measure for balancing both metrics effectively [29]. It combines precision and recall into a single value that captures model performance, taking into account both false negatives and false positives.

These performance metrics enable researchers to compare different sentiment analysis models objectively based on their ability to correctly classify sentiments within textual data. While these four metrics mentioned above are commonly employed, other evaluation measures such as specificity, area under ROC curve (AUC-ROC), or Cohen's Kappa coefficient may also be utilized depending on specific requirements or research goals.

It's important to note that selecting appropriate evaluation metrics depends on factors like class imbalance within datasets or specific application scenarios where certain types of errors might have more significant consequences than others.

The accuracy provides an overall assessment, while precision, recall, and F1-score offer more detailed insights into the performance of sentiment analysis models. These metrics collectively enable researchers to evaluate and compare different algorithms, facilitating advancements in the field of sentiment analysis.

Performance of different machine learning approaches in sentiment analysis

Several studies have conducted experiments using benchmark datasets. Specifically, Support Vector Machines (SVM), Recurrent Neural Networks (RNNs), and Transformer models have been widely evaluated. Here, we discuss the Performance of different machine learning approaches in sentiment analysis and analyze the strengths and weaknesses of each approach based on empirical findings.

Support Vector Machines (SVM)

Many studies have employed SVM for sentiment analysis due to its ability to handle high-dimensional feature spaces effectively [17]. SVM constructs a hyperplane that maximally separates positive and negative instances in the feature space. Experimental results suggest that SVM performs well when dealing with smaller datasets or datasets where linear separation is sufficient [18]. It often achieves competitive accuracy levels on benchmark datasets like SST, IMDb movie reviews, and Amazon product reviews. However, SVM may struggle with capturing complex linguistic patterns or long-range dependencies present in textual data.

Strengths

- Effective for smaller datasets.
- Suitable for linearly separable sentiment classification tasks.
- Good generalization performance when data is limited.

Weaknesses

- Limited capability to capture complex linguistic patterns.
- Difficulty handling long-range dependencies.
- May require extensive feature engineering for optimal performance.

Recurrent Neural Networks (RNNs)

RNNs are popular choices for modeling sequential data due to their ability to retain contextual information through recurrent connections [30]. They can capture dependencies between words within sentences by utilizing recurrent layers such as long short-term memory (LSTM) or gated recurrent units (GRU). Empirical results demonstrate that RNN-based models achieve promising results on various sentiment analysis benchmarks [31]. They excel at capturing sequential information and perform well when there are long-term dependencies involved in determining sentiments within text data. However, RNNs might suffer from vanishing or exploding gradient problems during training if not properly addressed.

Strengths

- Effective in capturing sequential dependencies.
- Suitable for sentiment analysis tasks involving long-term dependencies.
- Can learn representations that capture context and linguistic nuances.

Weaknesses

- Vulnerable to vanishing or exploding gradient problems.
- Computationally expensive, especially with longer sequences.
- May struggle with modeling very long-range dependencies.

Transformer Models

Transformer models have gained significant attention in recent years due to their ability to capture contextual information effectively using self-attention mechanisms [11]. The transformer architecture, as seen in models like BERT (Bidirectional Encoder Representations from Transformers), has achieved state-of-the-art performance on various natural language processing tasks, including sentiment analysis. Experimental results indicate that transformer-based models consistently outperform other approaches on several benchmark datasets. They excel at capturing global contextual information and have a strong capability to model complex relationships within text data. However, training large-scale transformer models can be computationally intensive and requires substantial computational resources.

Strengths

- Excellent at capturing global contextual information.
- Strong performance across diverse sentiment analysis benchmarks.
- Ability to model complex linguistic patterns effectively.

Weaknesses

- Computationally expensive during training and inference phases.
- Large memory requirements for storing parameters of the model.

The SVMs perform well when dealing with smaller datasets or linearly separable sentiment classification tasks but may struggle with complex linguistic patterns. RNNs are effective at capturing sequential dependencies but can encounter issues like vanishing/exploding gradients. Transformer models, such as BERT, exhibit excellent performance by leveraging self-attention mechanisms and encoding intricate relationships within text data; however, they require more computational resources compared to other approaches. It is important to note that the strengths and weaknesses mentioned here are based on empirical findings reported in the literature; however, further research is continually being conducted to explore enhancements or variations of these approaches for improved sentiment analysis performances.

RECENT ADVANCEMENTS IN NLP WITH MACHINE LEARNING

Recent advancements in natural language processing (NLP) with machine learning have transformed the field, enabling more accurate language understanding and processing. Here are some key advancements:

- **Transformer-Based Models**: The introduction of transformer models, which leverage self-attention mechanisms, has revolutionized NLP. The transformer architecture proposed in a study [11] has become a cornerstone for many NLP tasks, achieving state-of-the-art performance. Transformer-based models like BERT [32], GPT [33], and RoBERTa [34] have shown remarkable success in tasks such as text classification, named entity recognition, and machine translation.
- **Pre-training and Transfer Learning**: Pre-training large-scale language models on vast amounts of unlabeled data, followed by fine-tuning on specific tasks, has proven highly effective. The BERT model demonstrated the power of pre-training for a wide range of downstream NLP tasks. This approach has enabled models to achieve strong performance even with limited labeled data.
- **Contextual Word Embeddings**: Traditional word embeddings assign a fixed vector representation to each word, disregarding contextual nuances. Contextual

word embeddings, on the other hand, provide dynamic word representations based on the context. ELMo [35] and GPT are notable examples of models that generate contextual word embeddings, capturing the meaning and context-dependent nature of words more accurately.

- **Multi-Modal NLP**: Integrating multiple modalities, such as text, images, and audio, has gained attention in NLP. Multi-modal models combine visual and textual information for tasks like image captioning, visual question answering, and text-to-image synthesis. ViLBERT [32] and UNITER [36] are examples of models that fuse vision and language for improved understanding and generation of multi-modal data.
- **Few-Shot and Zero-Shot Learning**: Traditional machine learning requires a substantial amount of labeled training data. However, recent advancements in few-shot and zero-shot learning have made it possible to generalize to new tasks or classes with minimal training examples. Meta-learning techniques, as showcased in the work [37], have contributed to this advancement, enabling models to adapt quickly to novel tasks.
- **Explainability and Interpretability**: Ensuring the transparency and interpretability of NLP models has gained significance. Researchers have explored methods to understand and interpret model decisions. Attention visualization techniques, such as [38] and gradient-based saliency maps, have been used to provide insights into the model's decision-making process, enhancing its explainability.

These recent advancements in NLP with machine learning have significantly pushed the boundaries of language understanding and processing, enabling models to achieve remarkable performance across a wide range of tasks. Further research and development in these areas continue to drive progress in NLP and its applications.

Transfer Learning

In recent years, transfer learning has emerged as a powerful technique in natural language processing (NLP) that leverages pre-trained language models to improve generalization across tasks. One notable example of such pre-trained models is BERT (Bidirectional Encoder Representations from Transformers) [1].

Transfer learning involves training a model on one task or domain and then utilizing its learned knowledge to perform well on another related task or domain [39]. This approach has gained significant attention due to the scarcity of labeled data for specific tasks and the time-consuming nature of training deep neural networks from scratch. Pre-trained language models like BERT are trained on massive amounts of unlabeled text data using unsupervised methods, enabling them to learn rich representations capturing various linguistic patterns and semantic relationships within sentences [35]. These models can be fine-tuned by adding task-specific layers or additional training on labeled data for specific downstream tasks like sentiment analysis, named entity recognition, question answering, *etc*.

The use of pre-trained language models such as BERT has demonstrated remarkable improvements in several NLP benchmarks by providing contextualized word embeddings that capture both syntactic and semantic information effectively [33]. The key advantage lies in their ability to transfer knowledge from large-scale pre-training datasets, allowing them to generalize better across different domains and exhibit robust performance even with limited labeled data available for fine-tuning. By leveraging transfer learning techniques like BERT-based architectures, researchers have achieved state-of-the-art results across various NLP applications. These advancements have significantly reduced the need for extensive feature engineering efforts while improving accuracy levels compared to traditional machine learning approaches.

However, it is important to note that deploying pre-trained language models may come with computational challenges due to their large size and memory requirements during both the training and inference phases. Several techniques, such as knowledge distillation or model compression, have been proposed to address these challenges and enable the efficient deployment of transfer learning models.

Transfer learning methods like pre-trained language models (*e.g*., BERT) have revolutionized NLP by providing powerful tools for improving generalization across tasks. These models capture rich linguistic representations from large-scale unlabeled data and can be fine-tuned on specific downstream tasks, resulting in enhanced performance even with limited labeled data available. As research continues to advance, we can expect further improvements in transfer learning techniques and their application to a wide range of NLP problems.

Explainable AI

Explainable AI (XAI) has become a crucial aspect of natural language processing (NLP) models, aiming to improve transparency and interpretability in their decision-making process. In this section, we will discuss various approaches that have been developed to enhance the explainability of NLP models.

Interpretability approaches in NLP focus on providing insights into how a model arrives at its predictions or decisions. This is particularly important as complex deep learning architectures like neural networks can be considered black boxes due to their high dimensionality and non-linear transformations [40]. By improving the interpretability of these models, researchers aim to address concerns related to bias, fairness, ethics, and trustworthiness.

One approach towards achieving explainability in NLP is through attention mechanisms. Attention mechanisms allow the model to assign weights or importance scores to different parts of input text during processing [41]. These attention weights provide an indication of which words or phrases are most influential for making predictions, thus offering some level of interpretability. Another method for enhancing explainability is by utilizing rule-based systems or symbolic reasoning techniques alongside machine learning models. These systems incorporate prior knowledge encoded as rules or logical statements that guide the decision-making process [42]. By combining statistical modeling with explicit rules, it becomes possible to provide explanations based on predefined criteria.

Additionally, post-hoc explanation methods have gained popularity in NLP tasks. Post-hoc methods involve applying external tools or algorithms after the model has made its prediction [43]. Examples include generating heatmaps highlighting important words or phrases for classification decisions and using gradient-based techniques such as integrated gradients for feature attribution analysis. It is worth mentioning that there is ongoing research exploring hybrid approaches that combine multiple explanation methods for improved transparency and interpretability in NLP models' decision-making processes [44]. These hybrid approaches aim to leverage the strengths of different techniques and provide a more comprehensive understanding of model predictions.

However, explainable AI (XAI) is an important area of research in NLP that focuses on enhancing transparency and interpretability. Various approaches, such as attention mechanisms, rule-based systems, post-hoc explanations, and hybrid methods, have been developed to address this challenge. By improving the explainability of NLP models' decision-making processes, we can gain valuable insights into their inner workings and foster trust in their outputs.

FUTURE RESEARCH DIRECTIONS

The field of machine learning-based Natural Language Processing (NLP) is continuously evolving, and identifying emerging trends is crucial for driving future research. In this section, we will discuss potential areas that hold promise for exploration in the coming years.

Multilingual Sentiment Analysis

With the increasing globalization and diversity of online content, there is a growing need to develop models capable of analyzing sentiment across multiple languages. While sentiment analysis techniques have been extensively studied in English, extending these methods to other languages poses unique challenges due to variations in linguistic structures and cultural nuances [3]. Future research can focus on developing robust multilingual sentiment analysis approaches that can handle diverse language inputs effectively.

Fine-Grained Sentiment Classification using Deep Learning Architectures

Traditional sentiment analysis often categorizes texts into positive or negative sentiments. However, real-world scenarios demand a more nuanced understanding with fine-grained classification capturing various levels of sentiments such as strongly positive, weakly positive, neutral, weakly negative, *etc* [45]. Deep learning architectures like Convolutional Neural Networks (CNNs) and Recurrent Neural Networks (RNNs) have shown promising results in capturing contextual information for sentiment classification tasks. Further research could explore advanced deep learning models tailored specifically for fine-grained sentiment analysis.

Contextualized Word Representations

Pre-trained word embeddings like Word2Vec and GloVe capture distributed representations of words based on co-occurrence statistics within large corpora but lack context-specific information [20]. Recently developed contextualized word representations such as ELMo (Embeddings from Language Models), GPT (Generative Pre-trained Transformer), and BERT have revolutionized NLP by providing context-aware word embeddings that consider surrounding text when generating word representations. Future research could delve deeper into exploring novel architectures and training strategies for contextualized word representations to improve their performance across various NLP tasks.

Ethical Considerations in NLP

As machine learning-based NLP systems become more pervasive, it is vital to address ethical considerations associated with bias, fairness, privacy, and accountability [46]. Future research should focus on developing methodologies that ensure fairness and mitigate biases in NLP models' decision-making processes. Additionally, exploring ways to make NLP systems more transparent and accountable can help build trust among users.

Interdisciplinary Approaches

Collaboration between researchers from different fields, such as linguistics, cognitive science, psychology, and computer science, can lead to innovative breakthroughs in understanding language processing mechanisms [47]. Integrating knowledge from these disciplines could pave the way for novel approaches that combine linguistic insights with machine learning techniques for improved natural language understanding.

Hence, the future of machine learning-based NLP research will move in several exciting directions. Exploring multilingual sentiment analysis, fine-grained sentiment classification using deep learning architectures, advancing contextualized word representations, and addressing ethical considerations in NLP models' decision-making process while fostering transparency and accountability are potential areas for future exploration. By pushing boundaries in these areas through interdisciplinary collaboration and innovative methodologies, we can unlock new possibilities for enhancing language understanding applications.

CONCLUSION

Machine learning approaches have revolutionized natural language processing (NLP) and sentiment analysis, enabling us to extract valuable insights from textual data. In this article, we explored the key contributions of machine learning in these domains and highlighted their significance. By leveraging techniques such as supervised learning, unsupervised learning, and deep learning, machine learning models have achieved remarkable success in various NLP tasks. These include text classification, named entity recognition, sentiment analysis, machine translation, question answering, and more. Machine learning algorithms learn patterns and relationships from labeled or unlabeled data to make accurate predictions or generate meaningful representations of language.

Sentiment analysis has emerged as a prominent application of NLP powered by machine learning. It involves identifying subjective information like opinions and emotions expressed in text documents. With the advancements in machine learning algorithms like Support Vector Machines (SVM), Random Forests (RF), Recurrent Neural Networks (RNN), Convolutional Neural Networks (CNN), and Transformers-based models like BERT and GPT-3, sentiment analysis has reached new heights of accuracy.

The use of annotated datasets for training these models plays a crucial role in achieving high performance. Large-scale annotated corpora enable better generalization across different domains while also addressing challenges related to bias detection and fairness concerns. Moreover, transfer learning methods utilizing pre-trained language models such as BERT have shown significant improvements in generalization across various NLP tasks by capturing rich linguistic representations from large-scale unlabeled data. Fine-tuning these pre-trained models on specific downstream tasks has become a common practice with limited labeled data availability.

However promising the current state may be, there are still challenges that need attention for further advancement—areas such as multilingual sentiment analysis requiring robust models capable of handling diverse languages' linguistic structures effectively. Additionally, working towards explainable AI approaches that enhance transparency in decision-making processes is essential for building trust among users.

In conclusion, machine-learning-based approaches have greatly advanced NLP and sentiment analysis by enabling accurate predictions, efficient text processing, and the extraction of valuable insights from textual data. Continued research on machine learning techniques, dataset annotation, interpretability methods, and addressing challenges like multilingual sentiment analysis will pave the way for even more sophisticated language understanding systems in the future.

REFERENCES

[1] J. Devlin, M.-W. Chang, K. Lee, and K. Toutanova, "BERT: Pre-training of deep bidirectional transformers for language understanding," *Proc. Conf.*, vol. 1, pp. 4171-4186, 2018. [Online]. Available from: http://arxiv.org/abs/1810.04805.

[2] T. B. Brown, "Language models are few-shot learners," 2020. [Online]. Available: https://arxiv.org/abs/2005.14165.

[3] L. Zhang and B. Liu, *Sentiment Analysis and Opinion Mining*, Morgan & Claypool, 2012.

[4] A. L. Maas, R. E. Daly, P. T. Pham, D. Huang, A. Y. Ng, and C. Potts, "Learning word vectors for sentiment analysis," in *Proc. 49th Annu. Meeting Assoc. Comput. Linguistics*, Portland, OR, USA, 2011, pp. 142-150.

[5] A. Go, R. Bhayani, and L. Huang, "Twitter sentiment classification using distant supervision," 2009. [Online]. Available: https://www.researchgate.net/publication/228628979

[6] L. Bing, "Sentiment Analysis: Mining Opinions, Sentiments, and Emotions - Bing Liu - Google Books", *Comput. Linguist.,* vol. 42, pp. 595-598, 2015. [Online]. [Available: https://books.google.co.uk/books].

[7] T. Jaiswal, D. S. Jaiswal, and D. R. Shukla, "Soft computing techniques based image classification using support vector machine performance," *Int. J. Trend Sci. Res. Dev.*, vol. 3, no. 6, pp. 113-116, 2019. [Online]. Available: http://dx.doi.org/10.31142/ijtsrd23437

[8] T. Jaiswal, and S. Jaiswal, "Machine Learning-Based Classification Models for Diagnosis of Diabetes", *Recent Advances in Computer Science and Communications,* vol. 15, no. 6, p. e090522190936, 2022. [http://dx.doi.org/10.2174/2666255814666210201103252]

[9] http://arxiv.org/abs/1912.05911

[10] A. Sherstinsky, "Fundamentals of Recurrent Neural Network (RNN) and Long Short-Term Memory

(LSTM) network", *Physica D,* vol. 404, p. 132306, 2020. [http://dx.doi.org/10.1016/j.physd.2019.132306]

[11] A. Vaswani, *Attention is all you need,* 2017. https://arxiv.org/pdf/1706.03762.pdf

[12] Z. Lin, "A structured self-attentive sentence embedding," in *Proc. 5th Int. Conf. Learn. Represent. (ICLR)*, 2017. [Online]. Available: http://arxiv.org/abs/1703.03130

[13] A. Gulati, *Conformer: Convolution-augmented Transformer for Speech Recognition*, 2020. [http://dx.doi.org/10.21437/Interspeech.2020-3015]

[14] G. Angiani, L. Ferrari, T. Fontanini, P. Fornacciari, E. Iotti, F. Magliani, and S. Manicardi, "A comparison between preprocessing techniques for sentiment analysis in Twitter," CEUR Workshop Proc., vol. 1748, pp. 1–8, 2016. [Online]. Available: https://ceur-ws.org/Vol-1748/paper-06.pdf

[15] M. A. Attia, "Arabic tokenization system," in *Proc. 2007 Workshop Comput. Approaches Semitic Lang. Common Issues Res.*, Semitic '07, 2007, p. 65. [Online]. Available: [http://dx.doi.org/10.3115/1654576.1654588]

[16] N. Jindal and B. Liu, "Opinion spam and analysis," in *Proc. 2008 Int. Conf.* Web Search Web Data Mining, Palo Alto, CA, USA, 2008, pp. 219-230. [Online]. Available: [http://dx.doi.org/10.1145/1341531.1341560]

[17] T. Joachims, "Text categorization with support vector machines: Learning with many relevant features," in *Proc. European Conf. Mach. Learn.*, Freiburg, Germany, 1998, pp. 137-142. [Online]. Available: [http://dx.doi.org/10.1007/BFb0026683]

[18] B. Pang, L. Lee, and S. Vaithyanathan, "Thumbs up? Sentiment classification using machine learning techniques," 2002. [Online]. Available: http://arxiv.org/abs/cs/0205070

[19] T. Mikolov, K. Chen, G. Corrado, and J. Dean, "Efficient estimation of word representations in vector space," in Proc. Int. Conf. Learn. Represent. (ICLR), 2013. [Online]. Available: https://arxiv.org/abs/1301.3781

[20] T. Mikolov, I. Sutskever, K. Chen, G. Corrado, and J. Dean, *Distributed Representations of Words and Phrases and their Compositionality. arXiv e-prints, page*, 2013.

[21] J. Pennington, R. Socher, and C. Manning, "Glove: Global Vectors for Word Representation", *Proceedings of the 2014 Conference on Empirical Methods in Natural Language Processing (EMNLP),* 2014, pp. 1532-1543. [http://dx.doi.org/10.3115/v1/D14-1162]

[22] E. Cambria, "Affective Computing and Sentiment Analysis", *IEEE Intell. Syst.,* vol. 31, no. 2, pp. 102-107, 2016. [http://dx.doi.org/10.1109/MIS.2016.31]

[23] G. Salton, and C. Buckley, "Term-weighting approaches in automatic text retrieval", *Inf. Process. Manage.,* vol. 24, no. 5, pp. 513-523, 1988. [http://dx.doi.org/10.1016/0306-4573(88)90021-0]

[24] R. Socher, "Recursive deep models for semantic compositionality over a sentiment treebank", *Proceedings of the Conference,* 2013, pp. 1631-1642.

[25] J. McAuley, and J. Leskovec, "Hidden factors and hidden topics", *Proceedings of the 7th ACM conference on Recommender systems,* 2013, pp. 165-172. [http://dx.doi.org/10.1145/2507157.2507163]

[26] M. Sokolova, and G. Lapalme, "A systematic analysis of performance measures for classification tasks", *Inf. Process. Manage.,* vol. 45, no. 4, pp. 427-437, 2009. [http://dx.doi.org/10.1016/j.ipm.2009.03.002]

[27] D. M. W. Powers, "Evaluation: from precision, recall and F-measure to ROC, informedness, markedness and correlation," 2020. [Online]. Available: http://arxiv.org/abs/2010.16061

[28] R. Baeza-Yates and B. Ribeiro-Neto, *Modern Information Retrieval*, vol. 9, 1999.

[29] C.J. Van Rijsbergen, *Information retrieval.* 2nd ed. Butterworths: London, SE, 1979.

[30] T. Mikolov, M. Karafiát, L. Burget, J. Černocký, and S. Khudanpur, "Recurrent neural network based language model," in *Proc. Interspeech*, Makuhari, Japan, 2010, pp. 1045-1048. [Online]. Available: [http://dx.doi.org/10.21437/Interspeech.2010-343]

[31] K.S. Tai, R. Socher, and C.D. Manning, "Improved semantic representations from tree-structured long short-Term memory networks", *7th Int. Jt. Conf. Nat. Lang. Process. Asian Fed. Nat. Lang. Process. Proc. Conf.*, vol. vol. 1, 2015, pp. 1556-1566. [http://dx.doi.org/10.3115/v1/P15-1150]

[32] J. Lu, D. Batra, D. Parikh, and S. Lee, "ViLBERT: Pretraining task-agnostic visiolinguistic representations for vision-and-language tasks," *Advances in Neural Information Processing Systems*, vol. 32, 2019.

[33] A. Radford, K. Narasimhan, T. Salimans, and I. Sutskever, "Improving Language Understanding by Generative Pre-Training", *Homology Homotopy Appl.*, vol. 9, no. 1, pp. 399-438, 2018.

[34] Y. Liu, "RoBERTa: A robustly optimized BERT pretraining approach," 2019. [Online]. Available: http://arxiv.org/abs/1907.11692

[35] M. Peters, "Deep Contextualized Word Representations", *Proceedings of the 2018 Conference of the North American Chapter of the Association for Computational Linguistics: Human Language Technologies,* vol. Volume 1, vol. vol. 1, 2018, pp. 2227-2237. [http://dx.doi.org/10.18653/v1/N18-1202]

[36] Y.-C. Chen, "UNITER: UNiversal Image-TExt Representation Learning," 2020. [Online]. Available: https://arxiv.org/abs/1909.11740

[37] M. Yin, G. Tucker, M. Zhou, S. Levine, and C. Finn, "Meta-learning without memorization," 2019. [Online]. Available: http://arxiv.org/abs/1912.03820

[38] S. Wiegreffe, and Y. Pinter, "Attention is not not Explanation", *Proceedings of the 2019 Conference on Empirical Methods in Natural Language Processing and the 9th International Joint Conference on Natural Language Processing (EMNLP-IJCNLP),* 2019, pp. 11-20. [http://dx.doi.org/10.18653/v1/D19-1002]

[39] S. Panigrahi, A. Nanda, and T. Swarnkar, A Survey on Transfer Learning.*Smart Innovation.* vol. Vol. 194. Systems and Technologies, 2021, pp. 781-789.

[40] Z.C. Lipton, "The mythos of model interpretability", *Commun. ACM,* vol. 61, no. 10, pp. 36-43, 2018. [http://dx.doi.org/10.1145/3233231]

[41] D. Bahdanau, K. H. Cho, and Y. Bengio, "Neural machine translation by jointly learning to align and translate," in *Proc. 3rd Int. Conf. Learn. Represent. (ICLR)*, 2015. [Online]. Available: https://arxiv.org/abs/1409.0473

[42] M. Ridley, "Explainable Artificial Intelligence", *Research Library Issues,* no. 299, pp. 28-46, 2019. [http://dx.doi.org/10.29242/rli.299.3]

[43] M. Ribeiro, S. Singh, and C. Guestrin, "Why Should I Trust You?': Explaining the Predictions of Any Classifier", *Proceedings of the 2016 Conference of the North American Chapter of the Association for Computational Linguistics: Demonstrations,* pp. 97-101., 2016, . [http://dx.doi.org/10.1145/2939672.2939778]

[44] J. Chen, L. Song, M.J. Wainwright, and M.I. Jordan, "Learning to explain: An information-theoretic perspective on model interpretation", *35th International Conference on Machine Learning, ICML 2018,* vol. vol. 2, 2018, pp. 1386-1418.

[45] B. Pang, and L. Lee, "Opinion mining and sentiment analysis", *Comput. Linguist.,* vol. 35, no. 2, pp. 311-312, 2009.

[http://dx.doi.org/10.1162/coli.2009.35.2.311]

[46] A. Caliskan, J. J. Bryson, and A. Narayanan, "Semantics derived automatically from language corpora contain human-like biases," Science, vol. 356, no. 6334, pp. 183-186, 2017. [Online]. Available: [http://dx.doi.org/10.1126/science.aal4230]

[47] G. Weikum, "Foundations of statistical natural language processing", *SIGMOD Rec.,* vol. 31, no. 3, pp. 37-38, 2002.
[http://dx.doi.org/10.1145/601858.601867]

CHAPTER 9

From Data to Big Data: An Exploration of the Evolution and Impact of Large-Scale Data Analytics

Manish Kumar Gupta[1,*] and **Ashok Kumar Rai**[2]

[1] *Buddha Institute of Technology, Gorakhpur, India*

[2] *Galgotias University, Greater Noida, India*

Abstract: The epidemic growth of information has led to the big data era with vast volumes of diverse and complex data. This paper aims to provide a comprehensive overview of the transition from traditional data to big data, highlighting its transformative impact on various aspects of society, businesses, and scientific research. We begin by tracing the evolution of data, starting from structured data stored in traditional databases to the current era characterized by unstructured and semi-structured data from a wide range of sources. We delve into the technological advancements and challenges that have enabled the processing and analysis of big data, including distributed computing frameworks, scalable storage solutions, and advanced machine learning algorithms. Overall, this paper provides a comprehensive understanding of the transition from data to big data, elucidating the technological advancements, applications, and implications of large-scale data analytics. By examining the transformative power of big data, we hope to inspire further research and innovation in this rapidly evolving field, ultimately leading to a more data-driven and informed society.

Keywords: Big data, Structured data, Semi-structured data, Unstructured data.

INTRODUCTION

The digital revolution of the past few decades has brought about unprecedented growth in the amount and variety, leading to the emergence of the big data era. This transformation has had a profound impact on various aspects of society, businesses, and scientific research. The ability to collect, store, and analyze vast volumes of data has opened up new opportunities for understanding complex phenomena, making informed decisions, and driving innovation. The objective is to provide an overview of the evolution and impact of large-scale data analytics,

* **Corresponding author Manish Kumar Gupta:** Buddha Institute of Technology, Gorakhpur, India;
E-mail: manish.testing09@gmail.com

Vikash Yadav, Vimal Kumar, Sonam Gupta & Vandana Dixit Kaushik (Eds.)

from traditional data to the realm of big data. By examining the technological advancements, applications, and implications of big data analytics, we aim to shed light on its transformative power and inspire further research in this rapidly evolving field. To achieve this objective, we will explore the historical progression of data, from structured data stored in traditional databases to the diverse and unstructured data landscape of the big data era. We will discuss the challenges associated with collecting, storing, and processing big data and examine the technological solutions that have enabled its analysis at scale [1].

Moreover, we will delve into the applications of big data analytics in various domains, highlighting its impact on businesses and scientific research. In the business realm, organizations are leveraging big data to gain actionable insights into customer behavior, optimize operations, and drive innovation [2]. We will showcase real-world examples, such as personalized marketing, fraud detection, and supply chain optimization, to demonstrate the transformative potential of big data in decision-making processes. In scientific research, big data has revolutionized fields such as genomics, climate modeling, and particle physics. Researchers can now analyze massive datasets to uncover patterns, correlations, and anomalies that were previously unattainable due to limited data availability or computational constraints [3]. This has led to breakthroughs in understanding complex systems and has accelerated the pace of scientific discovery. However, along with the immense opportunities presented by big data, there are also challenges and concerns that need to be addressed. These include privacy and ethical considerations, data quality and veracity, and the need for robust security measures to protect sensitive information [4]. Understanding and addressing these challenges will be critical to harnessing the full potential of big data in a responsible and sustainable manner.

In summary, this paper aims to provide a comprehensive understanding of the transition from data to big data, elucidating the technological advancements, applications, and implications of large-scale data analytics. By examining the transformative power of big data, we hope to inspire further research and innovation in this rapidly evolving field, ultimately leading to a more data-driven and informed society.

EVOLUTION OF DATA

The evolution of data has witnessed a significant shift from structured data stored in traditional databases to the current era dominated by unstructured and semi-structured data from diverse sources. This transition has been driven by technological advancements and the exponential growth of digital information [5]. Structured data, characterized by well-defined schemas and organized in tables or relational databases, has long been the cornerstone of data storage and analysis. Traditional databases, such as those based on the relational model, provided a structured framework for capturing and managing data, ensuring consistency and integrity. The structured nature of the data facilitated efficient querying and analysis, making it suitable for well-defined applications and domains.

The shift towards unstructured and semi-structured data has been driven by various factors. The proliferation of social media platforms, online communication, and multimedia content has contributed to the exponential growth of unstructured data. Furthermore, the rise of IoT devices generating sensor data, machine logs, and telemetry data has further fueled the influx of semi-structured data. To effectively handle and derive value from this diverse and complex data landscape, new technologies and approaches have emerged. Distributed file systems, such as Apache Hadoop, have provided scalable storage and processing capabilities, enabling the storage and analysis of large volumes of unstructured and semi-structured data across clusters of commodity hardware [7]. The impact of this evolution in data has been profound. Organizations can now tap into vast amounts of unstructured and semi-structured data to gain deeper insights, make data-driven decisions, and unlock new business opportunities. Researchers can leverage diverse data sources to explore complex phenomena and drive scientific discovery. Table **1** shows the overview of the evolution of big data.

IMPACT OF BIG DATA ANALYTICS ACROSS DIFFERENT DOMAINS

The impact of big data analytics has been profound across various domains, revolutionizing decision-making processes, driving innovation, and enabling new discoveries [8-10]. This section explores some notable examples of the impact of big data analytics in different domains.

Finance

The finance industry has witnessed a significant impact from big data analytics. Financial institutions can leverage large-scale data analytics to detect fraudulent activities, assess risk, and make informed investment decisions. By analyzing diverse data sources, including transaction records, market data, social media sentiment, and news articles, organizations can identify patterns, anomalies, and market trends in real time, enabling proactive risk management and market insights [6]. Big data analytics has also enabled the development of algorithmic trading strategies and personalized financial services [11].

Table 1. Overview of the evolution of big data [5].

Era	Characteristics
Pre-Big Data	Structured data in traditional databases.
	Relational databases with predefined schemas.
	Limited data volume and variety.
Big Data (Current Era)	SQL-based querying and analysis.
	Unstructured and semi-structured data.
	Massive data volumes.
	Diverse data sources (social media, IoT, sensors, *etc.*)
	NoSQL databases for flexible storage and retrieval.
	Need for scalable and distributed computing.
Future Trends	Continued growth in data volume and variety.
	Advancements in data storage and processing technologies.
	Real-time and streaming data analytics.
	Integration of AI, machine learning, and big data.
	Enhanced data privacy and security measures.

Manufacturing and Supply Chain

Big data analytics has transformed manufacturing and supply chain operations by enabling predictive maintenance, optimizing production processes, and improving inventory management. By integrating data from sensors, production equipment, and supply chain systems, manufacturers can predict equipment failures, minimize downtime, and optimize maintenance schedules (Manyika *et al.*, 2011). Supply chain analytics leveraging big data provides real-time visibility into inventory levels, demand patterns, and logistics, facilitating more efficient inventory management and demand forecasting [12].

Transportation and Logistics

In the transportation and logistics sector, big data analytics has revolutionized route optimization, fleet management, and logistics planning. By analyzing vast amounts of real-time data, companies can optimize delivery routes, reduce fuel consumption, and enhance overall operational efficiency. Furthermore, big data analytics enables predictive maintenance of transportation assets, minimizing breakdowns and improving safety [13].

APPLICATIONS OF BIG DATA

We examine various applications, such as personalized marketing, fraud detection, and supply chain optimization, showcasing the immense potential of big data for enhancing decision-making processes. Big data analytics has transformed these domains by providing valuable insights and enabling more efficient and effective decision-making.

Personalized Marketing

Big data analytics has revolutionized marketing by enabling personalized and targeted campaigns. This allows for the delivery of highly personalized and relevant marketing messages, leading to increased customer engagement and conversion rates [14, 15]. The ability to leverage big data analytics in personalized marketing has been instrumental in driving customer-centric strategies and enhancing marketing ROI.

Fraud Detection

By analyzing vast amounts of transactional and behavioral data in real time, organizations can detect anomalies and patterns indicative of fraudulent activities [16]. Advanced machine learning algorithms, such as anomaly detection and predictive modeling, can identify suspicious activities and flag potential fraud cases [16]. The use of big data analytics in fraud detection has led to significant reductions in financial losses and improved security in various industries, including banking, insurance, and e-commerce.

Supply Chain Optimization

Big data analytics has transformed supply chain management by enabling real-time visibility, optimization, and predictive analytics. By integrating data from various sources, such as supplier information, transportation data, inventory levels, and demand patterns, organizations can optimize their supply chain operations [17]. Big data analytics allows for demand forecasting, inventory optimization, route optimization, and supplier risk management, leading to cost savings, improved customer satisfaction, and enhanced operational efficiency [18].

IMPLICATIONS OF BIG DATA FOR SCIENTIFIC RESEARCH

The implications of big data for scientific research are far-reaching, offering unprecedented opportunities for knowledge discovery, hypothesis generation, and advancements across various disciplines. Big data analytics enables scientists to leverage massive datasets, including genomics, climate data, social networks, and sensor data, to uncover patterns, identify correlations, and gain deeper insights [19]. This section explores the implications of big data for scientific research.

Accelerated Discovery

Big data analytics facilitates the analysis of large and complex datasets, enabling scientists to uncover hidden patterns and relationships that may have been difficult or impossible to detect using traditional research methods [20]. By leveraging advanced computational algorithms and machine learning techniques, researchers can extract valuable insights from vast amounts of data, leading to accelerated scientific discoveries. For example, in genomics research, the analysis of large-scale genetic datasets has enabled the identification of disease-related genes, personalized medicine approaches, and novel therapeutic targets [21].

Cross-Disciplinary Collaboration

Big data promotes collaboration among researchers from different disciplines. With the availability of diverse datasets, scientists can integrate information from multiple sources and domains, fostering interdisciplinary research and innovative approaches [22]. For instance, in climate science, the analysis of large-scale environmental data, coupled with socio-economic data, has led to a better understanding of climate change impacts and informed policy decisions (IPCC, 2014). The ability to integrate and analyze data from various fields paves the way for holistic approaches to complex research questions.

Reproducible and Transparent Research

Big data technologies facilitate reproducibility and transparency in scientific research. Researchers can share large datasets, computational models, and analysis workflows, allowing others to validate and reproduce research findings [21]. Open data initiatives and collaborative platforms enable the sharing and reuse of research outputs, enhancing scientific rigor and fostering a culture of transparency and accountability [26].

Data-Driven Hypothesis Generation

Big data analytics enables data-driven hypothesis generation by exploring large and diverse datasets for patterns and correlations [23]. Researchers can identify new research directions, formulate novel hypotheses, and generate testable predictions based on data-driven insights. This approach complements traditional hypothesis-driven research, providing a data-centric perspective that can uncover unexpected relationships and guide further investigation [24].

The implications of big data for scientific research are transformative, enabling scientists to tackle complex problems, generate new knowledge, and drive innovation. The ability to harness and analyze large-scale datasets has the potential to revolutionize research practices, enhance reproducibility, and foster collaboration across disciplines [25-27].

CHALLENGES AND CONCERNS

The utilization of big data in scientific research comes with various challenges and concerns that need to be addressed to ensure the reliability, privacy, and ethical use of data. This section discusses some of the key challenges and concerns associated with big data in scientific research.

Data Quality and Integration

Large datasets often contain noisy, incomplete, or inconsistent data, which can affect the accuracy and validity of research findings [28]. Integrating data from multiple sources also presents challenges, including data interoperability, standardization, and data cleaning. Researchers must employ rigorous data preprocessing and validation techniques to address these challenges and ensure the integrity of their analyses.

Data Privacy and Security

Big data in scientific research often includes sensitive and personally identifiable information, such as genomic data, health records, and social media data. Protecting the privacy and security of individuals' data is a critical concern [29]. Unauthorized access, data breaches, or inadequate anonymization techniques can lead to privacy violations and potential misuse of personal information. Researchers must comply with ethical and legal guidelines, implement strong data encryption and access controls, and employ privacy-preserving techniques to mitigate these risks.

Computational Infrastructure and Resource Requirements

The analysis of large-scale datasets requires significant computational power and infrastructure. Processing and storing massive volumes of data can strain existing computing resources, leading to scalability and performance issues [30]. Adequate resource allocation and management are essential to overcome these infrastructure challenges.

Ethical Considerations and Bias

Big data analytics can introduce ethical concerns and biases. The process of data collection, handling, and analysis may inadvertently perpetuate bias, discrimination, or unfairness if not carefully addressed. Biases may arise from biased sampling, algorithmic biases, or skewed representation of certain populations in the data. Researchers must be vigilant in addressing bias and ensuring fairness in their research design, algorithmic decision-making, and interpretation of results.

Data Sharing and Collaboration

While data sharing and collaboration are crucial for scientific progress, challenges arise regarding data ownership, intellectual property, and privacy regulations. Researchers may encounter barriers in accessing and sharing data due to legal restrictions, proprietary interests, or data protection regulations. Overcoming these challenges requires the development of data-sharing frameworks, standardized data-sharing protocols, and mechanisms for incentivizing data-sharing and collaboration.

Addressing these challenges and concerns requires a multidisciplinary approach involving researchers, policymakers, and technology experts. It necessitates the development of robust data governance frameworks, ethical guidelines, and technological solutions to ensure the responsible and ethical use of big data in scientific research.

CONCLUSION

In conclusion, the evolution of data from structured formats to the era of big data analytics has brought about significant advancements in decision-making processes and knowledge discovery. The impact of big data analytics spans across various domains, revolutionizing industries and enabling transformative outcomes. Examples include personalized marketing, fraud detection, supply chain optimization, improved patient outcomes in healthcare, proactive risk management in finance, predictive maintenance in manufacturing and supply chain, and efficient logistics planning in transportation. The immense potential of big data analytics for enhancing decision-making processes is evident, and as technology continues to advance and data continues to proliferate, the opportunities for innovation and insights are expected to grow even further.

REFERENCES

[1] T.H. Davenport, and D.J. Patil, "Data scientist: the sexiest job of the 21st century", *Harv. Bus. Rev.*, vol. 90, no. 10, pp. 70-76, 128, 2012.
[PMID: 23074866]

[2] T. Hey, S. Tansley, and K. Tolle, *The fourth paradigm: data-intensive scientific discovery.* Microsoft Research, 2009.

[3] D. Laney, "3D data management: Controlling data volume, velocity, and variety", *in Application Delivery Strategies,* vol. 5, no. 4, pp. 34-37, 2001.

[4] V. Mayer-Schönberger, and K. Cukier, *Big data: A revolution that will transform how we live, work, and think.* Houghton Mifflin Harcourt, 2013.

[5] V. Mayer-Schönberger, and K. Cukier, *Big data: A revolution that will transform how we live, work, and think.* Houghton Mifflin Harcourt, 2013.

[6] "Big Data: The Next Frontier for Innovation, Competition, and Productivity", *Capgemini Consulting,* 2012.

[7] H. Chen, R.H. Chiang, and V.C. Storey, "Business intelligence and analytics: From big data to big impact", *Manage. Inf. Syst. Q.,* vol. 36, no. 4, pp. 1165-1188, 2012.
[http://dx.doi.org/10.2307/41703503]

[8] H.M. Krumholz, "Big data and new knowledge in medicine: the thinking, training, and tools needed for a learning health system", *Health Aff. (Millwood),* vol. 33, no. 7, pp. 1163-1170, 2014.
[http://dx.doi.org/10.1377/hlthaff.2014.0053] [PMID: 25006142]

[9] Z. Li, L.T. Yang, J. Chen, J. Gao, and G. Min, "Internet of Things for Transport Logistics: State-o--the-Art and Prospects", *IEEE Trans. Industr. Inform.,* vol. 15, no. 1, pp. 40-49, 2019.

[10] J. Manyika, M. Chui, B. Brown, J. Bughin, R. Dobbs, C. Roxburgh, and A.H. Byers, *Big data: The next frontier for innovation, competition, and productivity.* McKinsey Global Institute, 2011.

[11] N. Shah, M.A. Hossain, and D. Kim, "Big data analytics in finance: A review and taxonomy of research", *Int. J. Inf. Manage.,* vol. 35, no. 4, pp. 401-414, 2015.

[12] C.S. Tang, J. Xie, and S.X. Zhou, "Big data and supply chain management research: A literature review and research agenda", *Int. J. Prod. Econ.,* vol. 208, pp. 298-313, 2019.

[13] S. Wang, J. Wan, D. Zhang, D. Li, and C. Zhang, "Towards smart factory for industry 4.0: a self-organized multi-agent system with big data based feedback and coordination", *Comput. Netw.,* vol. 101, pp. 158-168, 2016.
[http://dx.doi.org/10.1016/j.comnet.2015.12.017]

[14] B.K. Chae, Y.J. Lee, S. Han, and H. Park, "Personalized recommender system based on hybrid matrix factorization using big data analytics", *Sustainability,* vol. 10, no. 8, p. 2752, 2018.

[15] H. Chen, and K. Popovich, "Understanding customer relationship management (CRM) system adoption in small businesses", *J. Organ. End User Comput.,* vol. 30, no. 4, pp. 29-51, 2018. [JOEUC].

[16] A. Dal Pozzolo, O. Caelen, Y.A. Le Borgne, S. Waterschoot, and G. Bontempi, "Learned lessons in credit card fraud detection from a practitioner perspective", *Expert Syst. Appl.,* vol. 42, no. 10, pp. 5354-5368, 2015.

[17] W. Fan, and Y. Zhai, "Supply chain optimization in the big data era", *Ann. Oper. Res.,* vol. 270, no. 1-2, pp. 203-208, 2018.

[18] A. Gunasekaran, T. Papadopoulos, R. Dubey, S.F. Wamba, S.J. Childe, B. Hazen, and S. Akter, "Big data and predictive analytics for supply chain and organizational performance", *J. Bus. Res.,* vol. 70, pp. 308-317, 2017.
[http://dx.doi.org/10.1016/j.jbusres.2016.08.004]

[19] C. Phua, V. Lee, K. Smith, and R. Gayler, "A comprehensive survey of data mining-based fraud detection research", *Artif. Intell. Rev.,* vol. 33, no. 4, pp. 229-246, 2010.

[20] C.L. Borgman, J.C. Wallis, and N. Enyedy, "Little science confronts the data deluge: Habitat ecology, embedded sensor networks, and digital libraries", *Int. J. Digit. Curation,* vol. 7, no. 1, pp. 130-144, 2012.

[21] J.B. Buckheit, and D.L. Donoho, Wavelab and reproducible research*in Wavelets and Statistics*, 1995, pp. 55-81.
[http://dx.doi.org/10.1007/978-1-4612-2544-7_5]

[22] T. Hey, S. Tansley, and K. Tolle, *The fourth paradigm: Data-intensive scientific discovery.* Microsoft Research, 2009.

[23] Intergovernmental Panel on Climate Change (IPCC), *Climate change 2014: Impacts, adaptation, and vulnerability.* Cambridge University Press, 2014.

[24] D.B. Kell, and S.G. Oliver, "Here is the evidence, now what is the hypothesis? The complementary roles of inductive and hypothesis-driven science in the post-genomic era", *BioEssays,* vol. 26, no. 1, pp. 99-105, 2004.
[http://dx.doi.org/10.1002/bies.10385] [PMID: 14696046]

[25] Z.D. Stephens, S.Y. Lee, F. Faghri, R.H. Campbell, C. Zhai, M.J. Efron, R. Iyer, M.C. Schatz, S. Sinha, and G.E. Robinson, "Big data: Astronomical or genomical?", *PLoS Biol.,* vol. 13, no. 7, p. e1002195, 2015.
[http://dx.doi.org/10.1371/journal.pbio.1002195] [PMID: 26151137]

[26] V. Stodden, M. McNutt, D.H. Bailey, E. Deelman, Y. Gil, B. Hanson, M.A. Heroux, J.P.A. Ioannidis, and M. Taufer, "Enhancing reproducibility for computational methods", *Science,* vol. 354, no. 6317, pp. 1240-1241, 2016.
[http://dx.doi.org/10.1126/science.aah6168] [PMID: 27940837]

[27] K.A. Baker, A. Chiu, and S. Shoemaker, "Addressing computational challenges in big data analytics for neuroscience", *Curr. Opin. Neurobiol.,* vol. 52, pp. 24-30, 2018.

[28] P. Bryant, F. Coenen, and A. Patalano, "The challenge of big data in public health: An opportunity for visual analytics", *Health Inf. Sci. Syst.,* vol. 3, no. 1, p. 3, 2015.

[29] Y. Erlich, and A. Narayanan, "Routes for breaching and protecting genetic privacy", *Nat. Rev. Genet.,* vol. 15, no. 6, pp. 409-421, 2014.
[http://dx.doi.org/10.1038/nrg3723] [PMID: 24805122]

[30] M. K. Gupta, S. K. Pandey, and A. Gupta, "HADOOP- An open source framework for big data," in *Proc. Int. Conf. Innov. Eng. Manag. (ICIEM)*, 2022, pp. 1-5. [Online]. Available:
[http://dx.doi.org/10.1109/ICIEM54221.2022.9853179]

CHAPTER 10

Analysis Study on Blockchain Technology

Martand Ratnam[1], **Ayushi Prakash**[2,*] and **Sandhya Avasthi**[3]

[1] *AKTU, Lucknow, UP, India*

[2] *Ajay Kumar Garg Engineering College, Ghaziabad, India*

[3] *ABES Engineering College, Ghaziabad, India*

Abstract: Blockchain is a one-off innovation for the decentralized sharing of conditional information across a huge, distributed network, where non-believing individuals can cooperate with one another without a mediator in an undeniable way. A shared, unchangeable ledger called blockchain is used to record transactions, monitor assets, and establish trust. In this study, we examine the fundamentals of blockchain, including its uses, variations, and mode of operation. Behind this imaginative method, the security, protection issues, and agreement systems of this innovation are likewise significant and involve concern. In this chapter, we discuss the problems associated with blockchain technology, the pros and cons, and future aspects.

Keywords: Blockchain, Bitcoin, Consensus mechanism, Distributed, Security.

INTRODUCTION

Stakeholders in a wide range of sectors, including finance, medicine, utilities, property investment, and government, have recently become interested in blockchains. The centralized trusted party that underpins all conventional transactions creates several issues with efficiency, security, and transaction cost. The concept of blockchain technology is presented here to deal with these concerns and accomplish more secure, quicker, and clearer deals. We refer to the blockchain as enabling unreliable networks because transactions can occur even when parties do not trust one another. Transaction parties can reconcile more rapidly in the absence of a trustworthy mediator. Blockchain networks' heavy use of encryption, which grants all network interactions authority, is a significant aspect of these networks.

* **Corresponding author Ayushi Prakash:** Ajay Kumar Garg Engineering College, Ghaziabad, India; E-mail: prakashayushi@akgec.acin

Vikash Yadav, Vimal Kumar, Sonam Gupta & Vandana Dixit Kaushik (Eds.)

Satoshi Nakamoto introduced the blockchain technology [1]. Bitcoin is one application of the blockchain technology in the financial management industry. A distributed ledger system is all that the blockchain is. It conducts business dealings between individuals and organizations without the involvement of a third party.

Fig. (**1**) gives a graphical representation of the structure of blockchain technology. The components of blockchain innovation are:

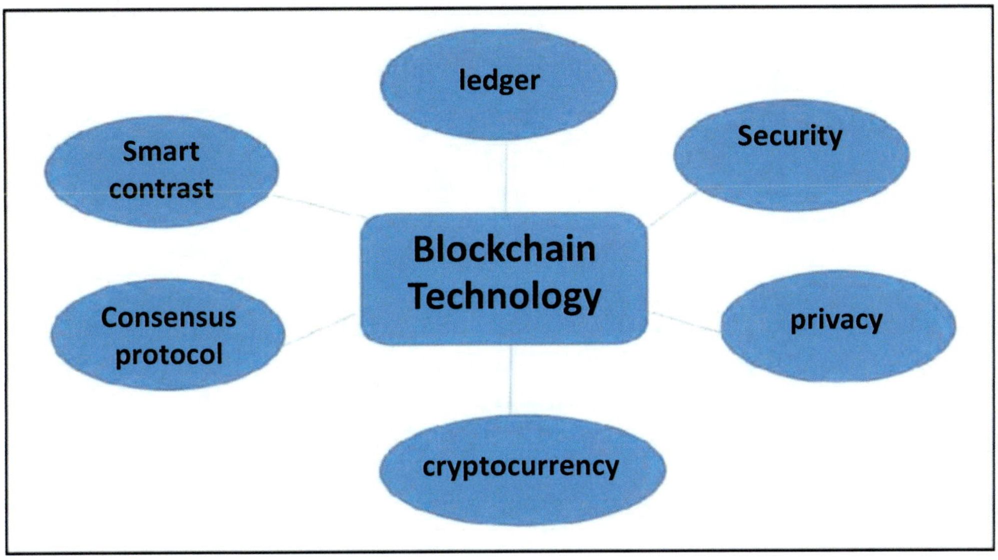

Fig. (1). Architecture of Blockchain Technology [1].

1. Ledger: Blockchain is a distributed ledger system that implies that everyone using the network has a copy of the same record. The blockchain lacks a centralized authority and a reliable third party.
2. Consensus Protocols: Exchange ought to be checked by all gatherings in an organization. Making a block and adding to its ledger is likewise a decentralized interaction. It is only a mining interaction. Every hub in the organization ought to settle on the exchanges recorded on the recently mined block.
3. Security: Blockchain makes use of public key cryptography and digital signatures to confirm the authenticity of network transactions.
4. It is created as a digital asset that functions as a medium of exchange for delivering safe transactions using encryption.
5. Privacy: The blockchain allows for the storage of any kind of data. If sensitive data, such as health information or citizen service, is being processed, the privacy regulations are relevant.

6. Smart contract: These agreements are actions having the capacity for self-execution and self-enforcement. These contracts rely on data from outside sources; thus, in order to prevent data tampering, cryptographic evidence should be given.

This is how the chapter is organized. Section II provides the definition of a blockchain; Section III discusses the technologies of a blockchain network and the types of blockchain; Section IV discusses the security concern of blockchain, followed by Section V, which discusses the privacy associated with blockchain and the applications of blockchain; the next section talks about the pros and cons, and the last section deals with the conclusion and future work that can be done.

LITERATURE REVIEW

According to Satoshi Nakamoto, bitcoin is a chain of computerized marks. The use of signatures can confirm the ownership chain. The Byzantine understanding and idea of the record in a conveyed setting were the creator's vital areas of interest [2]. Blockchain is a novel technology that is employed in applications like human enhancement, smart contracts, and artificial intelligence, among others, as the author [3] described in his work. An author [4] outlined Bitcoin's attributes as well as associated ideas like technical analysis of distributed currencies and proof of work. The author [5] developed an elliptic curve cryptographic paradigm for Bitcoin trading. A decentralized smart contract system's transactional privacy was investigated by the author [6] in this article.

BLOCKCHAIN TECHNOLOGIES

A block is a unit of the blockchain that contains all the transactions and, once they are complete, adds them to a permanent database. Transparent information sharing within a firm network is made feasible by a sophisticated database mechanism known as blockchain technology. In a blockchain database, information is kept in blocks that are connected to one another in a chain. The data is constant chronologically because it is impossible to break or alter the chain without the consent of the entire network. As a result, an unchangeable record for monitoring orders, payments, accounts, and other transactions may be made using blockchain technology. Blocks in blockchain are associated with a steady progression like a connected rundown. Each block comprises the hash of the past block, as displayed in Fig. (**2**) [7].

A network of nodes constructed like a peer-to-peer network makes up a blockchain. Users can communicate with one another on the blockchain by using public and private keys. They address the private key on the network with the public key and use it to sign their own transactions. In the network, it offers authentication, non-repudiation, and integrity. Before sending further, each node in the blockchain verifies that the incoming transaction is legitimate. Transactions that are not legitimate are declined [3]. There should be a set of rules for every database transaction in any blockchain network. Each blockchain client has these rules pre-programmed, which are used to determine if an incoming transaction is legitimate or not [8, 9].

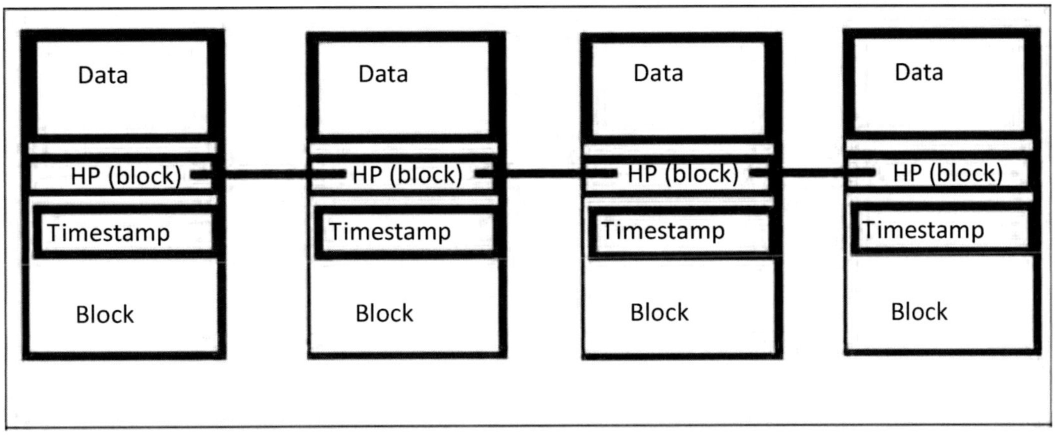

Fig. (2). Linked List of Blocks Connected by Hash Pointers: Blockchain [7].

Types of Blockchain

There are three different categories of blockchains.

1) Public Blockchain

In a public blockchain, everybody may contribute, and there are no trusted connections between the nodes. The transactions that are recorded in the public blockchain are irreversible. This blockchain uses the consensus algorithms Pos, Pow, and DPoS [10].

2) Private Blockchain

In a private blockchain, only the blockchain's owner has the power to change the data, while the other nodes only have restricted access. The private blockchain employs the PBFT consensus method.

3) Permission Blockchain

In a permission blockchain, based on a set of guidelines, each participant chooses his own consensus node. This one is appropriate for the semi-closed network created by several businesses.

Blockchain-related Technologies

One of the advancements used in blockchain innovation is public key cryptography, which is used for the encryption and decryption of sensitive data as well as message authenticity.

Encryption and Decryption

Asymmetric encryption uses sets of public and private keys. Data is encrypted using the public key and decrypted using the private key.

Digital signatures

Furthermore, PKC can be utilized for validation. The source's confidential key might be utilized to make the advanced mark, which the beneficiary can then approve utilizing the shipper's public key.

Hash function: It is just a numerical capability, known as a hash, that switches information of any inconsistent size completely to a specific set length. Hash functions are one-way operations that never return the original data; they are also deterministic operations since the same data always yields the same hash result.

Homomorphic Encryption

Homomorphic encryption is a cryptographic technique that allows operations on encrypted data to be performed. The encrypted result can then be decrypted to obtain the operation result, allowing sensitive data computations to be performed without disclosing it.

As a result of recent advancements and increased demand for data protection, homomorphic encryption is expected to become more relevant and used in a variety of industries.

SECURITY CONCERNS WITH BLOCKCHAIN SYSTEMS

The three security concepts of availability, confidentiality, and integrity are the major focus of blockchain technology. In essence, blockchain is a distributed system that depends on agreement among all nodes *via* a sequence of transactions to ensure availability and maintain data integrity. With the help of the appropriate cryptographic keys, transaction confidentiality can be preserved. Blockchain systems should primarily consider the following areas of security.

- Network level security.
- Associated surround system security.

- Transaction-level security.
- Smart contract security
- Ledger level security

Only authorized members are permitted to use the blockchain. Legitimate members start exchanges in the organization, and the members' transaction must be signed.

Network-level Security

From a network perspective, safe communication is required between components of different nodes. It needs to be safeguarded against a variety of network-wide internal and external attack vectors. The ledger needs to be able to survive denial-of-service assaults.

Transaction-level Security

PKI ideas must be used to encrypt transactions to prevent data breaches with unauthorized parties. Identification and protection of the permission that generates transactions are necessary so that only transactions using a certain name, such as "X", may be carried out. The blockchain's multi-signature capability is accessible for sensitive transactions, and the transaction information cannot be changed or altered.

Associated Surround System Security

Only authorized users should be able to access shadow databases and other pertinent surrounding system components. Authentication and authorization techniques are established to do this. It also entails document sharing to guard against malware, worms, and viruses.

Smart Contract Security

Legal agreements are governed by smart contracts, digital contracts, self-executing contracts, and blockchain contracts that may be pre-programmed to self-enforce. Contracts entered into the blockchain must abide by the fundamental guidelines established by the network. These contracts can call for data from an outside source, and data might be altered. To prevent this, a cryptographic proof that is obtained from a reliable source and is not altered must be added, as given in Fig. (**3**).

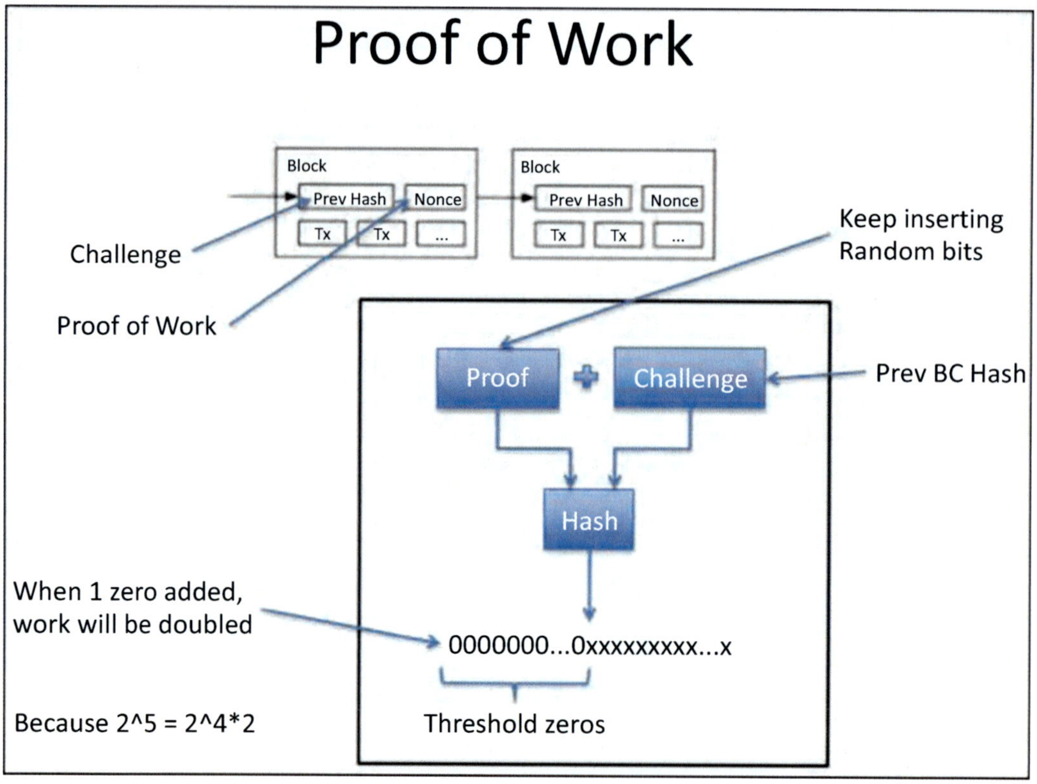

Fig. (3). Proof of work: Blockchain.

PRIVACY CONCERNS WITH BLOCKCHAIN TECHNOLOGY

The cryptocurrency Bitcoin is a prominent blockchain. It has a permission-less blockchain ledger, so everyone can view and verify every transaction. This appears to violate each user's right to privacy. In blockchain systems, the two categories that offer privacy mechanisms are transactional privacy and unlinkability.

Transactional Privacy

The only people who should have access to the transaction information are the parties to the transaction, regulators, and auditors. Participating nodes have a method for verifying transactions while taking the availability of funds into account, even when the transaction is completely encrypted.

Unlinkability

Unknowable entities have no access to the specifics of interactions between parties. In order to obtain information on the parties engaged in the transactions, it would be feasible to mine data from a number of transactions. It aims to prevent these inferences from being drawn.

CONSENSUS MECHANISMS IN BLOCKCHAIN

A consensus technique is used to keep decentralized networks secure. Every blockchain needs current records in order to function effectively. The blockchain can only be updated when all nodes agree on its current state. Errors are prevented, and malicious actors cannot affect the network by fabricating fake nodes, as in the case of double-spending and Sybil attacks.

To maintain the security of decentralized networks, a consensus mechanism is used, which is shown in Fig. (**4**). It can be modified only when all nodes are in agreement with the blockchain's present state.

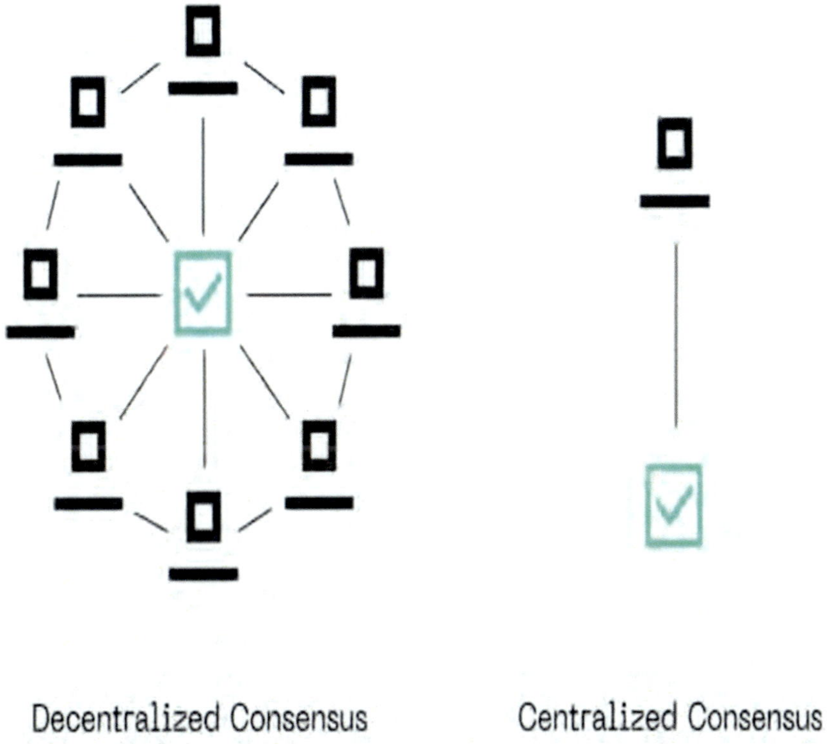

Fig. (4). Decentralized Consensus Mechanism.

Proof of Work (Pow)

A node known as a miner in this approach verifies new network transactions (blocks). The hashing algorithm is used by miners to combine the random number and the data in the block.

As seen below, if the calculated hash value falls within the permitted range, the miner who has generated it will receive reward points, and all other miners will cease operations on that block.

Proof of Stake (Pos)

Their percentage of coins in the network is the basis of this algorithm. If a node has more coins, it will have the opportunity to validate the block.

Delegated Proof of Stake (Dpos)

It is a Proof of Stake variant that focuses on reputation and the voting process. In the event the standing is higher and any remaining hubs vote in favor of this hub, a hub in the organization is picked as a designated hub. A user's vote will have greater weight when electing the delegate if they possess more coins.

Proof of Importance (Poi)

Each node in the network is given a significant score by this algorithm. The number of tokens owned, network activity, reputation, and the number of transactions performed to and from the specific account are among the variables that affect the significance score.

Proof of Activity (Poa)

Proof of Work and Proof of Stake algorithms have been merged in the PoA technique. Proof of work is used for initial mining, while Proof of stake is used for new blocks.

Proof of Elapsed Time (PoET)

The consensus technique employs a mechanism for choosing leaders at random. Any active node may be chosen as the leader, who then completes the block. With this approach, the system makes sure that the leader is selected freely, and each node will confirm this.

Practical Byzantine Fault Tolerance (PBFT)

The PBFT algorithm has addressed the Byzantine Generals' problem. It operates according to the replicated state machine theory. The replicas will cast ballots to change the state. Additionally, it offers improvements like message encryption and signing between clients and replicas, which automatically reduces the volume and quantity of messages sent and received. To tolerate "f" failed nodes, it requires "3f+1" replicas.

Stellar Consensus

Quorums and quorum slices are the foundation of this method. A certain number of nodes, known as a quorum, are required for agreement. Quorum slices are a subset of a quorum. A node may be present on more than one quorum slice. Each node chooses a subset of nodes in its slice for open participation, forming quorum slices. The system can reach a consensus at all levels by intersecting the quorums.

Ripple Consensus

A Unique Node List (UNL) is assigned to each node in this system. It is made up of other Ripple nodes in which the node has faith. Each node gathers transactions, which are then saved in a candidate set of data. When the competitor set gets over 80% of the UNL hubs' votes, it is viewed as a real block and is added to the chain.

BLOCKCHAIN USE

Decentralized Exchanges

Between the buyer and the selling, a broker is typically necessary. There is no third party when using blockchain technology. In a decentralized exchange, users establish their own digital assets, which are subsequently swapped when an agreement is reached.

Distributed Cloud Storage

Today, there are centralized cloud storage options, but you just need to rely on one storage provider. It will be decentralized thanks to blockchain technology.

Digital Identity

The following accompanying fields can utilize blockchain innovation for character applications: international IDs, e-residency, birth testaments, marriage declarations, and online record login.

Communication throughout the Supply Chain and Proof of Provenance

A business can proactively offer partners carefully long-lasting, undeniable records that mirror the item's condition at every valuation.

Smart Contracts

Blockchain-entered digital contracts are smart and legally binding since they are self-executing and automated.

Digital Voting

A voter may confirm their vote was successful and properly communicated to the rest of the globe with the use of blockchain.

PROS OF BLOCKCHAIN

i. Higher accuracy due to the lack of human verification: Blockchain allows for the recording of transactions, which eliminates human error and protects against data manipulation. Data is verified every time it is transferred from one blockchain node to another. Your records will be guaranteed to be accurate, and this method will also provide a very traceable audit trail.
ii. Saving money by not requiring third-party verification: Blockchain allows for significant reductions in transaction fees by removing the need for third-party middlemen when exchanging assets.
iii. Tampering is more challenging as a result of decentralization.
iv. Transactions are speedy, safe, and efficient.
v. Transparent technology: Due to the distributed nature of blockchain, each network participant shares the same data rather than having multiple copies of the same documents. Because the data is spread across a vast network of unrelated computers and systems, anyone can view, verify, and audit the data and transactions on the blockchain's ledger.
vi. Blockchain technology is intended to make it easier to identify and resolve problems. It also creates an audit trail that is permanent.

CONS OF BLOCKCHAIN

i. Bitcoin mining is expensive technologically: A Bitcoin transaction's average cost includes the cost of electricity. As a result, the inability to resolve energy issues may obviate the need for storage. Each Bitcoin network client now stores the entire transaction history, which can be up to 100GB in size. The size of the web grows faster as more transactions are processed.
ii. There are few transactions per second.
iii. Prior use in nefarious activities, such as on the dark web.

iv. Regulation varies by jurisdiction and is subject to change.
v. Storage space limitations.
vi. Many cryptocurrencies that run on decentralized blockchains are extremely volatile. Bitcoin prices, for example, frequently fluctuate by 20% or more in a single day.

CONCLUSION AND FUTURE SCOPE

Working blockchains enable trustworthy, verifiable peer-to-peer interactions as well as robust, distributed networks of peers. As businesses prepare to use blockchain technologies, government officials should create consistent regulations for this technology. Blockchain's main technology is its consensus procedure. Future scopes are the following:

i. Application in Digital Advertising: Blockchain technology is here to stay, even though it is still in its infancy, and all advertising firms are interested in learning how blockchain technology can help them improve their company's performance.
ii. Despite being a public ledger, all information on the blockchain is independently verified and protected with cutting-edge cryptography. This makes it less likely that the data or information will be compromised or altered without authorization.
iii. The blockchain will do away with the need for an intermediary. In conclusion, blockchain technology may have an impact on a wide range of processes and techniques. It eliminates the need for a trustworthy third party in business dealings.
iv. Blockchain technology has the power to completely transform research, consulting, analysis, and forecasting. Global dispersed prediction markets are developed through online platforms.
v. Internet of Things (IoT): With blockchain technology, several devices can use it as a public ledger, eliminating the need for a centralized website to manage device communication. The devices may communicate with one another in order to maintain energy efficiency, update software, and handle errors.
vi. Managing world trade: Customs agents can easily track down prohibited products such as counterfeit food items, counterfeit medications, counterfeit apparel, and counterfeit vehicle parts, electronics, and other pirate agents that attempt to sell inferior goods inside any country without breaching local laws by utilizing blockchain technology.
vii. Blockchain technology is poised to transform the travel Industry.
viii. Banking and Insurance Implementation.
ix. Managing the Supply Chain.
x. Cloud Storage Consolidation.

REFERENCES

[1] S. Nakamoto, "Bitcoin: A Peer-to-Peer Electronic Cash System," Available: https://bitcoin.org/bitcoin.pdf

[2] A. Gervais, G.O. Karame, V. Capkun, and S. Capkun, "Is bitcoin adecentralized currency?", *IEEE Secur. Priv.,* vol. 12, no. 3, pp. 54-60, 2014. [http://dx.doi.org/10.1109/MSP.2014.49]

[3] F. Tschorsch and B. Scheuermann, "Bitcoin and Beyond: A Technical Survey on Decentralized Digital Currencies," *IEEE Communications Surveys & Tutorials*, vol. 18, no. 3, pp. 2084–2123, 2016. Available: plore.ieee.org/document/7423672

[4] H. Wang, D. He, and Y. Ji, "Designated-Verifier Proof of Assets for Bitcoin Exchange Using Elliptic Curve Cryptography," *IEEE Transactions on Information Forensics and Security*, vol. 12, no. 8, pp. 1774–1785, Aug. 2017.

[5] A. Kosba, A. Miller, E. Shi, Z. Wen, and C. Papamanthou, "Hawk: The blockchain model of cryptography and privacy-preserving smart contracts", *2016 IEEE Symposium on Security and Privacy,* 2016, pp. 839-858. [http://dx.doi.org/10.1109/SP.2016.55]

[6] M. Swan, "Blockchain thinking: The brain as a DAC (decentralized autonomous organization", *Texas Bitcoin Conference,* 2015, pp. 27-29.

[7] Institute for Development and Research in Banking Technology, "Applications of Blockchain Technology to Banking and Financial Sector in India," Jan. 2017. [Online]. Available: https://www.idrbt.ac.in/wp-content/uploads/2022/07/BCT.pdf

[8] "Blockchain in Banking", In: *A Measured Approach.* Cognizant Reports, 2016.

[9] K. Christidis and M. Devetsikiotis, "Blockchains and Smart Contracts for the Internet of Things," *IEEE Access*, vol. 4, pp. 2292–2303, 2016. [Online]. Available: ieeexplore.ieee.org/iel7/6287639/6514899/07467408.pdf

[10] G. Greenspan, G. Greenspan, "Blockchains and Smart Contracts for the Internet of Things," 2015. [Online]. Available: http://www.multichain.com/blog/2015/11/avoiding

CHAPTER 11

A Study on Remote Sensing Image Segmentation and Classification

Vikash Kumar Mishra[1,*], **Abdul Aleem**[1], **Vimal Kumar**[1] and **Bosco Paul Alapatt**[2]

[1] *Galgotias University, Uttar pradesh, India*

[2] *Christ (Deemed to be University), Delhi NCR Campus, Ghaziabad, India*

Abstract: The image is a composition of many pixels. These pixels include two pieces of information: coordinate or position and intensity value. The image includes several objects; extracting the crucial objects from the image is critical. Based on the similarity of patterns, classes, groups, and segments of contained objects in the image can be created. Assigning the labels to the pixels is necessary to make the image more informative for analyzing features and decision-making. This study addresses segmentation techniques and classifying images pertaining to remote sensing images. Thereafter, Land Use Land Cover (LULC) mapping is discussed, which classifies the remote sensing images.

Keywords: Classification, Image segmentation, Remote sensing.

INTRODUCTION

The information contained in satellite photographs is sufficient to describe the geographical regions. Both quantitative and qualitative information is provided through remote sensing and satellite photographs, which minimizes the need for human effort in field surveys. The technique of classifying similar pixels into informative groups is known as image classification. The process of classifying satellite photos can also be thought of as information extraction. The ability to extract and decipher useful data from huge satellite photos requires effective and efficient processes and is the high need of the hour.

Segmentation further divides an image into its individual regions or objects [1, 2], depending on the problem being solved or how long it takes to isolate the object of interest. Image segmentation subdivides an image into well-distinguishable regions such that any newly formed region contains pixels with similar attributes.

* **Corresponding author Vikash Kumar Mishra:** Galgotias University, Uttar pradesh, India; E-mail: dr.vikash@gmail.com

Vikash Yadav, Vimal Kumar, Sonam Gupta & Vandana Dixit Kaushik (Eds.)

Fig. (**1**) constitutes three different objects with a uniform background. So, image segmentation is the process that will segment the image into four different regions, A, B, C, and D, based on either homogeneity of pixels or abrupt/ sharp local changes on boundaries of objects A, B, and C.

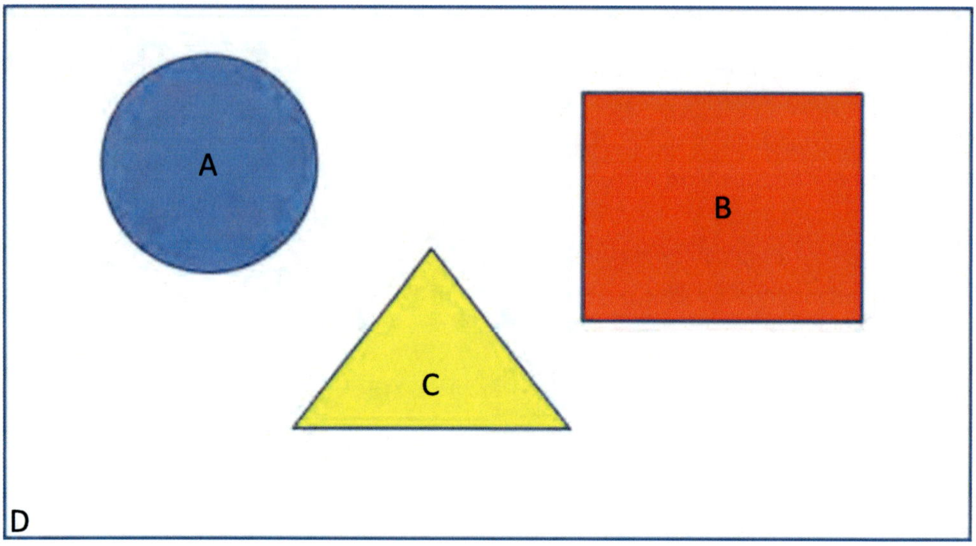

Fig. (1). Image with four different regions.

There are several applications of image segmentation, which are listed below:

a. Vehicle motion analysis [3] (object tracking).
b. Biometric/Thumb, signature [4, 5].
c. Arial image/ satellite image classification [6 .
d. Finding tumors, veins, *etc*., in medical images [7].
e. Finding people in surveillance images summarizing video, *etc* [8].

Segmentation Fundamentals

Let R be the entire image. Through the image segmentation, R is partitioned into n sub-regions, as R_1, R_2, R_3, R_4......... R_n [3], such that:

- R_1 U R_2 U R_3 U. . . . . R_n = R.
- R_is can be combined to generate R for i=1,2,3.... N, *i.e*., the set of R_is is connected.
- $R_i \cap R_j = \Phi \; \forall \; j \neq i$
- $Q(R_i)$=True [similarity of pixels in a particular region].
- Q(RiURj)=FALSE [dissimilarity of pixels in two different regions].

There are two segmentation approaches based on either of two basic properties of intensity value [4]:

- Discontinuity-based segmentation.
- Similarity-based segmentation.

DISCONTINUITY-BASED SEGMENTATION

This method detects sharp local changes in intensity. Predefined similarity criteria are partitioning an image into regions. Isolated points, lines, and edges are the three image features to find sharp changes. Derivatives, either of first-order and/or second-order, are utilized to find an image's difference or abrupt changes.

First Order Derivatives (FOD)

The FOD at point x of a one-dimensional function g(x) is produced by extending a function g(x+Δx) into a Taylor series about x while taking into account Δx=1 and keeping only the linear term as follows:

$$\frac{\partial y}{\partial x} = g'(x) = g(x+1) - g(x)$$

In an area of continuous intensity, FOD must be zero. However, it must be non-zero at the beginning of an intensity step or ramp and at certain locations along it.

Second Order Derivative (SOD)

SOD is obtained as follows:

$$\frac{\partial^2 g(x)}{\partial x^2} = \frac{\partial g'(x)}{\partial x^2} = g'(x+1) - g'(x)$$
$$= g(x+2) - g(x+1) - g(x+1) + g(x)$$
$$= g(x+2) - 2g(x+1) + g(x)$$

Our interest is in the second derivative about point x; hence, the expansion is around (x+1), *i.e.*,

$$= g(x+1) - 2g(x) + g(x-1)$$

- FOD usually produces a thicker edge corresponding to the image.
- SOD responds more strongly to little features like solitary points, thin lines, and

noise.

- At the ramp, SOD results in a double-edge response.
- A transition into an edge might either be from light to dark or vice versa, depending on the sign of SOD.
- Using a spatial filter is the preferred method for calculating the first and second derivatives at each pixel position in a picture.
- A 3*3 mask filter is employed to obtain the mask's response at the region's center, as shown in Fig. (**2**).

1	1	1
1	-8	1
1	1	1

Fig. (2). 3*3 mask filter.

$$R = w_1 z_1 + w_2 z_2 \text{..........} \text{..........} \ldots + w_9 z_9$$

Detection of Isolated Points

One pixel of a line can be seen as an isolated point. The Laplacian's second derivative serves as the foundation for point detection, as follows:

$$\nabla^2 f(x,y) = \frac{\partial^2 f(x,y)}{\partial x^2} + \frac{\partial^2 f(x,y)}{\partial y^2}$$

$$\frac{\partial^2 f(x,y)}{\partial x^2} = f(x+1,y) - f(x-1,y) - 2f(x,y)$$

$$\frac{\partial^2 f(x,y)}{\partial y^2} = f(x,y+1) - f(x,y-1) - 2f(x,y)$$

$$\nabla^2 f(x,y) = f(x+1,y) + f(x,y+1) - f(x,y-1) - f(x-1,y) - 4f(x,y)$$

If the absolute value of the mask's reaction at a given point exceeds a certain threshold, the position (x, y) on which the mask is centered is said to have identified a point. Fig. (**3**) depicts the mask used for point detection. The resulting image labels such points with 1 in this case. A binary image is created by labeling all others with 0. Fig. (**4**) depicts a point detection example.

$$g(x,y) = \begin{cases} 1 & \text{if } R(x,y) \geq T \\ 0 & \text{otherwise} \end{cases}$$

g(x, y)=output image, R=response of mask at centre point of region.

T= Non-negative threshold.

w_1	w_2	w_3
w_4	w_5	w_6
w_7	w_8	w_9

Fig. (3). Mask used for point detection.

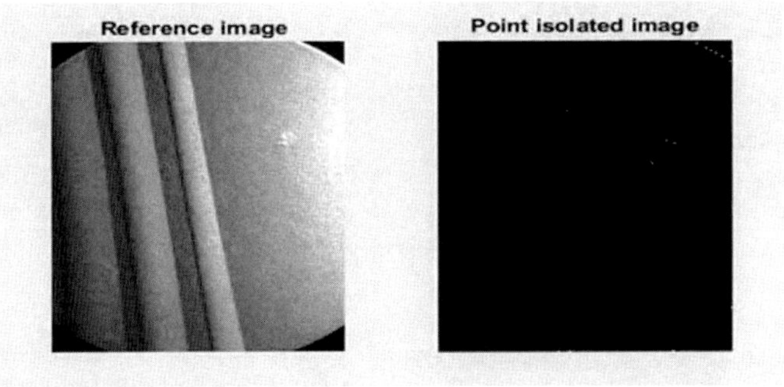

Fig. (4). Demonstration of point detection.

Line Detection

A line can be thought of as an edge segment where the background intensity is significantly higher or significantly lower than the intensity of the line pixel on either side of the line. If the mask is moved around an image, lines oriented horizontally and vertically at +45 and -45 will respond more strongly [3, 4]. Fig. (**5**) shows the mask used for differently oriented line detection, and Fig. (**6**) shows horizontal, vertical, and diagonal line segmentation.

−1	−1	−1	2	−1	−1	−1	2	−1	−1	−1	2
2	2	2	−1	2	−1	−1	2	−1	−1	2	−1
−1	−1	−1	−1	−1	2	−1	2	−1	2	−1	−1
Horizontal			+45°			Vertical			-45°		

Fig. (5). Mask used for differently oriented line detection.

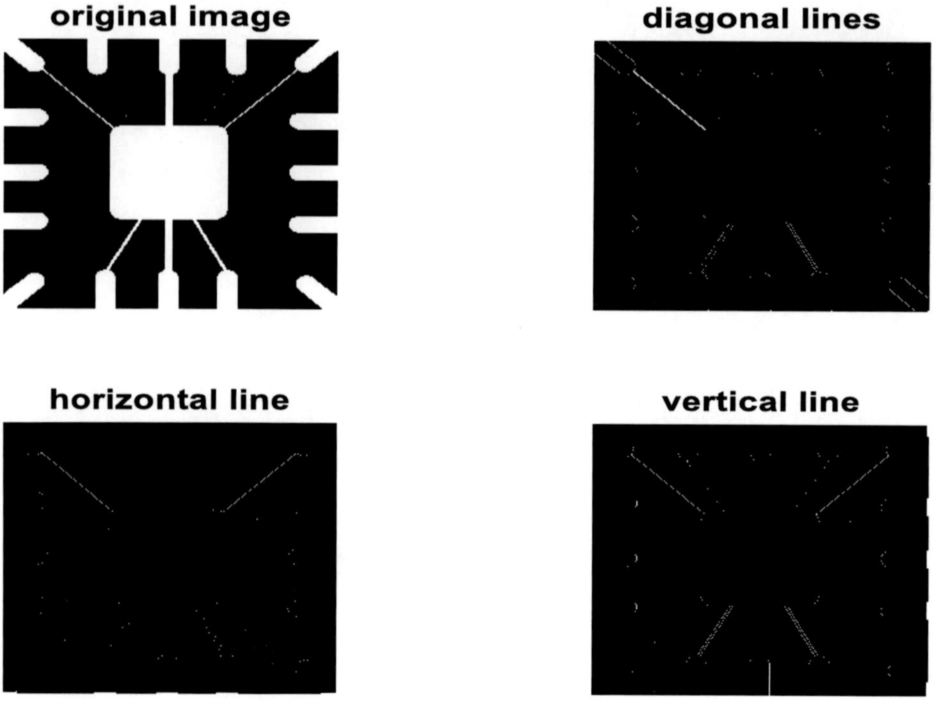

Fig. (6). Horizontal, vertical, and diagonal line segmentation.

Edge Detection

Edge is a boundary between two regions having distinct intensity or grey levels. We can use either the first or second derivative for edge detection, as shown in Fig. (7). The first derivative is preferred because [3]:

z_1	z_2	z_3
z_4	z_5	z_6
z_7	z_8	z_9

−1	0
0	1

0	−1
1	0

Roberts

−1	−1	−1
0	0	0
1	1	1

−1	0	1
−1	0	1
−1	0	1

Prewitt

−1	−2	−1
0	0	0
1	2	1

−1	0	1
−2	0	2
−1	0	1

Sobel

Fig. (7). Mask used for edge detection.

i. Second derivative is very sensitive to noise.
ii. It creates double edges.

Edge strength at location (x, y) of an image f can be found by gradient. Fig. (**8**) shows the result of different edge operators on the original image. The gradient is defined as a vector:

$$\nabla f = \begin{bmatrix} Gx \\ Gy \end{bmatrix} = \begin{bmatrix} \frac{\partial f}{\partial x} \\ \frac{\partial f}{\partial y} \end{bmatrix}$$

$$mag(\nabla f) = \sqrt{Gx^2 + Gy^2}$$

The direction of the gradient is given by:

$$\alpha(x, y) = \tan^{-1}(\frac{Gx}{Gy})$$

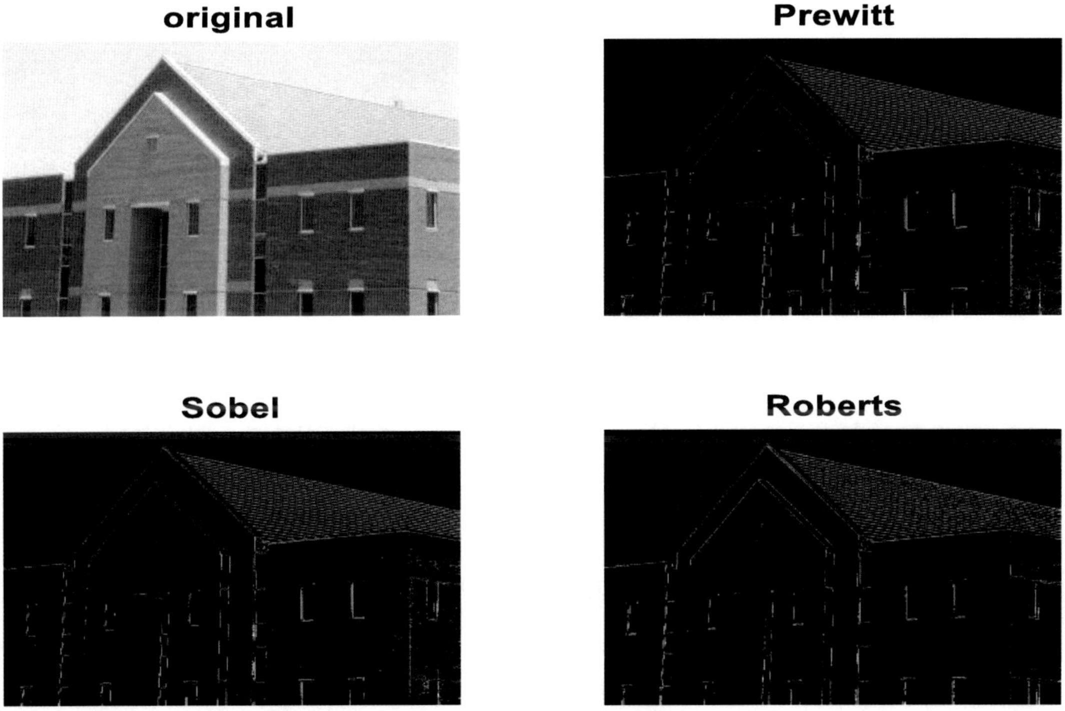

Fig. (8). The result of different edge operators on the original image.

Edge Linking

When applying the first or second-order derivatives, the unconnected edge points are obtained. It must link these edge points to get meaningful edges [9]. Two approaches for edge linking are:

Local Processing

We take an image that is already edge operated to give all edge points; we use some similarity measures to say whether two points are similar or not [10]. Two similarity measures are preferred:

1. Gradient (strength of edge point).
2. Direction.

If (x', y') ϵ Neighborhood (x, y), then we can find (x', y') and (x, y), which are similar if the following holds:

$$\nabla f(x,y) - \nabla f(x',y') \leq T$$

$$\alpha(x,y) - \alpha(x',y') \leq A$$

Global Processing

Global Processing of edge linking is also known as the Hough transform. It is the mapping of the spatial domain to the parameter domain [10, 11]. Hough transform is used in the following conditions:

i. Non-uniform illumination.
ii. Noise.
iii. If (x', y') is not a part of the defined neighborhood.

A line in the spatial domain is transformed to a point in the parameter domain, as shown in Fig. (**9**).

A point in the spatial domain is transformed into a line in the parameter domain, as shown in Fig. (**10**).

Two points joining a line are shown in Fig. (**11**):

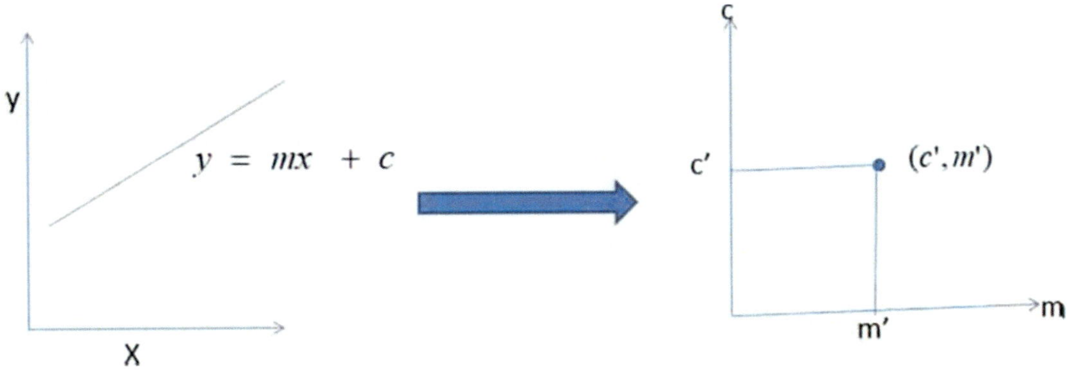

Fig. (9). Transformation of a line from the spatial domain to a point in the parameter domain.

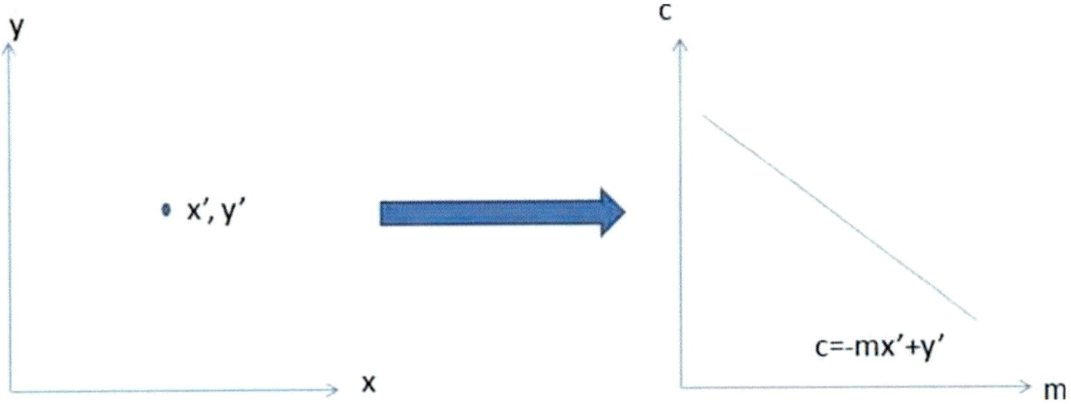

Fig. (10). Point to line transformation.

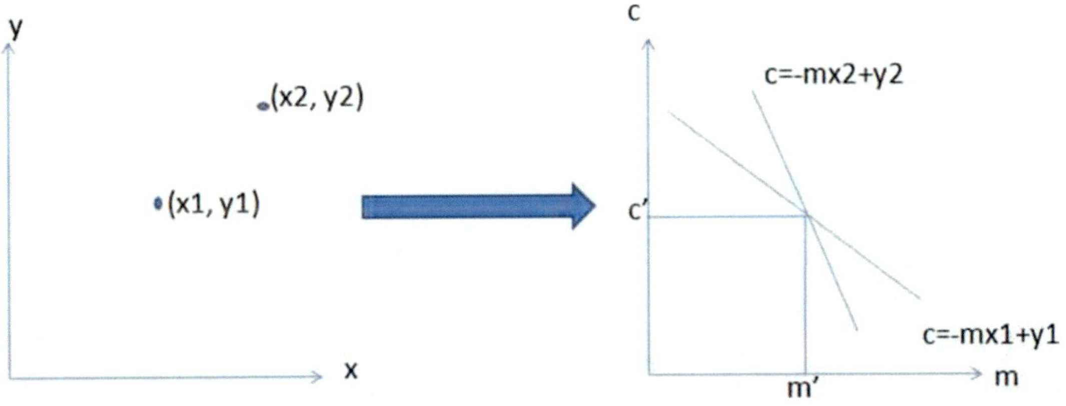

Fig. (11). Collinear point mapped to parameter space.

(c', m') defines the slope of the line passing through (x1, y1) and (x2, y2). If n points are mapped to the parameter domain on a line, they will represent n line with an intersecting point, giving the slope and intercept of the line passing through all n points.

These values of (c', m') are continuous, but the dealing is with discrete digital images in the reference. So, we need to compute values for (c', m') in the discrete domain instead of the continuous domain; to obtain this, accumulator sets are used, as shown in Fig. (**12**).

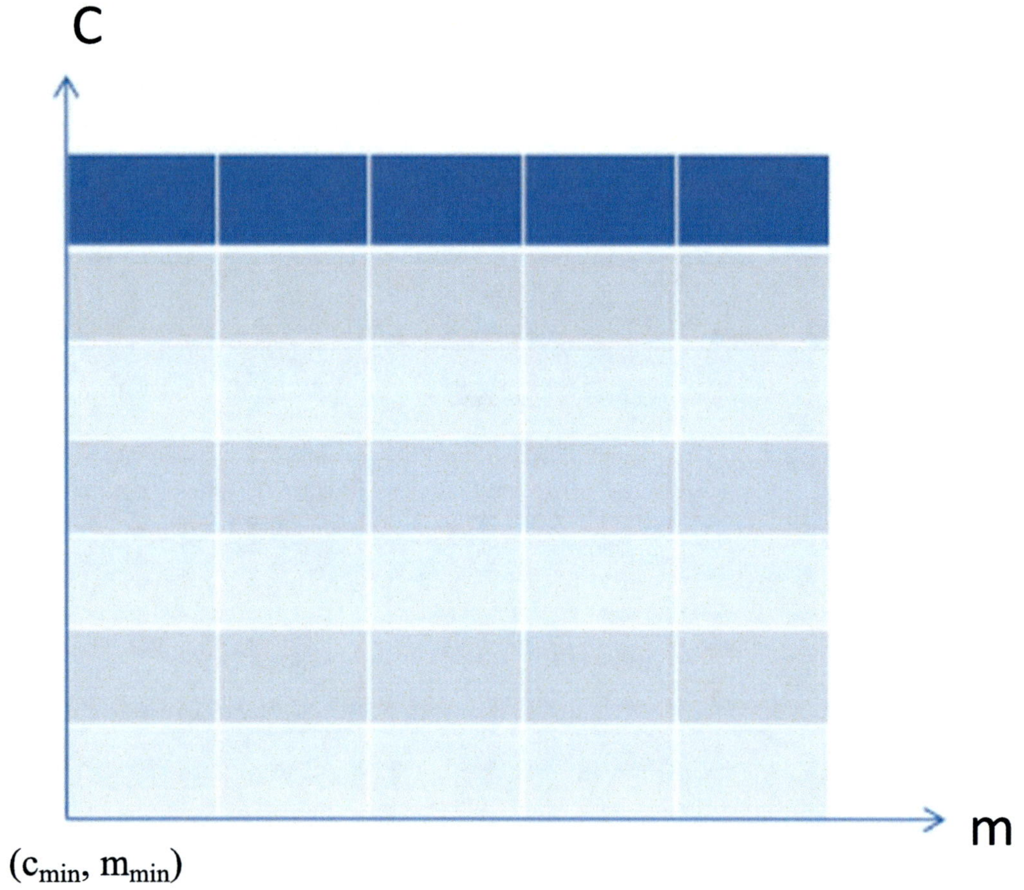

Fig. (12). Accumulator Set.

- The accumulator set is represented by A(i, j).
- Cell location (i, j) corresponds to the parameter value (m_i,c_i).
- We initialize the accumulator set with Zero A(i, j)←0.
- A point (x_k,y_k) in the spatial domain is mapped as a line in the parameter domain as:

$$c=-mx_k+y_k$$

- For all values of m, (m_{min}, m_{max}) compute the corresponding value of c:

  m_p■c_q

- And every accumulator set will be increased:

  A[p, q]→a[p, q]→1
- At the end of this A[p, q]→Q
- Q is the number of points lying on $y=m_i x+c_j$

If we talk about the range of (m_{min}, m_{max}) and (c_{min}, c_{max}), if (m_{min}, m_{max}) = (0, ∞) then (c_{min}, c_{max}) will also be (0, ∞) or for both (-∞ to $_+$∞). So, it is infeasible to compute such values. Instead of mapping the c-m plane, we will prefer to transform the x-y plane to α ρ –plane, as shown in Fig. (**13**).

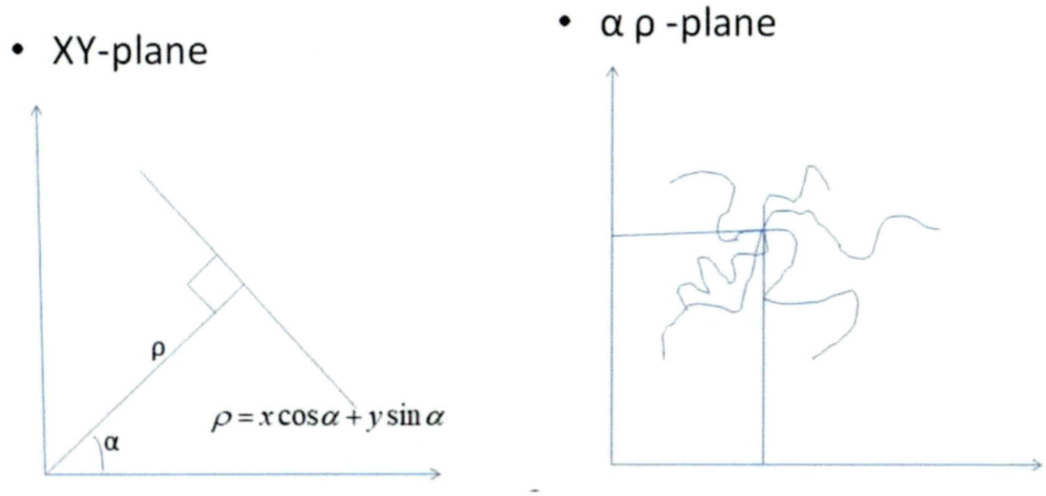

Fig. (13). Collinear points in the xy-plane mapped as a set of sinusoidal curves in the α ρ –plane intersecting at a point (α', ρ').

SIMILARITY-BASED SEGMENTATION

An image is partitioned into similar regions under predefined criteria. Similarity-based segmentation approaches [11] are as follows:

- Thresholding:
  a. Local.
  b. Global T.
  c. Dynamic/Adaptive.

- Region growth.

• Region merging and splitting.

Thresholding

Thresholding can be thought of as an operation involving comparisons to a function T of the following form:

T=T[(x, y), f(x, y), p(x, y)]

p(x, y) denotes some local property of this point.

• T = T[f(x, y)]→ Global.
• T = T[f(x, y), p(x, y)]→ Local.
• T = T[(x, y), f(x, y), p(x, y)]→Adaptive/Dynamic.

An Image f(x, y) comprises dark objects on a light background. In such a way that object and background pixels have grey levels grouped into two dominant modes. One obvious way to extract the objects from the background is to select a threshold 'T' that separates these modes [3, 4 - 7].

$$g(x,y) = \begin{cases} 1 & \text{if } f(x,y) \geq T \\ 0 & \text{otherwise} \end{cases}$$

Local Thresholding

Global Thresholding [11, 12] is the term used when T is consistent throughout the entire image. Thresholding is referred to as variable, local, or regional when the value of T varies across an image, as shown in Fig. (**14**). The following histogram can be used to segment the two different sorts of dark objects on a light background as follows:

$$g(x,y) = \begin{cases} a & f(x,y) > T2 \\ b & T1 < f(x,y) \leq T2 \\ c & f(x,y) \leq T1 \end{cases}$$

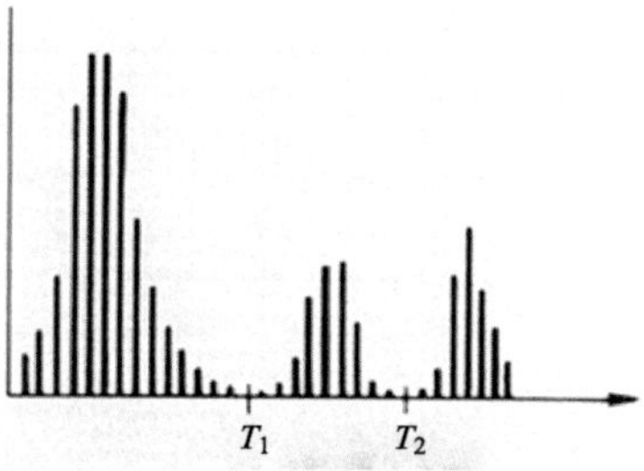

Fig. (14). Histogram of an image representing two dark objects on a light background.

Global Thresholding

The fundamental global threshold(T), shown in Fig. (**15**), is determined as follows:

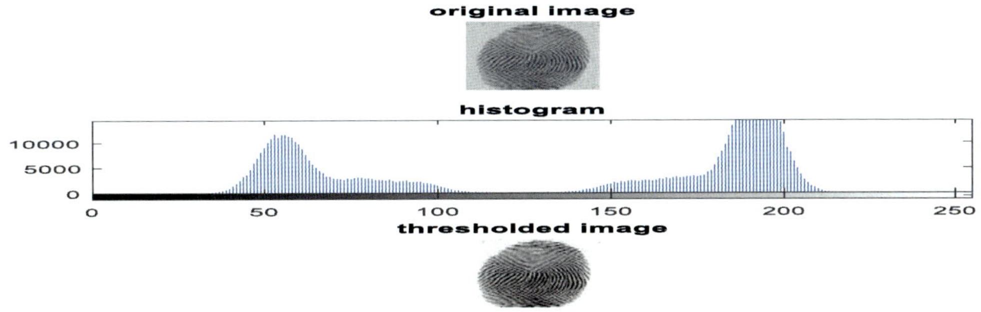

Fig. (15). Implementation of Global Thresholding.

1. Decide on a preliminary estimate for T (usually, the median image grey level).
2. Use T to divide the image into two sets of pixels: G1 for pixels with grey levels greater than T and G2 for pixels with grey levels lower than T.
3. Determine the average grey levels of pixels in G1 and G2 to get 1 and 2, respectively.
4. Determine a fresh threshold value:

$$T = \frac{\mu_1 + \mu_2}{2}$$

- Continue to follow steps 2 through 4 until the difference in T between iterations is smaller than a specified limit T.

Adaptive Thresholding

Images with uneven illumination make it difficult to segment using a histogram. This approach divides the original image into sub-images and uses the thresholding process for each sub-image [13].

Region Growing

Starting with a few pixels (seeds) that represent various image regions and expanding them until they encompass the entire image is a straightforward method of segmenting images. We require a rule outlining a growth mechanism for regions as well as a rule that checks the homogeneity of the regions at the conclusion of each growth phase [14]. Fig. (**16**) shows region growth using seed pixels and 3*3 neighborhoods.

Fig. (16). Region growth using seed pixel and 3*3 neighborhoods.

- The growth mechanism: We look for unlabeled pixels in the area's 8-neighborhood for each pixel at each stage k and for each region Ri(k), i = 1,..., N.
- Before assigning a pixel (x) to a region *i.e.* Ri(k), we check the following region homogeneity condition:

P(Ri(k) U {x}) = TRUE

If the above condition is satisfied, then it is valid; otherwise, it is invalid.

Region Splitting and Merging

It is based on the divide and conquer approach [15]. The following steps are used to segment an image:

STEP-I DIVIDE

1. Equally divide the input image into 4 sub-images;
2. Compute the characteristics of each sub-image, *e.g.*, intensity, color, texture, *etc.*;
3. Repeatedly divide sub-images into sub-sub-images if their characteristics are significantly different;

STEP-II MERGE (CONQUER)

1. Repeatedly merge adjacent sub-images if their characteristics are similar enough.

STEP-I DIVIDE

1. Divide the input image into 4 equal subimages
2. Determine the attributes of each subimage, such as its intensity, color, texture, *etc.*;
3. If two sub-images' traits are noticeably different, repeatedly split them into sub-sub-images;

STEP-II CONQUER (MERGE)

If two neighboring sub-images have enough similarities, repeatedly merge them.

REMOTE SENSING

The science and art of remote sensing involves interpreting data collected by a device without physical contact to learn more about a subject [16]. In remote sensing, the eyes act as sensors to detect the electromagnetic energy emitted by text and collect the resulting data, which is then processed by the mind to create the words. The various energy sources are detected using a variety of sensors. These sensors are used to gather information about things, processes, and phenomena that are remotely gathered and then evaluated to learn more.

Meteorology, climatology, oceanography, coastal studies, water resources, geology, archeology, and land use land cover (LULC) mapping are some of the applications of remote sensing.

The best electromagnetic energy source is the sun. When different earth surface features—such as vegetation, water, sand, buildings, *etc.*—reflect and emit electromagnetic energy, airborne or space-borne electromagnetic sensors collect data in pictorial or digital form. These data are then analyzed to provide details about the various earth sources that are the subject of the investigation. Two fundamental steps were involved in electromagnetic remote sensing of the Earth's surface [16, 17]:

Data Acquisition

The following components are needed to acquire data remotely: Energy sources, energy transmission through the atmosphere, energy interaction with the features of the earth's surface, and energy sources. Retransmission of energy through the atmosphere, airborne/space-borne sensor, and production of sensor data in the form of visual or digital information [16, 17] are shown in Fig. (**17**).

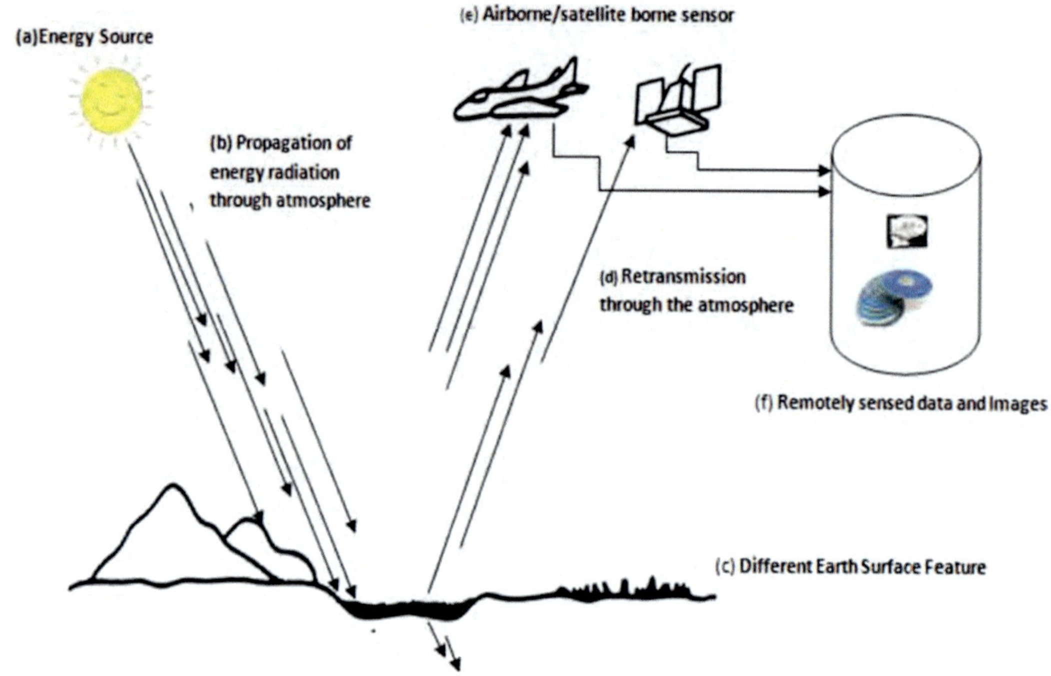

Fig. (17). The Remote Sensing Process.

Analysis of Acquired Data

The following steps are necessary for the analysis of acquired sensor data:

i. Various viewing and interpretation tools are used to review the data and extract information.
ii. Information is compiled in maps, tables, computer files, *etc*.
iii. Users are given information which they use in their decision-making process [16, 17].

Remote Sensing and Image Segmentation

Remote sensing data can be grouped or classified into different classes of regions using either discontinuity-based or similarity-based image segmentation. There are other methods than image segmentation to find the different regions of a remotely sensed image to give meaningful information for decision-making; such methods are known as classification methods. These classification methods are categorized into three categories [16]:

1. Supervised Methods.
2. Unsupervised Methods.
3. Hybrid Methods.

IMAGE CLASSIFICATION

Picture elements (Pixels) construct an image. Image classification is the process of collecting the pixels based on their spectral response. Image classification automates feature extraction and identification in an image and replaces the visual interpretation of image data with quantitative techniques. Satellite images have digital numbers (DNs) that are converted into categorical ranges. Satellite images are made up of a number of electromagnetic spectrum bands; these bands make up an image that only consists of spectral information. The process of categorizing image pixels into Land Use Land Cover (LULC) information or specific class information is called classification of an image [15]. Pixels can be classified into categorical categories according to their surface area, such as water, urban, forest, *etc*.

There are two stages involved in the process of image classification:

Stage I: Classification: In the context of land surface remote sensing, these categories or classes would be vegetation, water, sand, buildings, and other land cover types, depending on the geographic area and interest of the research.

Stage II: Labeling: Assign a label to the pixel based on spectral properties.

Land Cover Classification Steps

The following steps are used for the categorical interpretation of the data:

1. Determine the requirement of a classified image and also check how it will be used?
2. Determine how necessary it is to have a classified image.
3. Define the geographical area for the study.
4. Either select or develop a method to classify.
5. Select the imageries.
6. Preprocess the images for classification.
7. Collect additional data if required.
8. Implement the classification method and classify.

Classification Criteria

There are certain criteria fixed for the classification system to accurately and efficiently classify an image into the appropriate classes:

1. The minimum level of classification accuracy should be more than 85 percent.
2. The categorical accuracy for the different categories should be approximately equal.
3. The classification system can be extended to an extensive area as well.
4. The classification system shall be suitable for temporal data.
5. The small subclasses can be scaled up on larger areas if required.
6. The integration of subclasses into a larger class is also possible.
7. Time series or temporal analysis may also be possible.

Land use and Land Cover Classification System for use with Remote Sensor Data by the United States Geological Survey [18]

Level-I	Level-II
Urban or Built-up Land	Residential, Commercial and Services, Industrial, Urban or Built-up Land, Industrial and Commercial Complexes, Mixed Urban or Built-up Land, Other Transportation, Communications, and Utilities.
Wetland	Non-forested Wetland, Forested Wetland.
Barren Land	Strip Mines, Quarries and Gravel Pits, Beaches, Sandy Areas other than Beaches, Bare Exposed Rock, Dry Salt Flats, Transitional Areas, Mixed Barren Land.
Rangeland	Shrub and Brush Rangeland, Herbaceous Rangeland, Mixed Rangeland.
Forest Land	Evergreen Forest Land, Deciduous Forest Land, Mixed Forest Land.
Water	Streams and Canals, Bays and Estuaries, Reservoirs, Lakes.
Agricultural Land	Cropland and Pasture, other Agricultural Land, Confined Feeding Operations, Orchards, Groves, Vineyards, Nurseries, and Ornamental Horticultural Areas.
Perennial Snow or Ice	Glaciers, Perennial Snowfields.
Tundra	Wet Tundra, Herbaceous Tundra, Bare Ground Tundra, Shrub and Brush Tundra, Mixed Tundra.

Classification Methods.

Two approaches are generally used:

1. Supervised classification.

2. Unsupervised classification.

Supervised Classification

It is implemented in three steps as discussed below:

Training

Based on known data, also called "training data" or "sample data", another "numeric interpreter key" is calculated. Each numerically interpreted key describes a reflectance property of any terrestrial feature [1].

Classification

Each pixel from the unknown dataset is then categorically compared against the numerically interpreted key and classified in a similar class [1, 2].

Testing

Samples are taken from the classified image and compared to the pixel values of the original image to verify what number of pixels are classified correctly and what number of pixels are misclassified. The accuracy matrix is formed based on these figures. This accuracy matrix is used to determine the accuracy of the supervised classification method (in %), as shown in Fig. (**18**).

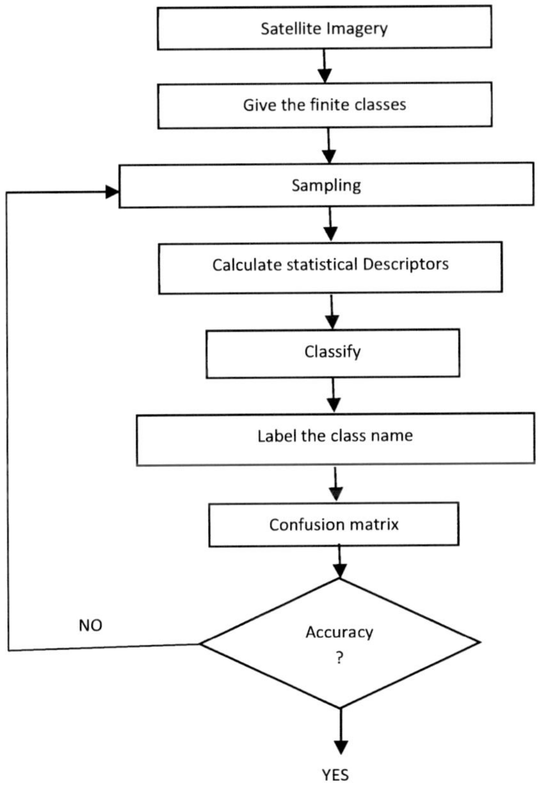

Fig. (18). Supervised Classification Scheme.

METHODS TO IMPLEMENT SUPERVISED CLASSIFICATION

The following are the different supervised methods that are utilized for the classification of satellite imageries into land use functional classes:

Minimum distance to mean classifier

The average or mean spectral value in each band for each class is calculated. The spectral value of the pixel is compared to the average of each category and assigned to the nearest class [19, 20].

Algorithm

1. Refer to the remotely captured imagery.
2. Identify and then define classes.
3. Select sample data for each defined class.
4. From the sample data, calculate the average for each defined class.
5. Take an unclassified pixel, find its distance from the average values, and classify it into a class with minimum distance from the average.
6. Iterate step 5 until all data is classified.
7. Give names to each class.

Parallelepiped Classification

This kind of classification scheme only requires a range of the spectral values in each class, and based on range, *i.e.* [minimum spectral value, maximum spectral value for a class], a particular pixel is classified into a class if its spectral value belongs to the range of that class [21, 22].

Algorithm

1. Refer to the remote sensing image.
2. Identify and then define the possible number of classes.
3. Select the training dataset for each class.
4. Based on the training dataset, find a range for each class, *i.e.*, [minimum spectral value, maximum spectral value].
5. Classify a pixel into a class if its spectral value falls within the range of that class.
6. Iterate step 5 until all data is classified.
7. Assign a label to each class.

Unsupervised Classification

This is a computer-automated methodology [23]. Two steps are used to implement this way of classification, viz., classification and testing, as shown in Fig. (**19**).

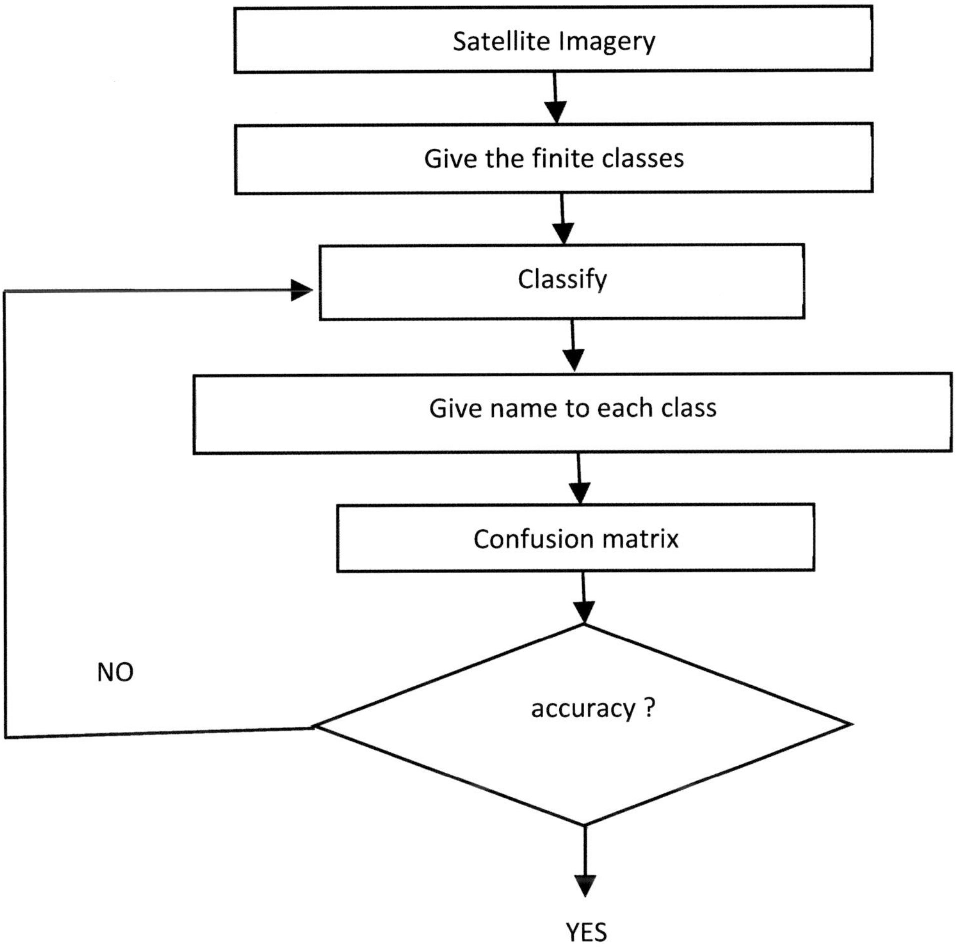

Fig. (19). Unsupervised Classification Scheme.

METHODS TO IMPLEMENT UNSUPERVISED CLASSIFICATION

The following are the different unsupervised methods that can be used for the classification of remote sensing images into land use functional classes:

K-MEANS

The classification steps for the K-means algorithm are written as follows [24, 25]:

ALGORITHM

1. Define the number of classes, say K, to classify the remotely sensed data into k number of classes.
2. From the data set, choose k random values as mean values.
3. Now, classify the remotely sensed data into K classes based on a randomly chosen mean based on the minimum distance to the mean.
4. Now calculate K number of means for newly classified K classes.
5. Reclassify the original remotely sensed dataset into K-classes based on the average calculated in step 4.
6. Iterate steps 4 and 5 to classify the original data set until the same means are not repeated.
7. Assign labels to classes.

CONCLUSION

Satellite images are rich enough to provide both qualitative and quantitative information and reduce human effort in field surveys. If we have an aerial or satellite image and we want to find vehicles on the road, instead of analyzing the entire image, we can focus only on the road and then on vehicles driving on the road. To do this, the image must be segmented or classified into different classes, constituents, or parts. Whether image segmentation or classification, both approaches aim to divide the image into meaningful areas, which can be further processed or analyzed for certain decision-making.

REFERENCES

[1] T. Lillesand, R. W. Kiefer, and J. Chipman, *Remote Sensing and Image Interpretation.* 7th ed. Hoboken, NJ: John Wiley & Sons, 2014.

[2] P.M. Mather, and M. Koch, *Computer processing of remotely-sensed images: an introduction.* John Wiley & Sons, 2011.
[http://dx.doi.org/10.1002/9780470666517]

[3] R. C. Gonzalez, R. E. Woods, and S. L. Eddins, *Digital Image Processing Using MATLAB.* 2nd ed. New Delhi, India: McGraw Hill Education, 2020.

[4] R. C. Gonzalez and R. E. Woods, *Digital Image Processing*, 3rd ed. New Delhi, India: McGraw Hill Education, 2018.

[5] A.D. Sappa, and B.X. Vintimilla, Edge point linking by means of global and local schemes.*Signal Processing for Image Enhancement and Multimedia Processing.* Springer US: Boston, MA, 2008, pp. 115-125.
[http://dx.doi.org/10.1007/978-0-387-72500-0_11]

[6] A.F. Brustolin, A. F. Brustolin, "Edge Detection Based on Global and Local Parameters of the Image," IEEE Access, vol. 5, pp. 17667–17678, 2017. [Online]. Available: https://ieeexplore.ieee.org/

document/7946452

[7] M. Weingart and O. Vascan, "Image Segmentation Processing – Some Techniques and Experimental Results," in Proc. IEEE Int. Conf. on Automation, Quality and Testing, Robotics (AQTR), Cluj-Napoca, Romania, May 2018, pp. 1–6. [Online]. Available: https://ieeexplore.ieee.org.

[8] Saini Rashmi, and Maitreyee Dutta And Robin Kumar, R. Saini, M. Dutta, and R. Kumar, "A Comparative Study of Several Image Segmentation Techniques," *J. Inf. Oper. Manage.*, vol. 3, no. 1, pp. 25–30, 2012.

[9] P. Roy, S. Dutta, N. Dey, G. Dey, S. Chakraborty, and R. Ray, "Adaptive thresholding: A comparative study", *2014 International conference on control, Instrumentation, communication and Computational Technologies (ICCICCT),* IEEE., pp. 1182-1186, 2014. [http://dx.doi.org/10.1109/ICCICCT.2014.6993140]

[10] A. Deshpande, P. Dahikar, and P. Agrawal, "An experiment with statistical region merging and seeded region growing image segmentation techniques", *International Conference on Recent Trends in Image Processing and Pattern Recognition,* pp. 493-506, 2018. Singapore.

[11] T. Zhang, G. Lin, W. Liu, J. Cai, and A. Kot, "Splitting *vs.* merging. Mining object regions with discrepancy and intersection loss for weakly supervised semantic segmentation. In Computer Vision–ECCV 2020: 16th European Conference, Glasgow, UK, August 23–28, 2020", *Proceedings,* vol. 16, no. Part XXII, pp. 663-679, 2020. [Springer International Publishing.].

[12] X. Cao, C. Wu, J. Lan, P. Yan, and X. Li, "Vehicle detection and motion analysis in low-altitude airborne video under urban environment", *IEEE Trans. Circ. Syst. Video Tech.,* vol. 21, no. 10, pp. 1522-1533, 2011. [http://dx.doi.org/10.1109/TCSVT.2011.2162274]

[13] N. Damodaram, and D.V.S. Reddy, N. Damodaram and D. V. S. Reddy, "Multi-Modal Biometric System Using Iris, Face and Fingerprint Images for High-Security Application," *in Proc. IEEE Int. Conf. on Computational Intelligence and Computing Research (ICCIC)*, Tamil Nadu, India, Dec. 2019, pp. 1–6. [Online]. Available: https://ieeexplore.ieee.org.

[14] R. Rangarajan, R. Rangarajan, "Attendance System in Third-Level Irish Institutions and Colleges Using Face Recognition Approach," *in Proc. IEEE Int. Conf. on Advanced Computing and Communication Systems (ICACCS)*, Coimbatore, India, Mar. 2023, pp. 1–5. [Online]. Available: https://ieeexplore.ieee.org.

[15] D. Lu, and Q. Weng, "A survey of image classification methods and techniques for improving classification performance", *Int. J. Remote Sens.,* vol. 28, no. 5, pp. 823-870, 2007. [http://dx.doi.org/10.1080/01431160600746456]

[16] A. Sundin, "Radiological and nuclear medicine imaging of gastroenteropancreatic neuroendocrine tumours", *Best Pract. Res. Clin. Gastroenterol.,* vol. 26, no. 6, pp. 803-818, 2012. [http://dx.doi.org/10.1016/j.bpg.2012.12.004] [PMID: 23582920]

[17] M.T. Maybury, *Multimedia Information Extraction: Advances in Video, Audio, and Imagery Analysis for Search, Data Mining, Surveillance and Authoring.* John Wiley & Sons, 2012. [http://dx.doi.org/10.1002/9781118219546]

[18] J.R. Anderson, *A land use and land cover classification system for use with remote sensor data,* vol. 964, US Government Printing Office, 1976. [http://dx.doi.org/10.3133/pp964]

[19] M. Congedo, P.L.C. Rodrigues, and C. Jutten, "The Riemannian minimum distance to means field classifier", *In BCI 2019-8th International Brain-Computer Interface Conference,* 2019.

[20] S. Bag, and G. Sanyal, "An efficient face recognition approach using PCA and minimum distance classifier", *2011 International Conference on Image Information Processing IEEE,* pp. 1-6, 2011. [http://dx.doi.org/10.1109/ICIIP.2011.6108906]

[21] F.G. Elfarra, M.A. Calin, and S.V. Parasca, "Computer-aided detection of bone metastasis in bone

scintigraphy images using parallelepiped classification method", *Ann. Nucl. Med.,* vol. 33, no. 11, pp. 866-874, 2019.
[http://dx.doi.org/10.1007/s12149-019-01399-w] [PMID: 31493203]

[22] P. Sathya, and V.B. Deepa, "Analysis of supervised image classification method for satellite images", *International Journal of Computer Science Research,* vol. 5, no. 2, pp. 16-19, 2017. [IJCSR].

[23] A. Olaode, G. Naghdy, and C. Todd, "Unsupervised classification of images: a review", *International Journal of Image Processing,* vol. 8, no. 5, pp. 325-342, 2014.

[24] G. Hamerly, and C. Elkan, G. Hamerly and C. Elkan, "Learning the k in k-means," *in Advances in Neural Information Processing Systems 16 (NeurIPS)*, S. Thrun, L. K. Saul, and B. Schölkopf, Eds. Cambridge, MA: MIT Press, 2004, pp. 281–288.

[25] M. Ahmed, R. Seraj, and S.M.S. Islam, "The k-means algorithm: A comprehensive survey and performance evaluation", *Electronics (Basel),* vol. 9, no. 8, p. 1295, 2020.
[http://dx.doi.org/10.3390/electronics9081295]

[26] M.E. Hoque, K. Kipli, T.M.A. Zulcaffle, D.A.A. Mat, A. Joseph, N. Zamhari, R. Sapawi, and M.Y. Arafat, "August. Segmentation of retinal microvasculature based on iterative self-organizing data analysis technique (ISODATA)", *In 2019 International UNIMAS STEM 12th Engineering Conference (EnCon) IEEE,* pp. 59-64, 2019.

[27] M. Vimal, S. Sandfeld, and A. Prakash, "Grain segmentation in atomistic simulations using orientation-based iterative self-organizing data analysis", *Materialia (Oxf.),* vol. 21, p. 101314, 2022.
[http://dx.doi.org/10.1016/j.mtla.2022.101314]

CHAPTER 12

Depression Detection on Social Media Using the CNN-LSTM Model

Lakshay Singh Mahur[1,*]

[1] *Raj Kumar Goel Institute of Technology, Ghaziabad, India*

Abstract: Depression is a disease that destroys the whole life of a person. Through this, that person creates their own zone so that she/he is alone and cannot talk to anyone. Some of the most common types of depression are major bipolar disorder, persistent depressive disorder, depression, and seasonal depressive disorder. Two types of depression that are mainly detected in women are perinatal depression and PMDD or premenstrual dysphoric disorder. Depression makes people lose their identity. When dealing with audio signals, CNN-LSTM models can be used to recognize emotions in speech. CNNs process audio spectrograms to capture acoustic features, and LSTMs capture the dynamics of speech over time, achieving better emotion classification. For tasks like recognizing hand gestures or sign language, CNN-LSTM models can effectively capture both the static hand positions (using CNNs) and the dynamic gestures over time (using LSTMs), leading to improved accuracy. In this paper, we can merge two algorithms to improve the accuracy. Firstly, we can find the individual accuracy of 6 algorithms and compare them with each other, then we can use the proposed model. When combining CNN and LSTM networks, there are two primary methods: Using the CNN output as the input to the LSTM. In this approach, the output of the CNN is passed as input to the LSTM. By doing so, the LSTM can learn and extract features from the input data that have been learned by CNN. Alternatively, the output of the LSTM can be used as the input to the CNN.

Keywords: CNN, LSTM, PMDD.

INTRODUCTION

Depression is a mental disease that is characterized by an enduring feeling of melancholy and a loss of curiosity in things and pastimes that you formerly loved. It can also impair cognitive abilities, including recall, dining, and resting. A mood illness, often known as mood disease, is a mental health problem that predominantly affects your feelings. It can generate long-lasting melancholy, elation, and/or fury. Treatment for emotional disorders is generally a mix of both

* **Corresponding author Lakshay Singh Mahur:** Raj Kumar Goel Institute of Technology, Ghaziabad, India; E-mail: lakshay2110007m@akgec.ac.in

Vikash Yadav, Vimal Kumar, Sonam Gupta & Vandana Dixit Kaushik (Eds.)

medication and psychotherapy/or talk therapy. Depression is not only difficult to deal with; it is also linked to the heart. "Depressive" illness or degeneration signs in adolescents can occur for a variety of reasons. If you notice mood or cognitive alterations that last more than a few weeks, it is a good idea to discuss this with your doctor or contact a psychologist. Dr. Nancy Donovan, a psychology professor at the Medical School of Harvard, suggested consulting a psychologist to help sort out possible causes. The most prevalent forms of mental illnesses are severe depression, chronic SAD, bipolar disorder, and major depression (previously known as dysthymia). According to the findings of the Pew Research Centre, 69% of grownups and 81% of teenagers in the US use online platforms. Recognizing a person's mental condition (stress, depression, or anxiety) is an essential subject of research to avert any negative events. Issues such as the failing economy, viral fear, and social estrangement have lately contributed to the increase in despair and anxiousness that has occurred since the pandemic's inception. In any given year, one out of 15 people (6.7%) suffers from melancholy. In addition, one out of every six persons (16.6%) will experience melancholy at some point in their life. Melancholy can hit at any age, although it occurs most commonly during the latter stages of adolescence and mid-20s. Women are more prone than males to suffer from depression. According to certain research, one-third of women will have a significant crisis of depression over their lifetime. There is a considerable degree of heredity factors (about 40%) when people in their immediate family (parents/children/siblings) suffer from melancholy. I used the LSTM and CNN models, which take just one number as an input and output. In this approach, the output of the CNN is passed as input to the LSTM. By doing so, the LSTM can learn and extract features from the input data that have been learned by CNN. Alternatively, the output of the LSTM can be used as the input to the CNN.

Related work

In a paper [1], the author suggests that depression has become a major issue that is impacting mental health. Furthermore, the rapid rise of social media allows for a wealth of information on one's online presence. Twitter is a 140-character-p-r-tweet program that allows users to convey their opinions and thoughts quickly and directly. The tagged Twitter messages are uploaded into a machine-learning system that classifies them into relevant groups. The selected machine learning algorithms, Naive Bayes and NBTree, are deployed on two different sizes of Twitter datasets to determine the algorithm's accuracy in identifying depressing Tweets and Tweets that are not depressing. NBT is an algorithm that classifies depressed and non-depressive tweets with an accuracy of 97.31% on the 3000 Twitter posts dataset as well as 92.34% on the one thousand Twitter posts dataset. Naive Bayes, in contrast, earns 97.31% on the 3,000 Twitter posts dataset and

92.34% on the 1000 Twitter posts dataset. By providing the same accuracy value in the investigation, both NB and NBT are effective in equal measure. The initiative, however, is confined to text alone. The work may be improved in the future by focusing on a certain user and their tweets at a specific moment and determining the condition of depression.

In another paper [2], the author divided depression into two categories and applied to a total of six algorithms, with each method providing the best accuracy on a typical basis. 90% of test information and 91% of the training information were used. The design was created and evaluated using the Bengali text as one characteristic. According to our manner and demonstration, a single data point is anticipated to be depressed, with 1 indicating depression. The extension of this unique work allows for the detection of the most frequent symptoms or features of depressive disease and the generation of an alarm for this mental condition and the common phenomenology of depression. Our DT correctness was 90% for CountVectorizer and 90.1% for Tf-Idf, for RF, the accuracy was 90.3% for CountVectorizer and Tf-Idf, and for NB and LR, the accuracy was 90.2% and 90.3% for CountVectorizer and Tf-Idf, respectively. The first poll was conducted in 2005. There is a proportion of 16.1% mental disorders in adults. In Bangladesh, 15.3% of individuals are relatives, 6.7% have a psychiatric disease, 4.5% have anxiousness, 2.1% have psychosomatic neuropsychiatric instability, and 0.9% have sleep-wake disorders. Moreover, 0.7% of people have OCD, which stands for obsessive-compulsive disorder, and 0.3% have developmental problems problem, while 0.3% have neuropsychological illness.

In a paper [3], the author suggests that conventional approaches are hindered by characteristics such as face-to-face communication and hesitancy to express oneself; therefore, machine learning used to identify suicide intention and depression in individuals is beneficial. In the future, I'd like to go deeper into context analysis using the retweet history and external connections. Although ML appears to be a superior method, it has specific constraints, such as the need for human involvement to validate the ML model's recommendations, it is restricted to diagnosing suicidal inclinations and depression, and the methodological approach since the data obtained lacks prior background explication. The findings can be enhanced by studying the data to see which terms appear the most frequently and what tendencies the postings follow. Thirty nine occurrences of Class 0 were discovered, indicating suicide tweets, 398 cases of Class 1 were identified (depressed tweets), and 3,393 instances of Class 6 were discovered (irrelevant tweets). The emphasis is on a limited subset of the data corpus. The detection of a higher propensity of suicide must be expanded by analyzing persons who send out these problematic Tweets. A dataset of 4443 tweets was utilized to develop the algorithms. They were gathered using Twint, an opensource tool that allows us to access Twitter data without utilizing its API, thus avoiding its drawbacks. Twint allows you to filter the generated tweets depending on numerous criteria, such as tweet content, username, time, geofencing, and so on. The tweets were acquired based on the substance of the tweets, which were developed based on interactions with psychotherapists.

In another paper [4], the author suggests that the initial aim of this study is to identify the translation for suicidal interpretation. As previously stated, social media has provided a venue for such speech, and research on the topic has been conducted. Twitter has a public API that allows the automated gathering of tweets based on particular parameters such as user ID, keyword, location, and other Twitter objects. With 300 million active users per month, it is an appealing platform for data mining. In the study by O'Dea, a set of 20 key phrases or keywords were found and utilized to extract tweets posted to Twitter by saving tweets containing one or more of the supplied sets of phrases. The retrieved tweets were analyzed by both human annotators and a computerized computer that was categorized into different levels of worry. Colombo expanded the 20 groups of phrases with 62 probable keywords discovered to investigate the depressive users' networks. Burnap and Voiles introduced classification measures such as POS and SS, in which the scores are used as a factor in post-categorization. However, one feature, TS, is suggested.

In a paper [5], the author evaluated numerous text categorization (TC) approaches. ML approaches include four BERT models, three RNN models, three essential pretreatment techniques, three reduction of features methods, and tuning of parameters. The following are some of the discoveries. An expert-provided collection of 50-word n-grams (mainly word unigrams) was discovered to be a decent basic detector. A heuristic technique based on the random forest ML method overcame computational explosion and resulted in a substantial improvement over a baseline result at a P = .01 level. The use of an iterative method that examines combinations of "k out of n0" (where n0 is the number of extracted features) and yields a 90.63% result. Using a dataset of post blogs composed in Hebrew that we created for this work, they ran lengthy and systematic trials for multiple TC models (*e.g.*, the half-interval search approach and the hill-climbing method). They created 28 feature sets and employed them in conjunction with five machine learning algorithms, preprocessing methods, three feature screening methods (Chi^2, ANOVA, and Mutual Information), and hyperparameters.

In another paper [6], the author suggests that the proposed approach, e-therapy immediate change tracking, can be utilized by psychiatrists and teenagers undergoing depression therapy. It allows psychologists to comprehend the status of individuals and aids them with the strategic planning of the therapy they deliver. Patients may also track their progress with each session, which helps them determine whether their condition is improving or whether they require extra assistance to improve more. Ultimately, this workaround will present teenagers with a substantial proof-featured application. The primary goal is to give an acceptable option for children who require melancholy therapy. The suggested solution comprises a mobile app that will aid clients and therapists in engaging in treatments online and monitoring the client's level of melancholy recovery after each therapy session. The movies from the training sample are used for training. These movies are supplied as input, which recognizes the human face, vision, and lips. The characteristics are then recovered using AAM and PCA to generate a parameterized approach, which is then used to characterize the new faces using the initial training paradigm. The aforementioned model generates a set of 72 non-rigid parameters, which are then fed into a set of 31 multiclass SVMs trained with the CK+ library for the classification of the 31 AUs. Previously, the facial action programming devices, which are used by many psychiatrists, were used to extract the required 31 AUs from the 46 core AUs observed to anticipate melancholy grades.

In a paper [7], the authors described a technique for real-time cardiac monitoring during depression bouts. With an effectiveness of more than 92%, they created a CNN-based machine learning method for categorizing ECG data into normal or ST-depression events of the heart. This method can detect ST depression episodes of varied lengths. The European ST-T database is used to assess the methodology. The top values found here are 0.95%, 0.98%, and 0.91% for correctness, responsiveness, and specificity, respectively. The proposed methodology is a powerful method for detecting ST depression episodes of varying lengths. For both subject-independent and subject-dependent situations, both specificity and sensitivity are more than 91%. A method for consistent ECG monitoring for ST depression is also described. When the filtering number is set to 16 for all convolution operations and the collection is made up of 40 successive rhythms, the best result is above 97 percent. Datasets are formed using 1108, 1098, 1088, and 1078 samples for 10, 20, 30, and 40 successive ECG beats, respectively. The ECG is a valuable tool for detecting coronary artery disease. A decrease or increase in the ST segment is a sign of IHD. In an ECG, the ST segment is defined as the time between the end of the QRS complex and the beginning of the T wave. A reference point must be identified to identify an ST segment variation. The PQ junction is recommended as the point of reference by the United States Academy of Cardiology/American Cardiac Federation.

In another paper [8], the authors trained a mental well-being classifier using SVM based on extracted individual difference variables from eye movement data to classify persons with melancholy and normal controls. The model achieved 77.0% accuracy, which is cutting-edge under the comparable information scenario. The model is intelligible, and the findings support the hypothesis of attention bias. Images are classified into three groups based on their emotional attribute values: positive, neutral, and negative. Positive pictures are those with positive themes that can elicit pleasurable emotions in people; negative images are the inverse, and neutral images have no evident emotional inclination. They used a Tobii eye tracker (60hz) to track the subjects' eyes throughout the laboratory exercise. The data set includes 29 melancholy males and 6 females (Mean age=24.23, SD=3.86) and 27 healthy controls (22 males and 5 females, SD=1.825 females) from hospitals and schools. The difference in the overall gaze time of favorable pictures produces the most significant results. Normal people have longer total gaze durations for positive images than those who suffer from depressive disorders, and the probability value of the t-test is 0.007, meeting the criteria for significance threshold; for unfavorable pictures, melancholy is somewhat greater for the typical individual, and the probability value is 0.038, meeting the metaphorical significance criterion as well.

In a paper [9], the author suggests that in this study, the facts were altered, processed, and reproduced. Further analysis was done by ensuring comprehensiveness, consistency, accuracy, and legibility (Neuman 2005). First, a code was created. Each question was assigned a letter and a numerical value; every query was coded sequentially using letters and numbers. Then, the information was put into an SPSS 24.0 data file. In this study, the proposed model investigated the association between SMA, psychological responses (anxiety, anxiousness, and melancholy), and scholastic achievement. According to the study findings, there was a favorable association between SMA and psychological responses among university students. The current study's findings validated the initial premise of this research, and a positive and substantial association between SMA and stress was discovered. For example, a rise in excessive social media use raises the amount of stress. Based on the findings, the second possibility of the study was confirmed, and a statistically significant positive link between SMA and students' anxiety-related behaviors was discovered, as was an association between inappropriate online platform use and feelings of anxiousness. Given the consequences of SMA on students' psychological reactions, the subject of social media addiction should be thoroughly addressed and explored. In addition, proper preparation should be undertaken to avoid addiction to social media, restrict its usage, and enhance its popularity. These developments provide opportunities while also posing risks. Allocating part of the research funds in this manner, the importance of the positive and negative effects of individual, societal, and academic uses of social media can be studied.

In a paper [10], the author suggests that data gathering is the first step of the approach. A large imbalanced Twitter data set was received from the Kaggle website. Before beginning data pre-processing, the data was cleaned and balanced. As part of the normalization procedure, the data was segmented, stemmed, and lemmatized. The information was then analyzed to provide a word score. Machine-learning classifiers were used to predict sad retweets that were not melancholy. The information was separated into two categories: training split sets and testing split sets. To guarantee that the classifier evolves, the training data was used to generate the sample framework. The test data was placed into the sample framework once it had been trained against the data for evaluation. They also used categorization metrics to analyze the outcomes. They compared the performance of the suggested model to that of other techniques. They acquired a mean accuracy of 97.21% for SVM and 97.31% for naive Bayes. They achieved 83% mean accuracy using a one-hot strategy on SVM, whereas the TF-IDf technique yielded 85% mean accuracy. The one-hot technique with decision trees achieved by CNN using the TF-IDf method had an average accuracy of 82%, and DBN with a one-hot method achieved 89% mean accuracy. The proposed approach enabled LSTM to achieve maximum accuracy. With a one-shot approach, you may achieve pinpoint precision. The epoch indicates the training data cycle and the obtained accuracy. As the period lengthens, so does the accuracy.

In another paper [11], according to the findings, social media use is linked to depression and secondary trauma, and it also predicts changes in health-related behavior. Nevertheless, no relationship was seen between health behavior change and psychiatric issues. Wuhan locals discovered that disseminating medical information *via* social media helped them with knowledge, emotional support, and peer support as the illness spread [12-20]. However, overuse of social media has culminated in psychological disorders. The research results show that taking a social media break during the global outbreak may improve wellness, which is crucial for reducing the pandemic's psychological burden. A public health crisis usually causes serious concern and worry among individuals who are affected. The COVID-19 pandemic, on the other hand, raised concerns about the lack of a vaccine or treatment, a scarcity of ventilators, enforcing social separation, wearing masks, rising economic troubles, and the welfare of those you love. Such concerns were understandable among Wuhan citizens, given that China was the first country to be hit by the COVID-19 pandemic, and Wuhan was the first epicenter of the worldwide health disaster. However, revealing certain unseen harms induced by the virus, such as sadness and subsequent trauma, was a difficult task.

Proposed Methodology

In this experiment, I deployed the CNN- LSTM model, which accepts a parameter and yields one particular result reflecting the chance that the tweet is depressing. The simulation substitutes every given sentence with its own. Extracted features are sent before passing the new wrapping. Through a neural layer, a vector is sent. CNNs are extremely proficient at acquiring spatial configuration from data; the convolution operation takes advantage of this by learning some architecture from the classification tasks before passing it into a normal LSTM layer. Finally, the LSTM layer output is input into a typical dense predicted model.

Fig. (**1**) depicts the suggested methodology's step-by-step approach. The following stages are described in detail:

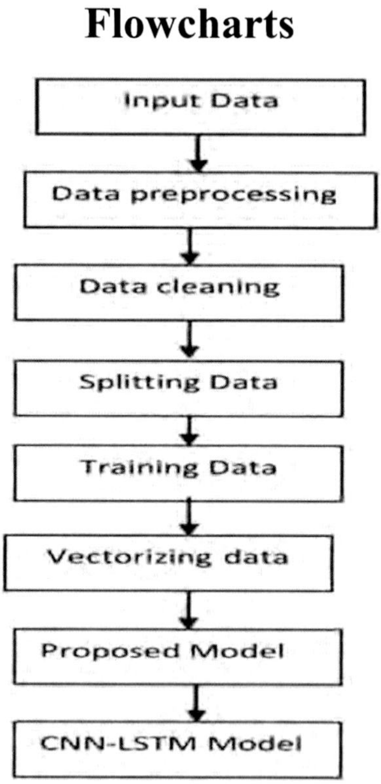

Fig. (1). Flowchart of CNN-LSTM.

DataSet

The depression and anxiety dataset, which is obtained from Kaggle, is used in this paper. The dataset is about 50000 rows and 2 columns.

Preprocessing

Here, we have cleaned the data so it is easy to read whether the caption of the dataset is positive or negative. Here, positive and negative are 25000 each.

Algorithm

In this paper, 7 algorithms are used, which are as follows:

LR

Logistic regression takes input data and calculates a weighted sum of the features. The logistical coefficient is used to transform it into probabilities and then classify the input based on that probability.

Bernoulli Naïve Bayes

The algorithm calculates the probabilities of an input belonging to each category based on the presence or absence of features. It then predicts the category with the highest probability.

CNN

CNN is a type of ANN that is particularly good at understanding, and data is processed using a grid-like structure, such as images or audio spectrograms.

SVM

SVM finds the optimal line or hyperplane. It can easily find fresh information that should be classified by identifying the end of the spectrum they tumble on. In a regression task, SVM tries to fit a line that best predicts the target values.

XG-Boost

The XGBoost machine learning algorithm takes a bunch of weak models (simple decision trees), combines their strengths, and corrects their errors to create a powerful predictive model [21].

Ada-Boost

For classification and regression tasks, an adaptive learning approach called Ada Boost is used. It is yet an additional prevalent ensemble learning approach that brings together the outputs of numerous inadequate models (usually basic classifiers) to produce a powerful prediction approach.

Proposed Model (CNN-LSTM)

CNN-LSTM is a hybrid neural network architecture that combines two powerful techniques. CNN: The initial part of the architecture involves using a CNN. CNNs are particularly good at capturing spatial features in data, like identifying patterns in images. LSTM: After the CNN extracts features from each element in the sequence, these features are passed to an LSTM network. LSTMs are a type of RNN that is well-suited for sequences because they can remember information over long sequences and capture temporal patterns. Integration of CNN and LSTM: The extracted features from the CNN serve as input to the LSTM. The LSTM's ability to capture sequential patterns then complements CNN's spatial feature extraction.

RESULT

As shown in the table, the accuracy of LR is 79%, BNB accuracy is 78%, CNN accuracy is 67.72%, SVM accuracy is 78%, XGB accuracy is 74%, and AdaBoost accuracy is 65%. Here, Bernoulli Naïve Bayes and SVM both have a common accuracy of 78%, and the highest accuracy of the proposed model (CNN-LSTM) is 85.18. CNN-LSTM models can yield excellent results in various tasks; designing and training such models require careful consideration of architecture design, hyperparameters, training data, and evaluation metrics. The success of a CNN-LSTM model depends on its appropriate application to the specific problem and thorough experimentation to achieve optimal performance. CNN-LSTM model can vary widely depending on the specific dataset, task, architecture, hyperparameters, and training process. When dealing with audio signals, CNN-LSTM models can be used to recognize emotions in speech. CNNs process audio spectrograms to capture acoustic features, and LSTMs capture the dynamics of speech over time, achieving better emotion classification. For tasks like recognizing hand gestures or sign language, CNN-LSTM models can effectively capture both the static hand positions (using CNNs) and the dynamic gestures over time (using LSTMs), leading to improved accuracy.

Table **1** provides a detailed overview of the evaluation metrics used to assess the performance of the proposed work's various machine learning (ML) models. These metrics are critical for determining the efficacy of ML models in the context of a research or project.

Table **1** contains a detailed description of the assessment criteria used for each ML model. Metrics like accuracy, precision, recall, F1 Score, and potentially others are often included in these criteria. Table **1** provides openness and clarity about how the ML models were extensively evaluated and compared, offering useful insights into their strengths and limitations by detailing the assessment matrix.

Table 1. Accuracy, Precision, Recall and F1-Score.

Model	Precision		Recall		F1-Score		Accuracy
	(0)	(1)	(0)	(1)	(0)	(1)	-
Logistic Regression	81%	79%	78%	81%	79%	80%	79%
Bernoulli Naïve Bayes	79%	76%	75%	80%	77%	78%	78%
SVM (Linear)	79%	77%	76%	80%	78%	79%	78%
XGBoost	79%	70%	65%	83%	71%	76%	74%
AdaBoost	80%	60%	40%	90%	54%	72%	65%

Fig. (**2**) depicts the accuracy values associated with models having the highest likelihood ratio (LR) values for both class labels 0 and 1. In this scenario, LR values are used to assess the model's capacity to distinguish between these two groups. By studying the accuracy values for these specific models, we obtain insight into their performance in properly detecting instances of class 0 and class 1, which is crucial for applications where precision is critical, such as binary classification tasks.

Fig. (**3**) depicts accuracy metrics for models associated with the greatest Likelihood Ratio (LR) values, with an emphasis on class labels 0 and 1. The LR values serve as a measure of the model's ability to differentiate between these two groups. Examining the accuracy scores in this context gives us a better idea of how well these specific models perform in reliably detecting examples from both classes 0 and 1. This analysis is especially important *in situ*ations when accuracy is required, such as binary classification jobs.

Fig. (**4**) depicts a full view of the F1 score metrics for models belonging to classes 0 and 1. Notably, the Likelihood Ratio (LR) model got the highest F1 score for class 0, reaching an astounding 79%. Similarly, the LR model did well in class 1 with an F1 score of 80%.

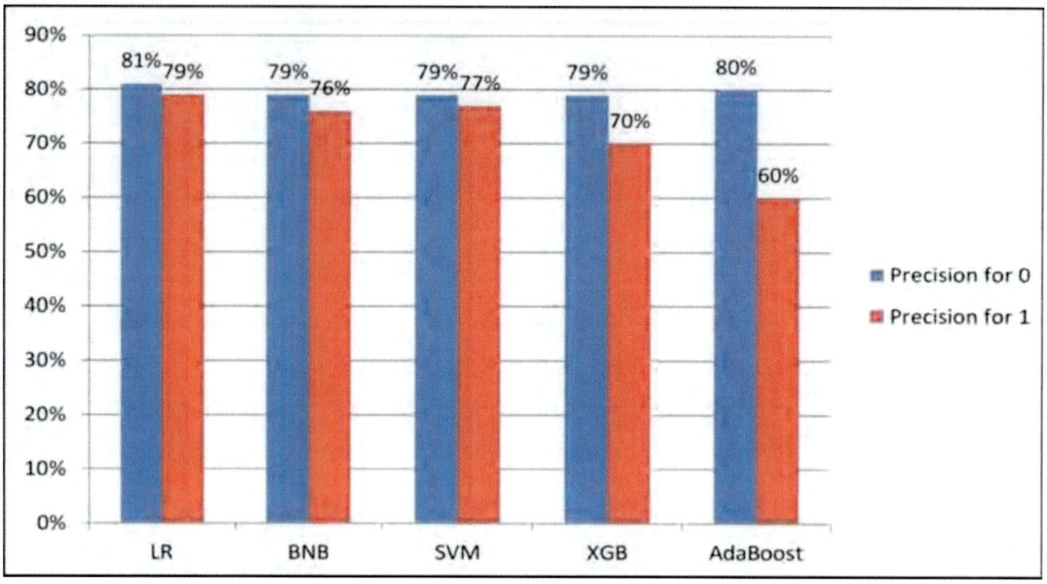

Fig. (2). Precision of models.

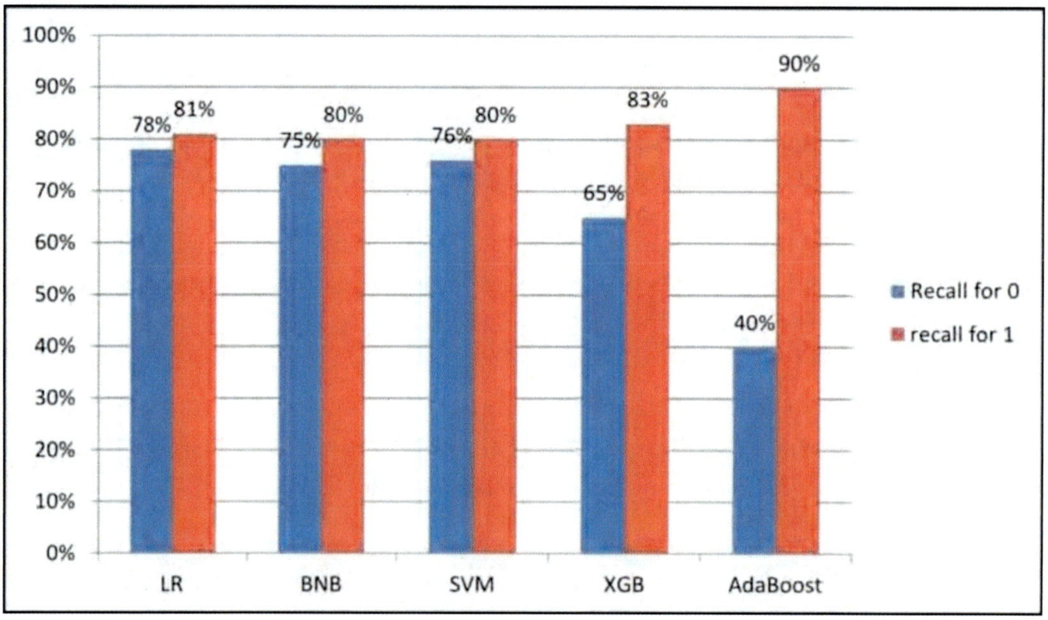

Fig. (3). Recall of model.

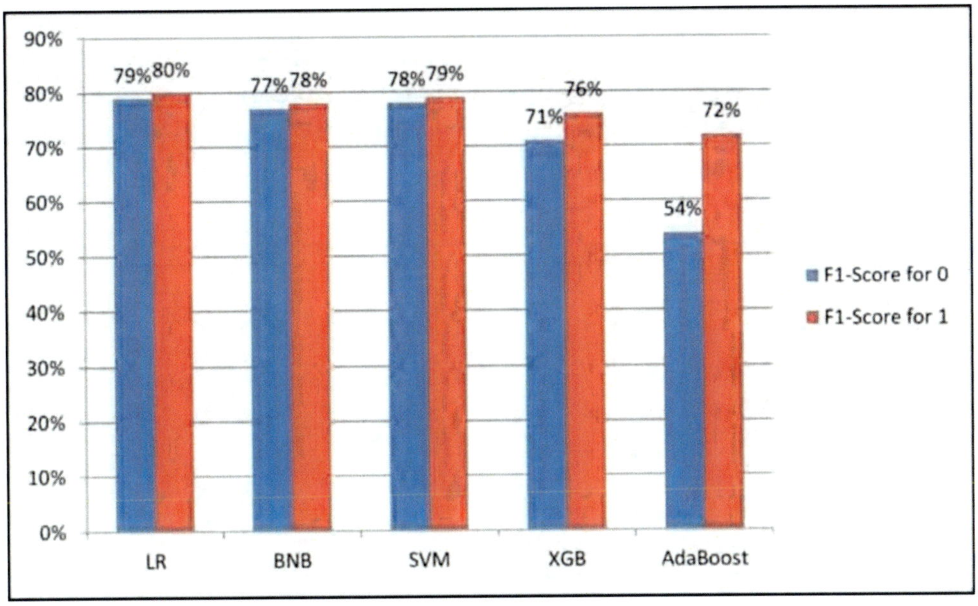

Fig. (4). F1-Score of models.

The F1 score is a useful metric that combines accuracy and recall to provide a fair evaluation of a model's ability to accurately identify cases for each class. Fig. (**4**) shows how efficient the LR model is in achieving this balance for both class 0 and class 1.

Table **2**: Comparison of Accuracy Scores Between Various Models and the Proposed Model, with CNN-LSTM Achieving the Highest Accuracy.

Table 2. Comparison of accuracies of various models with the proposed model.

Model	Accuracy (%)
Logistic Regression	79.00
Bernoulli Naïve Bayes	78.00
SVM	78.00
XGBoost	74.00
AdaBoost	65.00
CNN	67.72
Proposed Model (CNN-LSTM Model)	**85.18**

Fig. (**5**) shows a comparison of accuracy scores across various models, with a particular emphasis on highlighting the performance of the proposed model, CNN-LSTM. This statistic demonstrates that, among the models evaluated, CNN-LSTM is the best performer in terms of accuracy. This information is crucial for assessing the relative capabilities of different models and stresses the suggested CNN-LSTM model's greater accuracy [22].

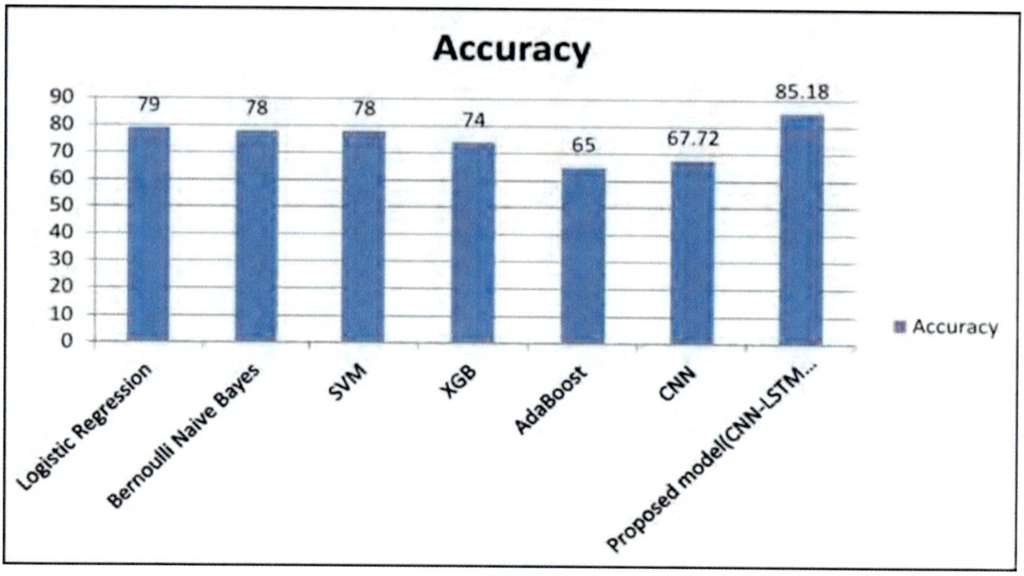

Fig. (5). Comparison of accuracies of various models with the proposed model.

CONCLUSION

The performance of the CNN-LSTM model must be increased. In CNN, the accuracy is 67.72%, and there is a loss, too, which is 95.72%. CNN is a type of network architecture for deep learning. It is basically used for image recognition. The accurateness of LR is 79%, the accuracy of the BNB Model is 78%, the accuracy of SVM is 78%, the accuracy of XGB is 74%, the sccuracy of AdaBoost is 75%, and the accuracy of the proposed model (CNN-LSTM Model) is 85.18%. When using a CNN and LSTM network in tandem, there are two primary methods. First is using the CNN output as the input to the LSTM. In this approach, the output of the CNN is passed as input to the LSTM. By doing so, the LSTM can learn and retrieve previously extracted characteristics based on the supplied information learned by CNN. The second is using the LSTM output as the input to the CNN.

FUTURE WORK

In the future, we can use other models to enhance the performance. There are many social media platforms other than Twitter *i.e.*, Facebook, Reddit, YouTube, and so on, in which we can find sentiments from comments, posts, *etc*. We can also use emoticons for sentiment analysis. After identifying sad people on social media, an online counseling service can be given to them, with free online counseling to keep them safe from this serious mental disease. To analyze the intelligence from our review dataset, we will create a framework based on the provided sentiment models.

REFERENCES

[1] K.A. Govindasamy, and N. Palanichamy, "Depression detection using machine learning techniques on Twitter data", *In 2021 5th international Conference on Intelligent Computing and Control Systems (ICICCS) IEEE,* pp. 960-966, 2021.
[http://dx.doi.org/10.1109/ICICCS51141.2021.9432203]

[2] D.B. Victor, J. Kawsher, M.S. Labib, and S. Latif, "Machine learning techniques for depression analysis on the social media-case study on bengali community", *In 2020 4th International Conference on Electronics, Communication and Aerospace Technology (ICECA) IEEE,* pp. 1118-1126, 2020.
[http://dx.doi.org/10.1109/ICECA49313.2020.9297436]

[3] A. Ramachandran, A. Gadwe, D. Poddar, S. Satavalekar, and S. Sahu, "Performance evaluation of different machine learning techniques using Twitter data for identification of suicidal intent", *2020 International Conference on Electronics and Sustainable Communication Systems (ICESC) IEEE,* pp. 223-227, 2020.
[http://dx.doi.org/10.1109/ICESC48915.2020.9155747]

[4] C. Lalrinmawii, and S. Debnath, "Analysis of Post centric suicidal expressions and classification on the Social Media Post: Twitter", *In 2020 11th International Conference on Computing, Communication and Networking Technologies (ICCCNT) IEEE,* pp. 1-5, 2020.

[5] Y. Hacohen-Kerner, N. Manor, M. Goldmeier, and E. Bachar, "Detection of Anorexic Girls-In Blog Posts Written in Hebrew Using a Combined Heuristic AI and NLP Method", *IEEE Access,* vol. 10, pp. 34800-34814, 2022.
[http://dx.doi.org/10.1109/ACCESS.2022.3162685]

[6] B. Vimaleswaran, and G.S. Ratnayake, "E-Therapy Improvement Monitoring Platform for Depression using Facial Emotion Detection of Youth", *2021 Third International Conference on Intelligent Communication Technologies and Virtual Mobile Networks (ICICV) IEEE,* pp. 950-955, 2021.
[http://dx.doi.org/10.1109/ICICV50876.2021.9388447]

[7] E. Tiryaki, A. Sonawane, and L. Tamil, "Real-time CNN-based ST depression episode detection using single-lead ECG", *in Proc. 2021 22nd Int. Symp. on Quality Electronic Design (ISQED),* pp. 566-570, 2021.https://ieeexplore.ieee.org

[8] R. Shen, Q. Zhan, Y. Wang, and H. Ma, "Depression detection by analyzing eye movements on emotional images", *in Proc. ICASSP 2021 - 2021 IEEE Int. Conf. on Acoustics, Speech and Signal Processing (ICASSP),* pp. 7973-7977, 2021.https://ieeexplore.ieee.org

[9] M.Z. Malak, A.H. Shuhaiber, R.M. Al-amer, M.H. Abuadas, and R.J. Aburoomi, "Correlation between psychological factors, academic performance and social media addiction: model-based testing", *Behav. Inf. Technol.,* vol. 41, no. 8, pp. 1583-1595, 2022.
[http://dx.doi.org/10.1080/0144929X.2021.1891460]

[10] A. Amanat, M. Rizwan, A.R. Javed, M. Abdelhaq, R. Alsaqour, S. Pandya, and M. Uddin, "Deep

learning for depression detection from textual data", *Electronics (Basel),* vol. 11, no. 5, p. 676, 2022. [http://dx.doi.org/10.3390/electronics11050676]

[11] B. Zhong, Y. Huang, and Q. Liu, "Mental health toll from the coronavirus: Social media usage reveals Wuhan residents' depression and secondary trauma in the COVID-19 outbreak", *Comput. Human Behav.,* vol. 114, p. 106524, 2021. [http://dx.doi.org/10.1016/j.chb.2020.106524] [PMID: 32836728]

[12] J. Li, and L. Qiu, "A sentiment analysis method of short texts in microblog", *in Proc. 2017 IEEE Int. Conf. on Computational Science and Engineering (CSE) and Embedded and Ubiquitous Computing (EUC),* vol. 1, pp. 776-779, 2017. [http://dx.doi.org/10.1109/CSE-EUC.2017.153]

[13] L.C. Cheng, and S.L. Tsai, "Deep learning for automated sentiment analysis of social media", *Proceedings of the 2019 IEEE/ACM international conference on advances in social networks analysis and mining,* pp. 1001-1004, 2019. [http://dx.doi.org/10.1145/3341161.3344821]

[14] J. Yang, and J. Yang, "Aspect-based sentiment analysis with self-attention and gated convolutional networks", In: *Proc. 2020 IEEE 11th Int. Conf. on Software Engineering and Service Science (ICSESS)*, 2020, pp. 146-149. [http://dx.doi.org/10.1109/ICSESS49938.2020.9237640]

[15] T. Marwa, O. Salima, and M. Souham, "Deep learning for online harassment detection in tweets", In: *Proc. 2018 3rd Int. Conf. on Pattern Analysis and Intelligent Systems (PAIS)*, 2018, pp. 1-5. [http://dx.doi.org/10.1109/PAIS.2018.8598530]

[16] K. Katchapakirin, K. Wongpatikaseree, P. Yomaboot, and Y. Kaewpitakkun, "Facebook social media for depression detection in the Thai community", In: *Proc. 2018 15th Int. Joint Conf. on Computer Science and Software Engineering (JCSSE)*, 2018, pp. 1-6. [http://dx.doi.org/10.29007/tscc]

[17] G. Geetha, G. Saranya, K. Chakrapani, J.G. Ponsam, M. Safa, and S. Karpagaselvi, "Early Detection of Depression from Social Media Data Using Machine Learning Algorithms", In: *Proc. 2020 Int. Conf. on Power, Energy, Control and Transmission Systems (ICPECTS)*, 2020, pp. 1-6. [http://dx.doi.org/10.1109/ICPECTS49113.2020.9336974]

[18] M.M. Tadesse, H. Lin, B. Xu, and L. Yang, "Detection of depression-related posts in Reddit social media forum", *IEEE Access,* vol. 7, pp. 44883-44893, 2019. [http://dx.doi.org/10.1109/ACCESS.2019.2909180]

[19] M. Deshpande, and V. Rao, "Depression detection using emotional artificial intelligence", *Proc. 2017 Int. Conf. on Intelligent Sustainable Systems (ICISS),* pp. 858-862, 2017. Available: https://ieeexplore.ieee.org

[20] M. Deshpande, and V. Rao, "Depression detection using emotion artificial intelligence", *In 2017 international conference on intelligent sustainable systems (iciss),* IEEE., pp. 858-862, 2017. [http://dx.doi.org/10.1109/ISS1.2017.8389299]

[21] S. Gupta, L. Goel, A. Singh, A.K. Agarwal, and R.K. Singh, "TOXGB: Teamwork Optimization Based XGBoost model for early identification of post-traumatic stress disorder", *Cogn. Neurodynamics,* vol. 16, no. 4, pp. 833-846, 2022. [http://dx.doi.org/10.1007/s11571-021-09771-1] [PMID: 35018201]

[22] S. Gupta, L. Goel, A. Singh, A. Prasad, and M.A. Ullah, "Psychological analysis for depression detection from social networking sites", *Comput. Intell. Neurosci.,* vol. 2022, pp. 1-14, 2022. [http://dx.doi.org/10.1155/2022/4395358] [PMID: 35432513]

[23] T. Varshney, S. Gupta, and L. Goel, "Literature Survey on Depression Detection Using Machine Learning", *Proceedings of the International Conference on Cognitive and Intelligent Computing: ICCIC 2021,* vol. Volume 1, pp. 313-321, 2022. Singapore. [http://dx.doi.org/10.1007/978-981-19-2350-0_31]

CHAPTER 13

Evaluating Twitter Sentiments *via* Natural Language Processing

Radhey Shyam[1,*], **Shilpi Khanna**[1], **Smita Singh**[1] and **Tanvi Jaiswal**[1]

[1] *Department of Information Technology, SRMCEM, Lucknow, India*

Abstract: Daily content sharing has increased significantly as a result of the quick expansion of user-created data on *social media* sites like *Instagram*, *Twitter*, and *Snapchat*. This content covers a wide range of topics as users express their opinions. This research aims to uncover the emotions hidden in these user posts, particularly focusing on sentiments related to product purchases, use of public services, and similar contexts. Sentiment analysis, a common method in research, seeks to reveal the emotional aspects of opinions in text. Recent research has looked at attitudes about a range of topics, including movies, consumer goods, and societal challenges. Users frequently communicate their ideas on Twitter among various channels. Analyzing sentiments through Twitter data has gained attention, and there are two main approaches: one based on existing knowledge and the other using machine learning. The feelings expressed in tweets about electronic items like laptops and smartphones are evaluated in this study using machine learning-based methods. The impact of domain knowledge on sentiment analysis can be tested by concentrating on particular regions. A novel method has been presented for categorizing tweets into positive or detrimental sentiments and for extracting individuals' viewpoints on various subjects. The study explores various techniques for sentiment analysis, encompassing machine learning and lexicon-based methods, along with the metrics employed to assess their performance. The suggested model attains an accuracy ranging from 52% to 67% in its outcomes.

Keywords: ANN, Assessment, Datasets, Emotions, ML techniques, NLP.

INTRODUCTION

A significant portion of the population engages with social networking platforms to express their feelings, thoughts, and daily experiences [1, 2]. This signifies that individuals possess the freedom to share their preferences and dislikes openly. Online platforms offer an avenue for individuals to communicate their view-

* **Corresponding author Radhey Shyam:** Department of Information Technology SRMCEM, Lucknow, India; E-mail: shyam0058@gmail.com

Vikash Yadav, Vimal Kumar, Sonam Gupta & Vandana Dixit Kaushik (Eds.)

points and impact others. Additionally, social media serves as a forum for companies to engage with their clients, whether through advertising or by actively seeking client comments and thoughts. Conversely, consumers have full autonomy over the content they wish to engage with and their subsequent responses.

The successes and setbacks of companies are disseminated through informal communication. Nevertheless, social media possesses the potential to shape consumer behaviors and choices. Surprisingly, a significant number of researchers in this domain assert that approximately 87% of "internet users are influenced by customer reviews" when they decide whether or not to purchase a product [3]. Consequently, if a company can swiftly grasp the sentiments of its customers, it gains a competitive edge by promptly adapting and devising effective strategies.

Despite the existence of technologies capable of capturing individuals' sentiments toward specific products or services, companies, and other data practitioners still encounter difficulties in data extraction. The expansive expansion of the World Wide Web has led to the widespread adoption of social media platforms like Twitter. This results in the generation of substantial volumes of opinion-based content, primarily in the form of tweets, which can serve as valuable resources for conducting sentiment analysis [4]. Considering the human perspective, this signifies a significant data load, posing challenges in efficiently extracting phrases, comprehending, assessing, analyzing, and structuring them into a coherent format within a reasonable time frame [4].

Informal communication is defined as the use of colloquialisms, slang, and other language features that deviate from the formal rules of spoken English, for instance, contractions like "wouldn't", "couldn't", *etc.* This informal communication may make it difficult for different algorithms to detect sentiment, which could impede analysis and decision-making [5]. Emoticons, which visually depict human facial expressions, play a role in drawing the recipient's attention to the emotional tone of a sender's written communication, compensating for the absence of body language and spoken cues, thus enhancing the receiver's understanding and interpretation of the message [6]. For example, an emoticon like a happy face conveys a positive mood. Currently, existing systems lack the necessary context to accurately interpret emotions conveyed through emoticons. Humans commonly resort to using emoticons when verbal expression is limited [7]. Failure to decipher emoticons leaves organizations without valuable insights. The use of short forms is pervasive, even in concise message services like Twitter, where the constraint of a 140-character limit encourages the frequent use of abbreviations to conserve space [8]. For instance, the abbreviation "Tba" is used to represent "To be announced."

The intention of this research is to delve into sentiment patterns within micro-blogging platforms, specifically focusing on analyzing the feedback provided by customers about a particular organization's product. The aim is to create an effective model that can categorize a substantial volume of tweets into meaningful classes for conducting *sentiment analysis*. The structure of the paper is as follows: the most popular micro-blogging platforms are presented in Section II. The common machine learning approaches for sentiment analysis are outlined in Section III. Methodologies for analyzing tweet sentiment are illustrated in Section IV. The result analysis of sentiment trends in tweets is presented in Section V. Lastly, Section VI presents a discussion of the findings and concludes the paper.

COMMON BLOGGING PLATFORMS

The most popular micro-blogging platforms that are widely used across the globe:

Sentiments Analysis

Sentiment analysis constitutes a crucial domain within natural language processing (NLP), computational linguistics, and text mining. It involves the computational examination of sentiments, perspectives, and emotions. The term "sentiment" denotes a standpoint or attitude that stems from emotions rather than pure logic [9], thus forming the basis of sentiment analysis or opinion mining. This field finds diverse applications, spanning disciplines, for instance, accounting, education, research, technology, politics, law, entertainment, and marketing [10]. Various online social platforms have emerged as avenues enabling internet users to openly express and engage in discussions regarding their viewpoints and thoughts [11].

Digital Social Networks

Online networking platforms comprise a group of web-based applications built upon the principles and technological foundations of Web 2.0. These platforms enable users to produce and share original material [17]. In the United States, the total amount of time spent on social media and mobile devices, including PC use, increased significantly by 37%. In 2011 and 2012, it was 88 and 121 billion minutes, respectively. Businesses use social networking sites to find and communicate with clients, yet it has been noted that social media might reduce productivity [18]. Rapid sharing of private information on social media can lead to potential harm [12]. The advantages of engaging with social media have expanded beyond mere social sharing, encompassing activities like enhancing an organization's reputation, fostering job opportunities, and financial gains [19]. Furthermore, social media finds applications in advertising for promotions by corporations, professional networking, recruitment, online education, and e-commerce [13, 17]. E-commerce can be enabled through social media platforms like Twitter, which provides 24/7 accessibility, straightforward customer service, and a global reach [18 - 20]. Businesses are increasingly embracing social media to gather market data, understand consumer behavior trends, and get client feedback.

Twitter

Twitter serves as a widely used real-time micro-blogging platform that enforces a character limit of 140 characters per tweet [3, 4, 12]. Twitter is a platform where users may voice their opinions on a range of issues that affect them in their daily lives. The platform also serves as a common ground for gauging public sentiment on specific matters [10, 11]. A corpus of tweets is used as the primary dataset in the context of sentiment analysis, which includes opinion mining and natural language processing (NLP) [1]. By gathering and evaluating sentiment expressed in public tweets regarding their products, services, and even competitors, Twitter has quickly become a crucial tool for businesses wanting to safeguard their reputation and brand [41]. An estimated 500 million people use Twitter, and millions of tweets are posted every day. The internet has witnessed significant growth, resulting in extensive volumes of opinion-laden content in forms like tweets, reviews, blogs, and discussions across various groups and forums. This abundance of data has positioned the internet as a swift, all-encompassing, and readily available channel for conducting sentiment analysis [21 - 24].

E-commerce Microblogging

A micro-blogging network, like Twitter, shares similarities with traditional blogging platforms, but distinctively, individual posts are shorter in length [14]. Twitter has imposed limitations on the word count in order to facilitate rapid information sharing and idea exchange [8]. Both small businesses and large organizations are progressively embracing micro-blogging as a strategy for e-commerce marketing [25 - 27]. Notably, a microblogging platform was developed a couple of years ago to promote a website for international trade, using a global microblogging network like Twitter for marketing [28]. The micro-blogging platform has empowered enterprises to manage brand perception, establish a crucial sales channel for products, enhance product sales, foster meaningful connections with consumers, and facilitate various other business operations [3, 4]. In fact, manufacturers of such products have begun to monitor these micro-blogs to gauge the overall sentiment surrounding their offerings [14]. These companies often track user responses and engage with them on micro-blogging platforms [29 - 31].

DOMINANT MACHINE LEARNING APPROACHES FOR ANALYZING SENTIMENT

The collective association of a set of items with a particular emotional polarity can be evaluated using the semantic notions of entities collected from tweets [41]. The idea of polarity revolves around determining whether a word or statement has a "positive" or "detrimental" meaning [32]. However, there are other methods for determining polarity within the context of sentiment analysis, including:

Support Vector Machine

Support vector machines (SVM) are used to categorize the emotions expressed in tweets. According to several studies [11] support vector machines have the capacity to extract and evaluate data on a test dataset with an accuracy ranging from 70% to 81.3%. Each of the three Twitter sentiment detection services combines data from pre-existing sentiment lexicons to classify each tweet as either "positive" or "detrimental" [33 - 36]. Based on their research, it has been found that an SVM trained on a dataset with noisy labels could accurately classify data up to 81.3% of the time.

Natural Language Processing

The foundations of NLP techniques are rooted in machine learning (ML), with a specific focus on statistical learning. This involves the utilization of a generalized learning algorithm in conjunction with a comprehensive dataset, referred to as a corpus, to derive patterns and principles [37]. The application of NLP extends to sentiment analysis, which is employed to discern the emotional tone within the text, and this application is executed across various granularities. Initially, it was employed at the broader document level for the purpose of categorization [38]. Following this, its scope was extended to operate at the level of individual sentences, enabling a more nuanced analysis of sentiment. More recently, this analysis has been pushed to even finer levels, down to the level of phrases and expressions [39].

In essence, NLP methods harness the power of ML to comprehend and interpret human language. The synergy between ML algorithms and extensive language datasets allows these techniques to identify patterns, extract meaning, and draw insights from text data. The process of sentiment analysis, a pivotal NLP task, exemplifies this convergence. Initially focused on entire documents to gauge overall sentiment, the methodology has progressed to dissecting sentences and phrases to capture nuances in an emotional context.

This evolution highlights the adaptability of NLP methods, which continually refine their approach to capture finer details in language usage. As technology advances and datasets expand, these methods are poised to unlock even deeper layers of meaning, enabling applications ranging from chatbots with heightened emotional intelligence to comprehensive analyses of public sentiment across diverse media. Ultimately, the marriage of NLP and ML epitomizes the marriage of linguistic understanding and computational prowess, fostering a new realm of possibilities for understanding and leveraging human language.

Case-based Reasoning

In the realm of ML, this technique finds extensive application for performing sentiment analysis. Referred to as case-based reasoning, it revolves around the retrieval of solutions from past resolved cases and their application to current issues that bear significant resemblance [40]. What sets this approach apart is its independence from a predetermined domain model, which in turn streamlines the collection of case histories. The framework of case-based reasoning continuously evolves as it incorporates novel information into its repository of cases. Leveraging this iterative process alongside database systems contributes to the efficient handling of large and complex datasets, simplifying their management [26]. This methodology proves especially effective for tasks like sentiment analysis, as it harnesses the collective knowledge embedded within historical cases. Discerning patterns and similarities empowers the system to make informed decisions about the sentiment associated with textual data. Its flexibility, rooted in real-world instances, renders it an adaptable solution capable of tackling a spectrum of problems without the need for rigid, predefined models. As ML advances, the integration of case-based reasoning stands as a testament to the significance of experiential learning from the past to enhance decision-making in the present [41].

Artificial Neural Network

The application of this mathematical framework lies in the interconnection of artificial neurons in order to create networks. These networks employ various methods of establishing connections between neurons. Their primary function revolves around the processing of extensive datasets. One of their key strengths is their ability to proficiently identify correlations that exist between the input and output elements of these datasets. Beyond that, these frameworks also excel in recognizing intricate patterns within datasets [42]. Through intricate connection techniques, these neural frameworks enable the translation of raw data into valuable insights. This process involves the propagation of signals through interconnected neurons, simulating the behavior of biological neural networks.

Consequently, these systems have become a cornerstone in ML, enabling technologies such as deep learning to thrive. Their efficacy in processing data and extracting meaningful relationships makes them a fundamental tool in various fields, ranging from image and speech recognition to complex data analysis tasks.

Python

Because it makes it easier to create solutions, this open-source programming language makes tackling problems simpler [32]. Python is often referred to as a scripting language, and its description encompasses its versatility across various systems [33]. Notably, it stands out as an excellent choice for prototyping due to its efficiency in producing functional prototypes compared to other programming languages [36]. Numerous researchers emphasize Python's efficiency, particularly for complex projects. Moreover, Python proves to be highly suitable for initiating social network or media streaming projects, especially those rooted in web-based environments that involve substantial data processing [34]. Additionally, Python is adept at memory management. It is worth mentioning that Python generates generators, allowing for an iterative process that handles items individually, acquiring source data one by one and guiding it through the entire processing sequence [36].

Application Programming Interface

Regarding both the quantity and quality of extracted elements, the Alchemy API demonstrates superior performance [15]. The Python Twitter application programming interface (API) has undergone advancements due to the compilation of tweets over time [31]. Python has the ability to rank the top 200 messages depending on how often they are retweeted, analyze the rate of retweeted messages at intervals of 100 seconds, and save the results in a database [41]. The "Python Twitter API" only supported tweets from the last six days; therefore, it was chosen to keep the data in a separate database [15].

TWITTER SENTIMENT ANALYSIS

Tweets and comments can contain sentiment, which can be used for a variety of purposes [21]. In addition, there are three fundamental types of moods: (i) positive, (ii) detrimental, and (iii) impartial [41, 39]. Sentiment analysis is a method for measuring the conveyed thoughts or attitudes within a collection of tweets [9]. Sentiment analysis, which refers to the strength of words and the polarity of text or phrases, is a general procedure of deriving polarity and subjectivity from semantic orientation [20]. Two key techniques for automating sentiment extraction are the lexicon-based technique and the machine learning-based approach [21 - 24].

- The terms that have already been associated with particular emotions are used in "lexicon-based approaches" [22]. Depending on the context in which they were created, these "lexical approaches" can vary, but they always involve identifying the orientation of documents by taking into consideration the semantic orientation of the sentences or phrases that compose those documents [20]. Lexical sentiment analysis's primary objective is to identify words that convey views within a dataset and then predict the stated sentiment in the text [25]. Lexical techniques often pre-process each tweet before removing "punctuation" [21].

– Initialize the total polarity scores to zero ($s = 0$) and then check to see if the token is contained in the dictionary.

- S will be positive (+) if the token is positive
- S will be detrimental (−) if the token is detrimental.

Look at the overall polarity score of the tweet. If it is above the threshold, it is positive. If it is below the threshold, it is detrimental.

An ML-based technique has a distinct benefit in that it may construct trained models that are specifically customized to different situations and uses. In contrast, the problem is the lack of labeled data, which can restrict the efficacy of this strategy for dealing with novel datasets due to the potentially high cost or impossibility of data labeling for some jobs [22].

- Machine learning-based approach—When using supervised classification approaches, ML algorithms frequently treat sentiment analysis as a binary process [43]. In this method, the classifiers must be trained using labeled data. When using this method, it is obvious that a word's local context should include both negative aspects (such as "Not beautiful") and intensifiers (such as "Very beautiful") [20]. A study [21] illustrated a fundamental method for creating a "feature vector" that involves applying a "part-of-speech tagger to each tweet post" that includes the phrase.

- Gather all adjectives for all tweets.
- Create a word list with the top N adjectives in it.
- Explore every tweet in the experimental set to produce the following:

* Number of uplifting words.
* Number of unfavorable words.
* The frequency, absence, or presence of specific words serves as an example of switch negation, a tactic that entails utilizing negation to flip a word's lexical

polarity. A word like ”lovely” (+3) becomes ”not beautiful” (-3) as a result of this shift [20].

To illustrate further, let’s consider additional instances:

She isn’t terrific ($6 - 5 = 1$), but she isn’t terrible either ($-6 + 5 = -1$).

In this example, negating a highly positive or detrimental value results in a nuanced viewpoint accurately captured by the shifted value. However, the ML-based approach is better suited for Twitter data compared to the lexicon-based method [22]. Additionally, ML approaches are able to produce a predetermined number of often occurring popular words, giving each expression an integer value based on how frequently it appears on Twitter [21].

Table 1. Performance of sentiment analysis for various keyword searches throughout the number of tweets.

Keyword Searched	Total Tweets Searched (#)	Positive (%)	Impartial (%)	Detrimental (%)
Flood	600	47.7	29.5	22.8
Iphone	270	22.6	67.8	9.6
Pollution	1400	32.6	41.4	26.0
Assignments	830	40.4	43.9	15.8
Death	320	24.7	15.0	60.3
Politics	175	32.6	37.1	30.3
Nuclear	580	22.9	36.6	44.5
Wedding	1130	44.7	43.5	11.8
Twitter	716	17.0	77.8	5.2
Reliance	2243	35.8	41.5	22.7

RESULT ANALYSIS

The Twitter API compiles the latest dataset each time we input a keyword to extract tweets. I is noteworthy that the dataset corresponding to the same keyword can vary across different time periods. In our study, we employed Twitter API data to conduct sentiment analysis. The prerequisites for conducting a comprehensive analysis of tweet sentiments comprise two main aspects: (i) Retrieval of Twitter Data and (ii) Sentiment Analysis. The sentiment analysis process utilizes information from the word cloud, as depicted in Fig. (**1**). Furthermore, Fig. (**2**) showcases both the original sampled tweets and their normalized counterparts that have been included in the analysis.

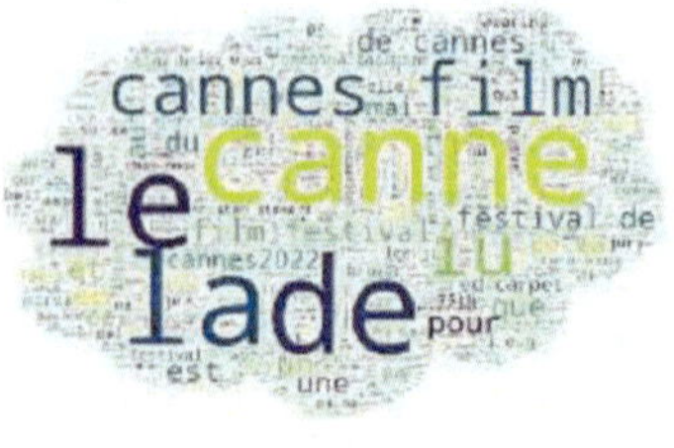

(a) All Tweets

(b) Positive Tweets

(c) Impartial Tweets

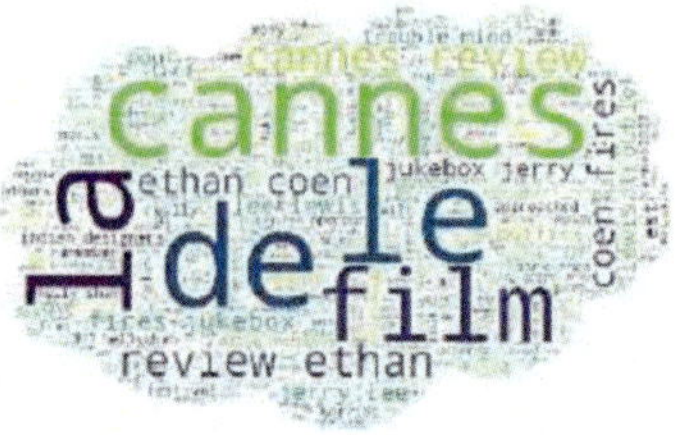

(d) Detrimental Tweets

Fig. (1). An illustration of data displayed as a word cloud: (a) All Tweets, (b) Positive Tweets, (c) Impartial Tweets, and (d) Detrimental Tweets [16].

	0
0	@Gplavallee72 Unless you can give us some insi...
1	RT @AlfonsGorina: A la roda de #CrimesOfTheFut...
2	RT @bellaxkristen: thank you cannes. ✨ □ https:...
3	RT @Variety: After earning dozens of walkouts ...
4	RT @KadinCinayeti: Cannes Film Festivali'nde k...
...	...
995	RT @hndmaidenonfire: Park Chan-wook on the red...
996	RT @Variety: Deepika Padukone strikes a pose a...
997	Laura Morante: «La Palma a Cannes? Nanni Moret...
998	RT @UNESCO: During the #Cannes2022 , @UNESCO w...
999	A l'affiche du nouveau film événement du réali...

1000 rows x 1 columns

(a) Tweet Samples

	0	text	polarity	subjectivity	sentiment	neg	neu	pos	compound
0	@Gplavallee72 Unless you can give us some insi...	unless you can give us some inside the board...	0.2	0.200000	positive	0.098	0.756	0.146	0.2716
1	RT @AlfonsGorina: A la roda de #CrimesOfTheFut...	a la roda de crimesofthefuture casi res da...	0.0	0.000000	neutral	0.000	1.000	0.000	0.0000
2	RT @bellaxkristen: thank you cannes. https:...	thank you cannes	0.0	0.000000	positive	0.000	0.444	0.556	0.3612
3	RT @Variety: After earning dozens of walkouts...	after earning dozens of walkouts and a 7 minu...	0.0	0.066667	negative	0.091	0.909	0.000	-0.1779
4	RT @KadinCinayeti: Cannes Film Festivali'nde k...	cannes film festivali nde k rm z hal ya ka...	0.0	0.000000	neutral	0.000	1.000	0.000	0.0000
...	...	...	...	...	...	...	...	...	...
994	[QUOTIDIENNE-CANNES] Jusqu'au 28 mai, les nuit...	quotidienne cannes jusqu au 28 mai les nuit...	0.0	0.000000	neutral	0.000	1.000	0.000	0.0000
995	RT @hndmaidenonfire: Park Chan-wook on the red...	park chan wook on the red carpet at cannes fi...	0.0	0.000000	positive	0.049	0.820	0.131	0.4588
997	Laura Morante: «La Palma a Cannes? Nanni Moret...	laura morante la palma a cannes nanni moret...	0.0	0.000000	neutral	0.000	1.000	0.000	0.0000
998	RT @UNESCO: During the #Cannes2022, @UNESCO w...	during the cannes2022 will highlight afr...	0.0	0.500000	positive	0.000	0.862	0.138	0.3400
999	A l'affiche du nouveau film événement du réali...	al affiche du nouveau film v nement du r ali...	0.0	0.000000	neutral	0.000	1.000	0.000	0.0000

676 rows x 9 columns

(b) Normalized Tweet Samples

Fig. (2). Examples of Tweet Samples Data: (a) Tweet Samples and (b) Normalized Tweet Samples [16].

Retrieval of Tweets

Developers must accept the "terms and conditions" of the "Twitter development platform" in order to access data *via* the "Twitter API". The resulting data is stored as a JavaScript object notation (JSON) file. JSON is chosen due to its lightweight nature, making it easily readable and writable. Additionally, it is easy to generate and parse for machines. JSON operates as a language-independent text format, adhering to the familiar paradigm of "C" family programming languages, which includes languages like Python.

The amount of output is determined by how long it takes to retrieve tweets from Twitter. The two categories of outputs are **(i)** encoded and **(ii)** un-encoded. In some cases, outputs, for security purposes in data access, may be expressed in the form of an ID, for instance, a string ID. A method for assessing a person's emotional tone is sentiment analysis. Each word in the tweets is assigned a value and classified as positive or detrimental using a lexical dictionary. The outcomes can be displayed in different file formats, including .txt, .csv, or HTML.

Analysis of Sentiments

In the context of processing tweets from a JSON file, each word's significance is determined by comparing it to a lexicon dictionary. However, due to the dictionary's limited coverage, assigning values to every single word in tweets is not feasible. Yet, leveraging Python's analytical capabilities, the scientific language can assess each tweet's essence and classify it as positive or detrimental, culminating in an outcome.

Although the lexicon dictionary's constraints prevent universal word valuation, Python's linguistic analysis empowers the categorization of tweets into favorable or unfavorable sentiments, yielding results. Word clouds for each tweet data frame and a pie chart displaying the hashtag distribution by sentiment (positive, detrimental, and null) are used to display the results. The category "null" designates "hashtags" with a value of 0.

The ten most uplifting and depressing "hashtags" are listed simultaneously by this application and are shown in Table **1**. These insights are visually presented through graphical representations in Figs. (**3** and **4**). Each visualization employs distinct colors to denote the percentages attributed to positive, detrimental, and null sentiment hashtags.

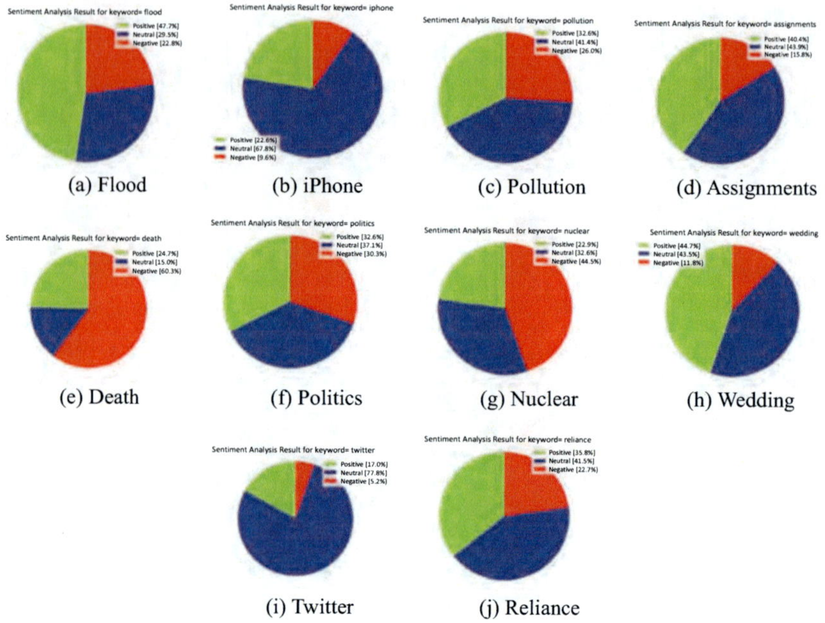

Fig. (3). Pie-chart-type-1 is used to visualize the effectiveness of tweet sentiments for the number of tweets that are searched using various keywords: (a) Flood, (b) iPhone, (c) Pollution, (d) Assignments, (e) Death, (f) Politics, (g) Nuclear, (h) Wedding, (i) Twitter, and (j) Reliance.

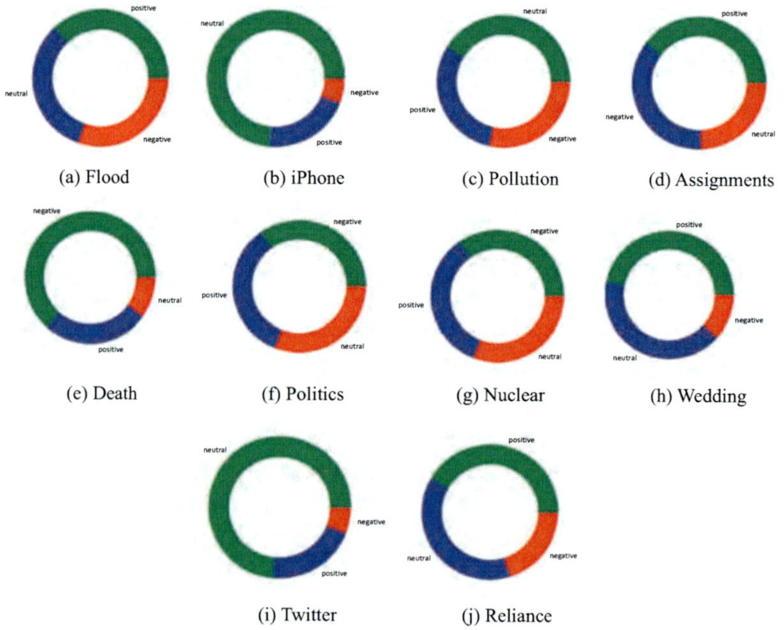

Fig. (4). Pie-char-type-2 is used to visualize the effectiveness of tweet sentiments for the number of tweets that have been searched using various keywords.

This analytical process amalgamates linguistic analysis with data visualization, offering a comprehensive portrayal of sentiment distribution in the tweet dataset. By discerning sentiment through Python's computational prowess and subsequently translating this analysis into illustrative forms, a deeper understanding of the dataset's emotional tone is attained. This synthesis of language processing and visualization affords insights into the prevailing sentiments and trends encapsulated within the tweets, serving as a valuable tool for sentiment analysis and communication analytics.

DISCUSSION AND CONCLUSION

The development of the Internet has revolutionized how people communicate their ideas and opinions today. Blog posts, online forums, product review sites, social media networks, and other comparable platforms are mostly responsible for making this possible. Massive social media platforms like Facebook, Twitter, and Google Plus, among others, have made it possible for millions of people to share their feelings, trade opinions, and freely discuss their everyday lives. Online communities offer a conversational setting where people can influence others through forums and participate in discussions. Social media generates a substantial amount of sentiment-filled data in the form of tweets, status updates, blog posts, comments, and reviews. Social media furthermore gives companies a way to communicate with their clients for marketing purposes. The internet-driven user-generated content significantly influences people's decisions. For example, when considering purchasing a product or availing a service, individuals tend to research and deliberate online, often engaging in discussions on social media before reaching a conclusion. However, the enormous amount of user-generated content makes a thorough analysis unfeasible for the average user. Numerous sentiment analysis approaches are routinely employed to automate this procedure in order to address this issue. We gather real-time tweets using the "Twitter API" and store them in a "Python dataframe". We utilize the "TextBlob library in Python" to compute the "polarity scores" of these tweets using "Naive Bayes". Following this, we create pie charts to visually represent the distribution of tweets as "positive", detrimental, or impartial (See Figs. **3** and **4**). Using Python's NLP library, we tokenize the tweets, apply lemmatization, and perform other data cleaning procedures to simplify the data frames (See Fig. **2**). Additionally, we produce word clouds for every tweet, each positive and detrimental tweet separately. (See Fig. **1**). It is worth noting that the accuracy of our model is influenced by the keywords we use for searching.

Positive keywords bias the results towards a higher positive percentage, while detrimental and impartial keywords influence the percentages accordingly. In this model, we achieved an accuracy range of 52% to 67%.

In this study, we created a compact ML module designed to analyze sentiment in Twitter posts. This module uses the "Twitter API" and basic Python models to quickly determine the overall sentiment of input text data. It provides users with both textual and graphical outputs, which improve understanding. We have shown how sentiment analysis may be used in a variety of contexts, including blogs, publications, customer reviews, social networks, and movie review websites. These applications entail evaluating opinions expressed by external sources. We explored various NLP and ML sentiment analysis techniques, emphasizing its extensive range of applications and its significance as a pioneering field of study.

The paper has presented a study that employs natural language processing (NLP) to analyze sentiment in tweets. The purpose of employing Twitter sentiment analysis is to comprehend how consumer views affect business success. The study combines NLP techniques with ML to enhance the accuracy of sentiment analysis. The sentiments expressed in tweets are classified into three folds: "positive", detrimental, and impartial. By analyzing these sentiments, one can derive overarching trends in public sentiment related to a specific topic. This information can then guide decision-making for improvement. The study utilizes the Twitter API to collect up-to-date datasets based on the keywords provided. Since the dataset obtained can vary over time, depending on when the keyword is entered, the results of the analysis may also differ accordingly.

REFERENCES

[1] M. Rambocas, and J. Gama, "Marketing Research: The Role of Sentiment Analysis", In: *Proc. 5th SNAKDD Workshop*, 2013. Available: https://www.aaai.org/ocs/index.php/SNAKDD/SNAKDD13/paper/view/6692

[2] Internet World Stats, "Usage and Population Statistics," 2013. Available: http://www.internetworldstats.com/stats.htm

[3] A.K. Jose, N. Bhatia, and S. Krishna, *Twitter Sentiment Analysis.* National Institute of Technology Calicut, 2010.

[4] P. Lai, *Extracting Strong Sentiment Trend from Twitter.* Stanford University, 2012.

[5] Y. Zhou, and Y. Fan, "A Sociolinguistic Study of American Slang", *Theory Pract. Lang. Stud.,* vol. 3, no. 12, pp. 2209-2213, 2013. [http://dx.doi.org/10.4304/tpls.3.12.2209-2213]

[6] M. Comesaña, A.P. Soares, M. Perea, A.P. Piñeiro, I. Fraga, and A. Pinheiro, "ERP correlates of masked affective priming with emoticons", *Comput. Human Behav.,* vol. 29, no. 3, pp. 588-595, 2013. [http://dx.doi.org/10.1016/j.chb.2012.10.020]

[7] A.H. Huang, D.C. Yen, and X. Zhang, "Exploring the potential effects of emoticons", *Inf. Manage.,* vol. 45, no. 7, pp. 466-473, 2008. [http://dx.doi.org/10.1016/j.im.2008.07.001]

[8] D. Boyd, S. Golder, and G. Lotan, "Tweet, tweet, retweet: Conversational aspects of retweeting on Twitter", In: *Proc. 43rd Hawaii Int. Conf. on System Sciences (HICSS)*, 2010, pp. 1-10. Available: https://ieeexplore.ieee.org/document/5422337

[9] T. Carpenter, and T. Way, "Tracking Sentiment Analysis through Twitter", *ACM Comput. Surv.,* 2010.

[10] D. Osimo, and F. Mureddu, "Research Challenge on Opinion Mining and Sentiment Analysis", *Conference of Fruct Association United Kingdom,* 2010.

[11] A. Pak, and P. Paroubek, "Twitter as a Corpus for Sentiment Analysis and Opinion Mining", In: *Special Issue of the International Journal of Computer Applications* vol. 10. , 2010, no. 11, pp. 1-10. Available: https://www.ijcaonline.org

[12] S. Lohmann, M. Burch, H. Schmauder, and D. Weiskopf, "Visual analysis of microblog content using time-varying co-occurrence highlighting in tag clouds", *Proc. Annual Conf. of VISVISUS,* pp. 1-8, 2012.
[http://dx.doi.org/10.1145/2254556.2254701]

[13] H. Saif, Y. He, and H. Alani, "Semantic sentiment analysis of Twitter", *Proc. Workshop on Information Extraction and Entity Analytics on Social Media Data,* pp. 1-8, 2011. Available: https://www.researchgate.net/publication/261870276

[14] A. Agarwal, B. Xie, I. Vovsha, O. Rambow, and R. Passonneau, "Sentiment analysis of Twitter data", *Proc. Annual Int. Conf. on Computational Linguistics (COLING),* pp. 1-9, 2012. Available: https://www.aclweb.org/anthology/C12-1016/

[15] J. Zhang, Y. Qu, J. Cody, and Y. Wu, "A case study of Microblogging in the Enterprise: Use, Value, and Related Issues", *Proceeding of the workshop on Web 2,* vol. 0, 2010.

[16] S. Singh, T. Jaiswal, R. Shyam, and S. Khanna, "ISI 2022. Smart Innovation", *Systems and Technologies,* vol. 333, pp. 225-238, 2023.

[17] G. Kalia, *A Research Paper on Social Media: An Innovative Educational Too,* vol. 1, pp. 43-50, 2013.

[18] A.M. Kaplan, "Users of the world, unite! The challenges and opportunities of social media", *Business Horizons,* vol. 53, no. 1, pp. 59-68, 2010.
[http://dx.doi.org/10.1016/j.bushor.2009.09.003]

[19] Q. Tang, B. Gu, and A.B. Whinston, "Content Contribution in Social Media: The case of YouTube", *2nd Conference of Social Media,* 2012 Hawaii.
[http://dx.doi.org/10.1109/HICSS.2012.181]

[20] M. Taboada, J. Brooke, M. Tofiloski, K. Voll, and M. Stede, *Lexicon Based Methods for Sentiment Analysis.* Association for Computational Linguistics, 2011.
[http://dx.doi.org/10.1162/COLI_a_00049]

[21] M. Annett, and G. Kondrak, "A comparison of sentiment analysis techniques: Polarizing movie blogs", *Proc. Conf. on Web Search and Web Data Mining (WSDM),* pp. 1-10, 2009. Available: https://dl.acm.org/doi/10.1145/1514954.1515014

[22] P. Goncalves, F. Benevenuto, M. Araujo, and M. Cha, "Comparing and combining sentiment analysis methods", *Proc. 2013 ACM Int. Conf. on Web Search and Data Mining (WSDM),* pp. 1-10, 2013.
[http://dx.doi.org/10.1145/2512938.2512951]

[23] E. Kouloumpis, T. Wilson, and J. Moore, "Twitter sentiment analysis: The good, the bad, and the OMG!", *Proc. 5th Int. Conf. on Weblogs and Social Media,* vol. 5, pp. 538-541, 2011. Available: https://www.aaai.org/ocs/index.php/ICWSM/ICWSM11/paper/view/2876

[24] S. Sharma, "Application of Support Vector Machines for Damage detection in Structure", *J. Mach. Learn. Res.,* 2008.

[25] A. Sharma, and S. Dey, "Performance Investigation of Feature Selection Methods and Sentiment Lexicons for Sentiment Analysis", *Association for the advancement of Artificial Intelligence,* 2012.

[26] J. Spencer, and G. Uchyigit, "Sentiment or: Sentiment Analysis of Twitter Data", In: *Second Joint Conference on Lexicon and Computational Semantics* University of Brighton: Brighton, 2008.

[27] A. Blom, and S. Thorsen, "Automatic Twitter replies with Python", *International conference Dialog,* 2012.

[28] B. Pang, and L. Lee, "Opinion mining and sentiment analysis", *Proc. 2nd Workshop on Making Sense of Microposts,* vol. 2, Cornell University, Ithaca, NY, pp. 1-10, 2008. Available: https://www.cs.cornell.edu/people/pabo/papers/2008-sentiment.pdf

[29] M. Hu, and B. Liu, "Mining and summarizing customer reviews", *Proc. ACM SIGKDD Int. Conf. on Knowledge Discovery and Data Mining,* pp. 168-177, 2004. [http://dx.doi.org/10.1145/1014052.1014073]

[30] P. Nakov, Z. Kozareva, A. Ritter, S. Rosenthal, V. Stoyanov, and T. Wilson, "Sem Eval-2013 Task2", *Sentiment Analysis in Twitter,* vol. 2, pp. 312-320, 2013.

[31] J. Wu, J. Wang, and L. Liu, "Kernel-based method for automated walking patterns recognition using kinematics data", *Proc. 5th Workshop on Natural Language Processing,* pp. 1-7, 2006. Available: https://ieeexplore.ieee.org

[32] T.D. Smedt, and W. Daelemans, "Pattern for Python", *Proc. COLING 2012,* pp. 1-7, 2012. Available: https://www.aclweb.org/anthology/C12-1020

[33] A. Sweigart, Invent Your Own Computer Games with Python, 2nd ed., 2012. Available: http://inventwithpython.com/

[34] C. Seberino, "Python: Faster and easier software development", In: *Proc. Annual Conf.* California, 2012, pp. 1-15.

[35] R. Shyam, and R. Singh, "A Taxonomy of Machine Learning Techniques", *Journal of Advancements in Robotics,* vol. 8, no. 3, pp. 18-25, 2021.

[36] A. Lukaszewski, *MySQL for Python, Integrate the flexibility of Python and the power of MySQL to boost the productivity of your applications.* Birningham, Packt Publishing Ltd.: UK, 2010.

[37] V. Nareyko, "Why Python is perfect for startups", 2014. Available: http://opensource.com/business/13/12/why-python-perfect-startups

[38] R. Shyam, and R. Chakraborty, "Machine Learning and its Dominant Paradigms", *Journal of Advancements in Robotics,* vol. 8, no. 2, pp. 1-10, 2021.

[39] A. Hawkins, "There is more to becoming a thought leader than giving yourself the title," 2013. Available: http://www.thesocialmediashow.co.uk/author/admin/

[40] R. Prabowo, and M. Thelwall, "Sentiment Analysis:A Combined Approach", *International World Wide Web Conference Committee (IW3C2),* 2009.

[41] H. Saif, Y. He, and H. Alani, *Alleviating Data Scarcity for Twitter Sentiment Analysis.* Association for Computational Linguistics, 2012.

[42] R. Shyam, "Convolutional Neural Network and its Architectures", *Journal of Computer Technology & Applications,* vol. 12, no. 2, pp. 6-14, 2021.

[43] R. Shyam, S. Khanna, P. Verma, and S. Maurya, "Assessing the Performance of DL Methods in Handwritten Digit Recognition", *International Journal of Data Structure Studies,* vol. 1, no. 1, pp. 25-32, 2023.

SUBJECT INDEX

A

B

C

Vikash Yadav, Vimal Kumar, Sonam Gupta & Vandana Dixit Kaushik (Eds.)

D

E

F

G

H

I

K

L

T

V

Made in United States
Orlando, FL
05 November 2026

90200370R10145